Praise for *iPad*™ *& iPhone*™ *Administrator's Guide*

"The must-have book for administrators of iPad and iPhone devices. A complete and precise guide to all the steps of administration in the corporate environment."

—*Peter Winkler, Sr. Software Engineer, Epitec Group*

"Guy Hart-Davis' knowledge of the subject is surpassed only by the clarity with which he explains it. The concise, step-by-step instructions, handy tips, and illustrations from both the Mac OS and Windows inspire confidence. If I were mass-deploying iOS devices in an enterprise setting, I'd have this book by my side."

—*Dave Caolo, Editor, The Unofficial Apple Weblog*

"This is a must-have book for iPhone/iPad administrators. There are tons of tips and step-by-step instructions that are well-illustrated with graphics and screenshots. If you want to deploy iPhones and iPads, this book is the answer."

—*Harold Hisona, iPhone/iPad "how-to" guide writer, MakeTechEasier.com, and SEO Consultant of PhilippineAlmanac.com*

iPad™ & iPhone™
Administrator's Guide

About the Author

Guy Hart-Davis is the author of more than 60 computer books about Mac OS X, iPads and iPhones, Windows, and other topics. His recent books include *Integrating Macs into Windows Networks* and *Mac OS X System Administration*.

About the Technical Editor

John W. Turner is an Infrastructure Architect for the Ford Motor Company. An IT professional for 20 years, he has worked in automotive, medical, multimedia, and financial systems for medium and large companies. He co-authored *The Definitive Guide to Linux Network Programming* (Apress, 2004) and *The Apache Tomcat Security Handbook* (Wrox, 2003). He holds a Bachelor's degree in Information Systems and recently earned a Master's degree in Information Assurance from the University of Maryland.

iPad™ & iPhone™
Administrator's Guide

GUY **HART-DAVIS**

New York   Chicago   San Francisco
Lisbon   London   Madrid   Mexico City   Milan
New Delhi   San Juan   Seoul   Singapore   Sydney   Toronto

The **McGraw·Hill** Companies

Cataloging-in-Publication Data is on file with the Library of Congress

iPad™ & iPhone™ Administrator's Guide

1234567890   DOC DOC   109876543210

ISBN   978-0-07-175906-9
MHID   0-07-175906-9

Sponsoring Editor
  Megg Morin

Editorial Supervisor
  Jody McKenzie

Project Manager
  Tania Andrabi,
  Glyph International

Acquisitions Coordinator
  Stephanie Evans

Technical Editor
  John W. Turner

Copy Editor
  Bob Campbell

Proofreader
  Laura Bowman

Indexer
  Karin Arrigoni

Production Supervisor
  Jim Kussow

Composition
  Glyph International

Illustration
  Glyph International

Art Director, Cover
  Jeff Weeks

Cover Designer
  Jeff Weeks

This book is dedicated to Rhonda and Teddy.

At a Glance

Contents

Acknowledgments

My thanks go to the following people for making this book happen:

- Megg Morin, for getting the book approved and signing me to write it
- Stephanie Evans, for handling the administration, schedule, and finances
- John Turner, for performing the technical review and providing helpful suggestions and encouragement
- Tania Andrabi, for coordinating the project
- Bob Campbell, for editing the text with care and a light touch
- Glyph International, for laying out the pages
- Laura Bowman, for proofreading the book
- Karin Arrigoni, for creating the index

Introduction

In six short months, the iPad has become an indispensable business tool as well as a must-have consumer gadget, following the trail blazed by its smaller sibling, the iPhone. Go into pretty much any company or organization today, and you'll find people using iPads and iPhones to get their jobs done—more easily, more quickly, and wherever they happen to be.

Here are four quick examples:

■ Carrying an iPad instead of a clipboard, the doctor can not just make a bedside visit and see how the patient is doing—she can connect to the database, double-check the details of how esoteric medications interact, and then prescribe new meds for the patient on the spot.

■ Instead of returning to the dispatch desk and grabbing a paper order sheet, the warehouse picker pulls up the next order on his iPhone. He piles each item into a dispatch tray, marks it complete with a tap on the iPhone, and moves on to the next order—saving time, effort, and shoe leather (okay, rubber).

■ On her iPad, the real-estate agent can instantly pull up details of alternative properties to the one the client is shaping up to reject, show full-color pictures of them on an easily viewed screen, and then press-gang the client to visit the most promising prospect immediately.

- In the staid underwriting room of global insurer Lloyd's of London, insurance brokers still queue in orderly lines to meet with the underwriters—but nowadays some of the insurance brokers have iPads under their arms rather than slipcases containing insurance slips.

The iPad and iPhone are great for streamlining business workflows like this—but to work their magic, the iPad and iPhone need to hook deep into your systems. So you must allow them to connect to your network . . . tap into your e-mail servers . . . access your network from the outside . . . and much more.

All this means that you need to manage the iPads and iPhones just as you manage notebooks and desktop computers. In fact, you must manage the iPads and iPhones much more tightly—your desktops won't leave the office without significant human intervention, but your company's iPads and iPhones are designed to carry your corporate data into the wilds of the urban jungle day in and day out.

So—how do you get the iPads and iPhones connected, configured, and secured? Let me tell you . . . .

Is This Book for Me?

Yes.

If you need to add iPads and iPhones to your company's or organization's networks, pick up this book so that you can learn the best way to add them and keep them under control.

If you've already added iPads and iPhones—or if users have added them to the network without your say-so—get this book to find out how to bring the devices under your control and avoid untold depths of administrative grief.

You'd probably like some specifics. Read on.

What Will I Learn in This Book?

Here's what you will learn from this book:

- Chapter 1, "Planning Your Deployment and Choosing the Right iPads and iPhones," explains why you need to manage the iPads and iPhones, suggests ways of deciding which services you'll provide to the devices, and tells you how to choose the right model for each company or organization member who needs one.

- Chapter 2, "Activating and Setting Up iPhones and iPads," takes you through the process of activating iPhones on a carrier network and setting both iPhones and iPads up so that you can configure them for users. In this chapter, you'll learn how to get the latest version of iTunes, how to switch iTunes to its activation-only mode, and how to update the carrier settings on an iPad or iPhone.

■ Chapter 3, "Configuring an iPad or iPhone Automatically," shows you how to use Apple's configuration tool, iPhone Configuration Utility, to create configuration profiles containing payloads of settings for iPads and iPhones—and how to load those profiles onto the devices. iPhone Configuration Utility is the tool that'll save you the most time in managing your network's iPads and iPhones, and this chapter digs into it in depth.

■ Chapter 4, "Setting Up Wireless Networks on the iPad and iPhone," covers connecting the iPads and iPhones you manage to wireless networks. You can make a wireless connection manually if necessary, or have the users make it manually, but to save time, you'll probably want to put a Wi-Fi payload in a configuration profile you load on the device. You may also need to reinforce your wireless network before adding iPads and iPhones to it.

■ Chapter 5, "Equipping the iPad and iPhone with the Apps That Users Need," shows you how to identify and install the best-of-breed business apps that your network's iPad and iPhone users need. The chapter suggests apps you may want to try, ranging from Microsoft Office–compatible productivity suites to remote-access and remote-control apps that make administrators' lives easier.

■ Chapter 6, "Connecting the iPad and iPhone to Your Mail Servers," takes you through connecting the iPad and iPhone to your e-mail system so that users can send and receive messages. The chapter covers Microsoft Exchange first, other mail servers next, and then how to troubleshoot common problems with both.

■ Chapter 7, "Putting Documents on the iPad and iPhone," explains how to make sure the iPad and iPhone are equipped with the documents they need. You'll learn first how iOS (the iPhone operating system) handles documents—in brief, oddly—and meet the tools you use for transferring documents from computer to iPad or iPhone and back. Then we'll talk about how to deal with documents in the iWork applications, and how to get Microsoft Office documents synchronized between iOS devices and computers.

■ Chapter 8, "Securing Your Company's iPads and iPhones," goes through the measures you can take to keep valuable and sensitive data safe without locking the iPad and iPhone users in a lead-lined room. You'll learn how to secure iOS devices with a passcode either directly or through policy, how to apply data protection, and how to encrypt the backups iTunes keeps of vital data. And for when the iPad or iPhone goes astray, you'll learn how to wipe its contents remotely—wherever it is.

■ Chapter 9, "Giving iPad and iPhone Users Remote Access to the Network," shows you how to let users access the network from the outside by using virtual private networking (VPN). You can create VPN payloads in configuration profiles, but you may also need to set up VPN connections manually—or dig into the settings by hand to troubleshoot problems such as those this chapter discusses.

■ Chapter 10, "Troubleshooting iPad and iPhone Hardware and Software Problems," gives you the skills and techniques you need to deal with hardware and software problems that occur with the iPad and iPhone. These range from everyday maneuvers you'll want to teach users to keep them off your back—dealing with things like app freezes and Wi-Fi sulks—to heavy-duty fixes you'll probably keep to yourself to maintain your superhero status. You'll also learn how to get the best performance out of the battery, and how to replace it when it fails.

■ The Index—okay, you know about the index. It's not exciting unless you go for orderly arrangements, but it's useful enough to be essential.

Conventions Used in This Book

To make its meaning clear and concise, this book uses a number of conventions, five of which are worth mentioning here:

■ The pipe character or vertical bar denotes choosing an item from the menu bar. For example, "choose File | New" means that you should click the File menu, and then click the New item on the menu that opens.

■ The phrase "select the check box" means putting a check mark in the check box (or making sure the check mark is already there), and "clear the check box" means removing a check mark from the check box (or making sure there's no check mark in it).

■ Note, Tip, and Caution paragraphs highlight information that's worth extra attention. Notes answer the questions you were about to ask, Tips save you time and effort, and Cautions save you grief and hair.

■ Sidebars provide extra information on important topics.

■ The ⌘ symbol represents the Mac Command key.

CHAPTER 1 | Planning Your Deployment and Choosing the Right iPads and iPhones

If you run a network—whether on Windows Server or Mac OS X Server—you no doubt have users who want to connect their iPads and iPhones to the network. You could refuse—maybe. But when the requests are coming from VPs and managers, high-revenue sales folk, and the knowledge workers who keep the company ticking, you may not have the leverage to stem the tide for long.

Besides, you may want to connect your own iPad or iPhone to the network. Connecting via VPN can help you troubleshoot problems remotely, saving you those midnight journeys to the office to coddle a balky server.

Once you commit to allowing iPads and iPhones to connect to the network, you have a choice. You can either plan your deployment and keep the iPads, the iPhones, and your network in general under control, or open the floodgates to a rush of users who may swamp your wireless network, stomp on your DHCP servers, and trample like browsing buffalo around parts of the network they're not supposed to be able to see.

You don't need me to tell you it makes sense to plan your deployment and retain control of the network. This chapter shows you how to start that planning and—assuming you have the choice—choose the right iPads and iPhones for the people in your company or organization. The chapter also outlines the problems that can occur if you don't keep the iPads and iPhones under control.

We'll start with a question that your company's or organization's VPs may well ask—why do you need to manage the iPads and iPhones? Can't you just tap in the details of the wireless network and let the users get on with their work (and play)?

Understanding Why You Need to Manage the iPads and iPhones

With their built-in Wi-Fi capabilities, the iPad and the iPhone are easy to connect to a wireless network. If the wireless network is open, broadcasting its network name (the SSID—service set identifier), the network pops up on the Wi-Fi Networks screen of the iPhone or iPad, where the user can touch it and then enter the password. Even if the wireless network is closed, the user can connect by tapping in the network's name and the password.

For home use, or for connecting at the coffee shop, this is great. But when you're adding iPads and iPhones to your managed network, you'll likely want to keep them under closer control to avoid problems. Harmless as they may seem to management and users alike, the iPad and iPhone can threaten the security of your network and your valuable data, cause traffic problems, and increase your and your colleagues' workload by requiring configuration and support.

To get the most out of the iPad and iPhone, you'll also need to connect them to your network in the right way. For example, to enable users to get e-mail from your Microsoft Exchange system on their iPads, you'll need to set up the iPads to connect to your mail servers. Just glomming onto the wireless network won't cut the mustard.

Let's dig into this a bit, starting with the potential problems and what you can do about them.

Reducing the Security Threats from the iPad and iPhone

The iPad and iPhone seem friendly devices, but they pose several threats to the security of your network and its data.

First, if you allow users to connect their own iPads or iPhones to the computers within your network, you expose the computers to any malware the users have picked up on their home computers. Malware can transfer itself from an infected computer to a USB device such as the iPad or iPhone easily enough, and it can propagate itself from there to the computers in your network. If you're unlucky, a disgruntled user could bring in an attack program on purpose rather than by accident.

To avoid this threat, you'll probably want to lock down the USB ports of your network's computers so that users can't casually connect iPads, iPhones, or other USB devices.

Second, even if the iPad or iPhone contains no malware, the user can copy confidential or other sensitive data from his PC or Mac to the device and take it outside the network. You then lose control over the data, which can end up anywhere—especially if the iPad or iPhone gets lost or stolen.

You can avoid this threat too by locking down the USB ports of computers to which you don't allow users to connect iPads and iPhones. For those computers to which you do allow the devices to connect, you can manage the types of data that users can synchronize. And you can set up each managed iPad and iPhone so that you can wipe it remotely if it is lost or stolen.

Third, if you allow unmanaged iPads and iPhones to connect to your wireless network from within, you may find them able to access areas of the network you don't want them to reach from the iPhone or iPad even though you allow them to access those areas using a PC or Mac.

You can avoid this problem by controlling which devices can connect to your wireless access points and by making sure that any sensitive information on approved devices is secured for when it leaves the building or campus.

 NOTE You may also want to provide guest access to the Internet for unapproved devices. See the end of the chapter for details.

Avoiding Traffic Problems from Connecting the iPad and iPhone to the Network

All other things being equal, adding extra wireless devices to the network takes extra bandwidth and can cause congestion. Adding just a few iPads and iPhones to a large wireless network should make little difference (but see the nearby Note). But bringing in a slew of new devices can cause traffic problems, especially when multiple wireless users connect from the same area of the building or campus—for example, a phalanx of marketing executives using iPads in a meeting, or a squad of students descending on a lecture room equipped with iPhones.

NOTE   Early versions of the iPad firmware gave DHCP servers grief by clinging for dear life onto the IP address the iPad had grabbed even though the DHCP lease had expired. If you're getting mystery IP address conflicts, check for iPads running early versions of the firmware. Update any culprits you find.

To avoid these problems, plan your deployment of iPads and iPhones rather than just letting it happen. Work out the following:

- **How many extra devices will connect to the wireless network**   This should be easy enough to figure out, especially if your company or organization is supplying the devices.

- **How much the users will use the iPads and iPhones**   This can be much harder to establish—but you will normally know which users compute only on the iPad or iPhone and which spend most of their time on a desktop or laptop computer; which apps you have permitted the iPads and iPhones to run; and roughly which types of data you'll expect them to be hauling across the wireless network to the devices.

- **Where the users will use the iPads and iPhones**   If the users will be spread out all over your wireless network, your existing infrastructure may be able to handle the extra load. But if you'll often have groups of users joining the wireless network (for example, in meeting rooms or lecture halls), you may need to provide more capacity in particular areas—for instance, by adding access points.

NOTE   To work out where users will use the iPads and iPhones, you'll probably want to consult both representative users and your crystal ball. Monitor the load on your wireless access points, and be prepared to adapt your network further if you find that traffic is heavier in certain areas than you anticipated.

Minimizing Configuration and Support Problems Caused by iPads or iPhones

If you allow more than a handful of iPads and iPhones onto your network, you'll want to minimize configuration and support by automating setup. For managing both iPads and iPhones, Apple provides the free iPhone Configuration Utility, which you'll meet in detail in Chapter 3. You use iPhone Configuration Utility to create configuration profiles specifying the setup you want for the devices, and then install a configuration profile on each device.

To reduce support headaches, write up an iPad and iPhone support policy that sets down clearly what you do support and what you don't. For example, for managed iPads and iPhones, list the apps and services (discussed next) that you support. For unmanaged iPads and iPhones, you may choose to provide only Internet access and nothing more, stating clearly that anything to do with apps or hardware grief is the owner's responsibility.

Deciding Which Services You'll Provide to the iPad and iPhone

At this point, you've decided to permit iPads and iPhones to join the network. Next, decide which services you'll provide to the iPad and iPhone.

These are the services you're most likely to need to provide:

■ **Internet access**   Many users will want to be able to access the Internet, either through your main wireless network or through a guest network (as discussed at the end of the chapter).

■ **POP and IMAP e-mail**   Users can access e-mail on POP or IMAP servers.

■ **Exchange ActiveSync**   Users can connect to your Exchange server for e-mail, scheduling, and contacts.

■ **LDAP directories**   Users can connect to LDAP directories to look up data.

■ **Calendaring**   Users can access data on servers that use the CalDAV standard for calendaring.

■ **Files and documents**   Users may need to copy files and documents to their iPads and iPhones, either to work with the files on the device or to use it as an easy means of getting large files from A to B.

■ **Remote access to the network**   Users may need to access the network securely via VPN.

■ **Remote control to network computers**   Administrators (okay, maybe some power users too) may need to take remote control of computers on the network.

Choosing the Right iPads or iPhones

If you'll provide your company's or organization's workers with iPads or iPhones, your next task is to choose the right models for their needs. In this section, we'll look at the decisions you'll normally need to make.

NOTE   You can also use the iPod touch as a corporate networking device using most of the same techniques described in this book. But because the iPod touch has neither cellular data access nor enough screen space to display larger apps and documents, it tends to be less useful than the iPhone and iPad.

Choosing Between the iPad and the iPhone

First, decide whether the user needs an iPad or an iPhone. In most cases, this is a straightforward decision depending on what the user will do with the device.

You'll probably have extra criteria of your own, but here are four standard criteria to get you started:

- **Phone functionality**   If the user will need to make phone calls on the cellular network, get an iPhone.

- **Portability**   If the user needs a device that will fit in his pocket, get an iPhone (or maybe an iPod touch).

- **Screen size**   If the user needs a larger screen for data input, reading, or other tasks, get an iPad.

- **Apps**   If the user needs apps that run only on the iPad, go for that device. The usual offenders here are productivity apps—anything from Apple's Pages, Keynote, and Numbers to custom big-screen apps you've built in-house—but other apps may also be a consideration. (For example, some games run only on the iPad, or run much better on the iPad; and some VPs run faster, smoother, and quieter with games on their iPad.)

Choosing Among Different Models of iPads

When you've decided that a particular person needs an iPad, you have two further decisions to make:

- **3G or not 3G**   If the user will need to connect to the 3G network, get a 3G model. Otherwise, if the user will connect only to Wi-Fi networks, you don't need to spend the extra money upfront on a 3G iPad or shoulder the ongoing expense of a data plan.

NOTE   For your 3G iPad users, you need to get a data plan as well. Check out your phone company's data plans and estimate how much data users will need to shift via 3G. For example, at this writing, AT&T's smaller plan gives only 250MB per month, which forces many users to go for the 2GB per month plan instead. Make sure that iPad 3G users use safe wireless networks when they're available (for example, in the office and at home), rather than 3G.

- **Capacity**   At this writing, the iPad comes in 16GB, 32GB, and 64GB models; the higher the capacity, the higher the price. Unless users need large amounts of music and video on the iPad for business uses, 16GB should be adequate, and 32GB should be more than enough—even if you add a load of apps and documents.

Choosing Among Different Models of iPhones

When you've decided that a user needs an iPhone, your main decision is which capacity of iPhone 4 to get.

> **NOTE**   At this writing, Apple and the phone companies are still selling the iPhone 3GS as well as the iPhone 4. The iPhone 3GS is a fine phone, especially when you upgrade it to iOS4 (iPhone OS 4)—but the iPhone 4 is so much better that it's barely worth buying a new iPhone 3GS anymore.

At this writing, the iPhone 4 comes in 16GB and 32GB capacities. As with just about everything else in computing, having more space is usually helpful—but if the user doesn't need to carry large amounts of songs and videos with her, the 16GB iPhone provides plenty of space for documents, pictures, mail, and other data.

For the iPhone, you need to choose a carrier—unless you're in the U.S., where the only carrier is AT&T at the moment—and a suitable data plan. Make sure the data plan will meet the user's needs, as the bargain-basement data plans tend to cover only the lightest of use. For example, AT&T's Data Plus plan provides a meager 200MB of data per month, encouraging you to pay the extra money for the 2GB Data Pro plan.

> **TIP**   Use the Data Calculator on the AT&T web site (www.att.com/standalone/data-calculator/index .html) or a similar online tool to get an idea of how few e-mail messages, attachments, web pages, and downloads it typically takes to gobble up a 200MB data allowance.

Choosing Accessories for the iPad or iPhone

If only the iPad or iPhone itself were the end of the expense—but no such luck. The odds are high that you'll need to buy accessories as well: a case to protect the device from damage, a physical keyboard that'll let the user whack in text faster, a dock or stand, and perhaps an extra charger. You may also decide to buy an AppleCare extended warranty for the iPad or iPhone.

You can find iPad and iPhone accessories at many stores, both online and offline. When shopping online, the Apple Store (http://store.apple.com) is a good place to start, as it has both Apple's own accessories and third-party accessories that Apple considers worthy of reselling. Other sites worth investigating include Griffin Technology (www.griffintechnology.com), Digital Lifestyle Outfitters (www.dlo.com), and the stores you can search through iLounge (http://ilounge.pricegrabber.com).

Protecting the iPad or iPhone with a Case

Apple's sleek industrial designs look great but tend to be more susceptible to damage than some of their homelier rivals. So you'll probably want to armor up your iPads and iPhones with protective cases—and manufacturers have conspired to produce a wide enough range of options to reduce most people to indecision. You can get everything from Apple's minimalist iPhone Bumpers (for the iPhone 4) to lush leather cases (for most iPhone models and the iPad) to armored cases apparently designed to survive a cross between the *Die Hard* movies and *Waterworld*.

> **NOTE**   Many online stores include user reviews that cover cases' strong points and weak points honestly, but you'll often do better to shop for cases in the flesh (or leather, or rubber—whatever you prefer). Or you may find it more practical to let users choose cases for their devices up to firm price limits you set.

Adding a Dock or Stand for Easy Charging

Next on the list of accessories for making users' lives easier while increasing the iPad's or iPhone's survival rate, a dock or stand is often a good idea. A dock or stand gives the user a place to park the iPad or iPhone when it's not in use, reducing its chance of getting knocked off the desk. Most docks and stands also provide an easy way of recharging the iPad or iPhone, which helps users avoid forgetting to charge the device and running out of juice at a critical moment.

> **NOTE**   For the iPad, consider getting the Keyboard Dock for iPad, as discussed in the next section.

Adding a Keyboard to Speed Up Text Entry

As far as "soft" keyboards go, the iPad's onscreen keyboard is pretty good—Apple has made it a decent size, especially in landscape mode, and it's easy to press the keys accurately without bumping into the other keys. But you still need to look at where you're placing your fingers, as there are no physical keys to tell them they're in the right places. For anyone who doesn't touch-type, this seems a minor annoyance; but for any touch-typist, it's a killer.

Because the iPhone's screen is that much smaller, its keyboard is necessarily that much worse. Again, Apple has made it as good as possible—but few people want to be tapping out long documents with a finger (or a couple of thumbs).

So for any user who will need to enter serious amounts of text on the iPad or iPhone, you'll probably want to add a keyboard.

For the iPad, the best choice is usually a keyboard with a built-in Dock Connector and stand, which turns the iPad into a form of mutant laptop. Look first at the Apple iPad Keyboard Dock ($69; http://store.apple.com), which includes extra keys for iPad-specific commands, and then see if any competitors provide more features or better value.

For either the iPad or the iPhone, you can also use most Bluetooth keyboards, though it's wise to double-check compatibility before buying a third-party keyboard. Using Bluetooth gives you a far wider choice of keyboards—and you may even be able to dig an old keyboard out of your hardware closet.

Keeping the iPad or iPhone Going with an Extra Charger or Battery Pack

Both the iPad and the iPhone do pretty well for battery life, but even so, heavy users will benefit from being able to recharge the devices either at home (without carrying off the charger from the office) or on the go. To keep them going, you can get wall chargers, car chargers, or battery packs.

CAUTION   When buying a charger or battery pack, double-check that it's compatible with the device you're intending to use it with. Even though all iPhones and iPads use the same Dock Connector, different models have different power requirements.

Covering Your Bets with an AppleCare Protection Plan

Finally on the accessories front, decide whether to buy an AppleCare Protection Plan for the iPad ($99) or iPhone ($69). The AppleCare Protection Plan extends the standard 90-day telephone support period to one year and the hardware repair coverage from one year to two years.

Even though extended warranties are a waste of money in general, they're worth considering for the iPad and iPhone for two reasons:

- **Life's tough and may be short**   For a handheld mobile device such as the iPad or iPhone, daily life is a contact sport that provides all too many opportunities for injury. Falls and immersions are usually the worst hazards, but you may find that your company's users find more inventive ways to maim or terminate their devices.

- **Medicine is expensive**   Most types of serious damage to an iPad or iPhone need a pro's skills to fix them. And in most cases, replacement will cost even more.

NOTE   Instead of AppleCare, you may prefer to get a third-party insurance plan to cover your iPads and iPhones.

Providing Guest Internet Access for Unmanaged iPads and iPhones

So far in this chapter we've been assuming that you'll be providing the iPads or iPhones to the people in your company or organization. After all, this is a great way to keep them happy while retaining control of the network.

Depending on your situation, though, you may have people bringing their own iPads and iPhones into work (or onto campus) and wanting to connect to the Internet but not to your network.

In this case, you don't need to set the iPads or iPhones up as managed devices—in fact, you probably don't want to. Instead, you can provide Internet access for them by setting up a guest wireless network that they can use freely, but which leads only to the Internet rather than to the internal parts of your network.

If you can marshal the hardware and time to set up a guest wireless network, it can be a great way to keep users happy and off your back. As a bonus, you can restrict the bandwidth allocated to the guest wireless network so that the iPad and iPhone users can't eat too far into your Internet connection—and of course you can block unapproved sites to prevent users from accessing unsuitable material on the company's dollar.

NOTE   Various wireless routers, such as Apple's AirPort Extreme models, can run a secondary wireless network for guest access. But if your wireless routers can't do this, add another router that can.

CHAPTER 2 | Activating and Setting Up iPhones and iPads

Once you've got your iPhones and iPads, you'll need to set them up and get them ready for use. You'll probably want to perform initial setup yourself rather than delegate it to the users, both so that you can help users avoid problems and so that you can configure the iPads or iPhones as described in the next several chapters before handing them over.

iTunes is the primary management tool for iPhones and iPads (not to mention iPods, including the iPod touch), and you need to use iTunes to get the devices set up. First, you'll need to install a SIM card and activate each iPhone before its phone functionality will work; also, depending on your carrier, you may need to install a SIM card in each 3G iPad before it can connect to the cellular network.

In this chapter, we'll go through what you need to do to get the iPhones and iPads set up so that you can configure them for users. We'll start by making sure you have an up-to-date version of iTunes installed on your computer, because you won't get far without one. Next, we'll look at how to switch iTunes to its activation-only mode. Then, for the meat of the chapter, we'll examine how to actually activate the iPhones and set up both iPhones and iPads. And finally, we'll glance quickly at how to update the carrier settings on an iPad or iPhone.

Installing the Latest Version of iTunes

To set up an iPad or iPhone, you must have iTunes installed on your computer. Macs normally come with iTunes installed, although you can remove it; PCs don't normally include iTunes, but some manufacturers do install it. Either way, it's a good idea to update iTunes to the latest version to avoid any bugs that Apple has already knocked on the head and given concrete boots.

Downloading the Latest Version of iTunes

To get the latest version of iTunes, steer your web browser to the iTunes Download page (www.apple.com/itunes/download/) and download the distribution file. This page automatically gives you the Windows version of iTunes if your PC is running Windows and the Mac version of iTunes if you're using a Mac, so visit it using the appropriate operating system.

 NOTE When downloading iTunes, you'll probably want to clear the check boxes for iTunes news and special offers and Apple news and information.

Updating iTunes to the Latest Version

If your PC or Mac already has iTunes installed, make sure you've got the latest version. Open iTunes and give the appropriate command:

- **Windows** Choose Help | Check For Updates.
- **Mac** Choose iTunes | Check For Updates.

If iTunes announces that the version you've got is the current version, as shown in the top part of Figure 2-1, you're all set. If iTunes tells you a new version is available, as in the bottom part of Figure 2-1, click the Download iTunes button, and then follow the prompts to install it.

Understanding the Software Components You Get with iTunes

The iTunes distribution file for Windows is pretty hefty—nearly 100MB at this writing. Apart from software's general tendency to grow alongside hardware's capabilities, the distribution file is large because it includes several items other than iTunes itself. These are the other items:

■ **QuickTime** QuickTime is Apple's multimedia player, and it shares features with iTunes. Because iTunes actually uses QuickTime features for playing back audio and video, you can't dispense with QuickTime.

■ **Bonjour for Windows** Bonjour is Apple's zero-configuration networking technology that provides an easy way for consumers to share items such as music (using iTunes), printers (using the Bonjour Printer Wizard), and photos (using iPhoto on Macs) without having to configure networking. You may well not want Bonjour running on a corporate or enterprise network—in which case, either don't install Bonjour or (if you've installed it) remove Bonjour as described later in this chapter.

■ **Apple Software Update** Apple Software Update is a utility that automatically checks both for updated versions of iTunes and other Apple programs already installed and for Windows versions of other Apple programs you may want

Figure 2-1. Make sure you've got the latest version of iTunes by choosing Help | Check For Updates on Windows or iTunes | Check For Updates on the Mac. If a new version is available, download it, and then install it.

to install. For example, after you install iTunes (and QuickTime), Apple Software Update prompts you to install Safari for Windows. You may well not want to run Apple Software Update on a corporate or enterprise network.

■ **Apple Mobile Device Support**   Apple Mobile Device Support is a service that enables iPhones and iPads to connect to iTunes on Windows. Apple Mobile Device Service is required if you want iPhones and iPads to work with iTunes.

If you go ahead with a default installation of iTunes, the installer automatically installs Bonjour and Apple Software Update as well as QuickTime and Apple Mobile Device Service. If you prefer not to have Bonjour and Apple Software Update components on a Windows PC, you need to open up the iTunes distribution file and extract the files you actually need, and then run them individually.

The following subsections tell you what you need to know about each installation type.

Installing iTunes for Windows with All Its Components

The normal way to install iTunes on Windows is with all its components, including Bonjour and Apple Software Update. This type of installation is fine for consumers and for other standalone installations, but for a corporate or enterprise installation, you'll probably want to omit Bonjour and Apple Software Update, as discussed in the next section.

If you go with the full installation, it's straightforward with no surprises. After you double-click the distribution file (or set it to run itself automatically after the download), your browser usually makes you confirm that you want to install iTunes. You then need to accept the license agreement before making four decisions on the Installation Options screen (Figure 2-2 shows the Windows version of this screen):

■ **Add iTunes And QuickTime Shortcuts To My Desktop**   Clear this check box unless you actually want the installer to create the shortcuts, as it tries to do by default.

■ **Use iTunes As The Default Player For Audio Files**   Leave this check box selected if you want iTunes to be the default player for audio files such as MP3 and WAV files. If you prefer to use Windows Media Player or another player, clear this check box.

■ **Default iTunes Language**   In this drop-down list, choose the language to use for the iTunes user interface—for example, English (United States).

■ **Destination Folder**   The installer suggests installing iTunes in the iTunes folder in the Program Files folder—for example, C:\Program Files\iTunes\ in a vanilla setup. Usually, this is the best place; if you need to use a different folder, click the Change button, use the Change Current Destination Folder dialog box to pick the folder, and then click the OK button.

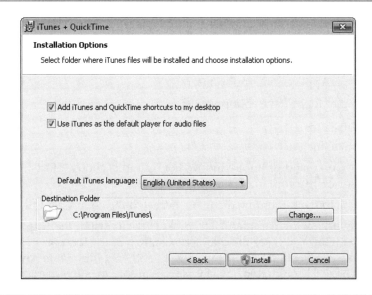

Figure 2-2.   On the Installation Options screen, choose whether to create shortcuts for iTunes and QuickTime, whether to make iTunes the default player, the language, and the destination folder.

Once you've made your decisions, click the Install button to run the installation. On Windows 7 and Windows Vista, you'll need to click the Continue button in the User Account Control dialog box to confirm that you want to install the programs.

When the installation is complete, the installer displays the Congratulations screen. If you want to launch iTunes, leave the Open iTunes After The Installer Exits check box selected; if not, clear it. Then click the Finish button.

Installing iTunes on Windows Without Bonjour and Apple Software Update

If you want to install iTunes for Windows without Bonjour and Apple Software Update, follow these steps:

1. Download the iTunes distribution file from Apple's web site (www.apple.com/itunes/download/) if you don't already have it. Choose to save the file to a convenient location rather than letting the installer run automatically.

2. If you don't already have an unarchiving utility, download one. Here are three examples:

   ■ IZArc (www.izarc.org; free)

   ■ WinZip (www.winzip.com; $39.99; evaluation version available)

   ■ WinRAR (www.rarlab.com; $24.99; trial version available)

3. Run the unarchiving utility and open the iTunes distribution file (which is called iTunesSetup.exe unless you rename it). Figure 2-3 shows the iTunesSetup.exe file open in IZArc.

4. Extract the following files to a convenient folder:

   ■ AppleApplicationSupport.msi

   ■ AppleMobileDeviceSupport.msi

   ■ iTunes.msi

   ■ QuickTime.msi

5. Open a Command Prompt window. For example, choose Start | All Programs | Accessories | Command Prompt.

6. Navigate to the folder to which you extracted the component files.

7. Type the following command and press ENTER to install the Apple Application Support item. You'll see the dialog box shown in the top part of Figure 2-4 as Apple Application Support installs; the other components have similar dialog boxes. Each dialog box closes itself automatically when the installation finishes.

```
AppleApplicationSupport.msi /passive
```

NOTE   The **/passive** parameter runs the installer without prompting you to choose options for the installation—for instance, the installation folder. (The regular type of installation is presumably aggressive.)

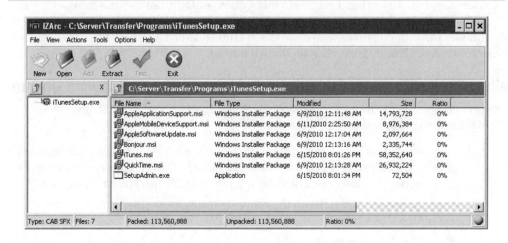

Figure 2-3.   To install iTunes on Windows without Bonjour and Apple Software Update, use an unarchiving tool such as IZArc to extract the files you need from the iTunes distribution file.

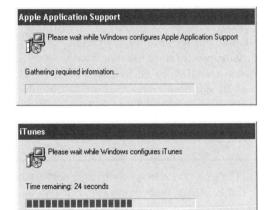

Figure 2-4. The installer displays a dialog box showing the progress of the installation—in this case, installing Apple Application Support (above) and iTunes (below).

8. Type the following command and press ENTER to install QuickTime:

```
QuickTime.msi /passive
```

NOTE On 64-bit Windows versions, you need to give these 64-bit program names in place of the regular names: AppleApplicationSupport64.msi, iTunes64.msi, and AppleMobileDeviceSupport64.msi.

9. Type the following command and press ENTER to install iTunes:

```
iTunes.msi /passive
```

10. Type the following command and press ENTER to install Apple Mobile Device Support:

```
AppleMobileDeviceSupport.msi /passive
```

11. Close the Command Prompt window. For example, click the Close button (the × button) or press ALT-F4.

NOTE If you've already installed iTunes with Bonjour and Apple Software Update on a PC, you can remove Bonjour and Apple Software Update by opening Control Panel and using the Programs And Features applet (in Windows 7 or Windows Vista) or the Add Or Remove Programs applet in Windows XP.

Switching iTunes to Activation-Only Mode

If you need to activate lots of iPhones or iPads, it's a good idea to switch the copy of iTunes you're using to its hidden activation-only mode.

The difference in activation-only mode is that once you've finished activating an iPhone or iPad, iTunes automatically ejects it so that you can get right along with activating the next device. By contrast, in normal mode (or consumer mode, if you like), iTunes assumes that you're activating the device for your own use with the PC or Mac you're working on. So once activation is finished, iTunes prompts you to synchronize your data with the iPhone or iPad.

 TIP To check whether iTunes is in activation-only mode or normal mode, choose Help | About iTunes on Windows or iTunes | About iTunes on the Mac. In the About iTunes dialog box, look below the iTunes version number in the scrolling readout. If **Activation-only** appears, iTunes is in activation-only mode; if not, iTunes is in normal mode.

Switching iTunes to Activation-Only Mode on Windows

To switch iTunes to activation-only mode on Windows, follow these steps:

1. If iTunes is running, close it. For example, choose File | Exit or press ALT-F4.

2. Open a Command Prompt window. For example, choose Start | All Programs | Accessories | Command Prompt.

3. Type the following command and press ENTER to switch to the PC's Program Files folder:

   ```
   cd %programfiles%
   ```

   Type the following command and press ENTER to turn on activation-only mode:

   ```
   iTunes\iTunes.exe /setPrefInt StoreActivationMode 1
   ```

 NOTE Two things here. First, it's fine to use all lowercase for the **setPrefInt** command. Second, when you give the command, there's no response—you just see the command prompt again. This is fine. If you get the command wrong, Command Prompt returns an error.

4. Close the Command Prompt window unless you need to leave it open for other purposes.

When you need to turn off activation-only mode, repeat the preceding procedure, but use the command **iTunes\iTunes.exe /setPrefInt StoreActivationMode 0** instead. (Again, using lowercase is fine.)

Creating Shortcuts to Launch iTunes in Activation-Only Mode and Normal Mode

If you need to switch frequently between activation-only mode and normal mode, create a Windows shortcut for each. You can then switch easily from one mode to the other without messing about in Command Prompt.

To create the activation-only shortcut, follow these steps:

1. Right-click the desktop and choose New | Shortcut to launch the Create Shortcut Wizard.

2. On the What Item Would You Like To Create A Shortcut For? screen, enter the iTunes path and filename in one of these ways:

   ■ Type **%programfiles%\iTunes\iTunes.exe** in the Type The Location Of The Item text box.

   ■ Click the Browse button to display the Browse For Files Or Folders dialog box. Navigate to the \Program Files\iTunes\ folder, click the iTunes.exe file, and then click the OK button.

3. Click the Next button to display the What Would You Like To Name The Shortcut? screen.

4. In the Type A Name For This Shortcut box, type a name such as **iTunes (activation-only mode)**, and then click the Finish button. Windows creates a shortcut on the desktop and gives it the name you specified.

5. Right-click the shortcut and click Properties on the context menu to display the shortcut's Properties dialog box with the Shortcut tab at the front, as shown here.

(Continued)

6. In the Target text box, type the **setPrefInt StoreActivationMode 1** parameter after the program path and filename.

7. Click the OK button to close the Properties dialog box.

Now create the normal-mode shortcut. Follow these steps:

1. Click the iTunes shortcut you just customized.

2. Press CTRL-C to copy the shortcut.

3. Press CTRL-V to paste the shortcut. iTunes adds *Copy* to the name.

4. Press F2 to open the copy's name for editing.

5. Type the name you want—for example, **iTunes (normal mode)**—and press ENTER.

6. Right-click the renamed shortcut and click Properties on the context menu to display the shortcut's Properties dialog box. Again, the Shortcut tab appears at the front.

7. In the Target text box, change **StoreActivationMode 1** to **StoreActivationMode 0**.

8. Click the OK button to close the Properties dialog box.

Now test that each shortcut works.

Switching iTunes to Activation-Only Mode on the Mac

To switch iTunes to activation-only mode on the Mac, follow these steps:

1. If iTunes is running, quit it. For example, CTRL-click or right-click the iTunes icon in the Dock and then click Quit on the context menu.

2. Open a Terminal window. For example, click the desktop, choose Go | Utilities, and then double-click the Terminal icon.

3. Type the following command and press RETURN to turn on activation-only mode:

```
defaults write com.apple.iTunes StoreActivationMode -integer 1
```

 NOTE When entering the **defaults write** command, you need to get the capitalization of the **StoreActivationMode** parameter right. If you put the parameter's name in lowercase or otherwise mess it up, the parameter goes into the com.apple.itunes file, but iTunes ignores it. As in Windows, when you give the command, there's no response—you just see the command prompt again. This is what's supposed to happen. If you get the command wrong, Terminal lets you know by displaying the help screen.

4. Quit Terminal (unless you need to keep it open). For example, choose Terminal | Quit Terminal or press ⌘-Q.

When you need to turn off activation-only mode, repeat the preceding procedure, but use the command **defaults write com.apple.iTunes StoreActivationMode –integer 0**. Alternatively, use the command **defaults delete com.apple.iTunes StoreActivationMode** to delete the StoreActivationMode setting. Either way, you need to get the capitalization right for the **StoreActivationMode** parameter.

> **NOTE**   Instead of using the **–integer 1** parameter, you can use **–boolean yes** or **–boolean true** to turn on StoreActivationMode. And you can use **–boolean no** or **–boolean false** to turn it off. The **defaults read** command still returns **0** or **1** for the StoreActivationMode parameter, so usually it's easiest to stick with **–integer**.

Activating and Setting Up Your iPhones and iPads

Before you can use any of the iPhone's telephony features, you must activate the iPhone. This involves installing a SIM card, connecting the iPhone to a computer that's running iTunes, and then walking through the activation process. Once, you've done that, you can set up the iPhone using iTunes.

Similarly, for a 3G iPad, you may need to install a micro-SIM card if you want to use the cellular network. This depends on the carrier you're using, as some carriers (such as AT&T) install the micro-SIM for you. And you use iTunes to set up the iPad (3G or not).

The setup process for the iPad and the iPhone is the same, so we'll look at the two devices together. First, though, we'll deal with activating the iPhones.

Choosing Who Will Activate Your iPhones

Normally, you have three main choices for activating your iPhones:

- Have whoever sells you the iPhone activate it.
- Activate the iPhone yourself.
- Have whoever will use the iPhone activate it.

Let's look at each option in turn.

Activating the iPhone at the Point of Sale

For a consumer, the standard way of activating an iPhone is at the point of sale. If you walk into an Apple Store and buy an iPhone, the Apple staff will set you up with a suitable calling plan and provide you with a convenient way to make your chosen carrier that much richer each month. Then they'll offer to install the SIM card and activate the iPhone for you to eliminate the chance of your messing up the process.

If you turn down this kind offer, you can activate the iPhone by using your computer at home (or work, or wherever). We'll look at how to do this in the next section.

For a business, activating iPhones is more complicated. First, you probably won't want to go into your local Apple Store and clear the shelves of iPhones; nor will you want the VPs and power users stampeding to retail outlets, charging unsuitable consumer plans on their corporate cards, and then demanding you clean up the mess.

Instead, you'll likely want to talk to your country's carriers and pore through the details of the plans they provide, comparing their costs, advantages, and drawbacks just as you would when considering buying other equipment or services. If the carrier can provide iPhones with SIM cards installed and already activated, that'll save you time and effort. Otherwise, you'll need to activate the iPhones yourself.

Activating the iPhone Yourself

In many cases, the best option is to activate each iPhone yourself. This takes more effort, but it enables you to set up each iPhone with the certificates and configuration profiles it needs, thus avoiding support issues later on.

NOTE   If you need to activate a whole bunch of iPhones, put iTunes into activation-only mode, as described earlier in this chapter.

See the section "Installing the SIM Card and Activating the iPhone," a little later in this chapter, for details.

Having the User Activate the iPhone

The third option is to have the user activate the phone as a regular consumer does. This is a sensible option when the user works at a remote location and needs the iPhone before you can get it to her, or when you're managing the iPhones only loosely—for example, in a campus environment where the students buy the devices themselves.

Installing the SIM Card and Activating the iPhone

To start the process of activating the iPhone, install the SIM card if it's not already installed:

- **iPhone 4**   The iPhone 4 takes a micro-SIM that fits in its right side.
- **iPhone 3G and 3GS**   The iPhone 3G and 3GS take a SIM that fits into the top.

Whichever model you have, use the SIM eject tool (which comes folded cutely into the front of the cardboard information pack in the iPhone box) to open the SIM card tray: Press the end of the tool into the round hole gently but firmly until the tray comes open, then pick the tray out with your fingernails.

NOTE   The SIM eject tool is nearly as easy to lose as a needle in a haystack—but if you have a whole stack of iPhones to activate, you'll have plenty of eject tools to lose. Tether one to a convenient corner of your desk to keep it safe; or, if you lose them all, grab a paper clip instead, and pull the outside end free so that you can insert it in the hole on the iPhone.

Once you've removed the SIM card tray, insert the SIM or micro-SIM card in it. The card has an angled corner so that it'll fit in only one way (unless you force it really hard). Then slide the SIM card tray back into the iPhone. On the iPhone 4, you'll find the tray goes at a slight downward angle (when the iPhone's screen is facing up); just press the tray in until its edge is flush with the iPhone's case.

If you don't know whether the iPhone you're dealing with has a SIM card installed or not, you can either open the SIM card tray and find out, or simply turn the iPhone on. If the iPhone contains no SIM card, it displays the "No SIM card installed" message shown on the left in Figure 2-5. In this case, turn the iPhone off, open the SIM card tray, and insert a suitable SIM card.

When the iPhone notices the SIM card, it displays the "Connect to iTunes" screen, shown on the right in Figure 2-5.

Connect the USB end of the iPhone's cable to your PC or Mac, and then connect the Dock Connector end to the Dock Connector port on the iPhone. When the iPhone notices the computer, it displays the "Waiting for activation" message (shown on the left in Figure 2-6). As soon as it gets a grip on the network and manages activation, it displays the "iPhone is activated" message (shown on the right in Figure 2-6).

At this point, if you're running iTunes in activation-only mode, iTunes displays a message box telling you that the iPhone is activated and that you can eject it. Click the Eject button next to the iPhone's entry in the Source list in iTunes to eject the iPhone. You can then disconnect the Dock Connector from the iPhone.

 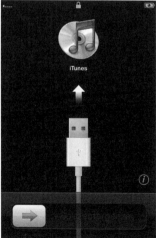

Figure 2-5.   The iPhone tells you if it has no SIM card installed (left). Once you've installed a SIM card, the iPhone prompts you to connect it to iTunes (right).

Figure 2-6.   The iPhone lets you know clearly when it is trying to activate itself (left) and when it has succeeded (right).

   NOTE   You may want to keep the iPhone connected so that you can configure it using iPhone Configuration Utility, as discussed in Chapter 3.

If you're running iTunes in normal mode, as you'd do when setting up an iPhone on your own computer, proceed as described in the next section.

Installing the SIM Card in the iPad

If the iPad is a 3G model, you'll normally want to install a SIM card in it so that you (or the user) can connect to the cellular network. You can install the SIM card either when you're first setting up the iPad or at any convenient point thereafter. You don't need to install a SIM card in order to get the iPad set up, but you can't connect the iPad to the cellular network until you do install a SIM card.

Like the iPhone 4G, the iPad uses a micro-SIM card and comes with a SIM eject tool cunningly hidden in the front of the cardboard information pack in the box. If you've lost the SIM eject tool and don't have another handy, straighten out the end of a paper clip and use that instead.

Press the end of the tool into the round hole on the left side of the iPad gently but firmly until the tray comes open, and then pick the tray out with your fingernails. Insert the micro-SIM card with the angled corner in the right place, and slide the SIM card tray back into the iPad. As on the iPhone 4, the tray goes in at a slight downward angle when the iPad's screen is facing up. Push the tray in until its edge is flush with the iPad's case, and you'll be in business.

Connect the iPad to the computer using its USB cable, and then set it up as described in the next section.

Setting Up the iPad and iPhone

After activation, the iPhone is ready to be set up. The iPad also needs to be set up, but it's ready for setup the moment you take it out of the box.

This section takes you through the steps involved in setting up an iPad or iPhone. Depending on the situation, you may want to set it up yourself (for example, because it's your iPad or iPhone), or you may prefer to have the user who will use the iPad or iPhone set it up so that he can use his own iTunes Store account for purchases.

To set up the iPad or iPhone, follow these steps:

1. At first, iTunes displays the Welcome To Your New iPad screen (see Figure 2-7).

NOTE You can skip the registration process by clicking the Register Later button on the Welcome To Your New iPad screen or the Welcome To Your New iPhone screen.

2. Click the Continue button to display the iPhone Software License Agreement screen.

3. Read as much as you dare (click the Save button if you want to save the agreement to a file for reference), and then select the I Have Read And Agree To The iPad Software License Agreement check box or the I Have Read And Agree To The iPhone Software License Agreement check box.

Figure 2-7. Once iTunes has recognized the iPad or iPhone, click the Continue button to start the registration process.

4. Click the Continue button to display the iTunes Account (Apple ID) screen (see Figure 2-8). From this screen, you can set up the iPad or iPhone to use an Apple ID. Unless you've set up users with individual iTunes accounts as part of a corporate account, you will normally want to have each user create his or her own account (or use his or her existing account).

5. From the iTunes Account (Apple ID) screen, take one of the following actions:

    ■ **Cancel the account setup**   If you don't want to associate the iPad or iPhone with an iTunes account at this point, click the Cancel button. iTunes may display an error message box such as that shown in Figure 2-9, telling you that it could not complete your iTunes Store request. Click the OK button.

    ■ **Set up the iPad or iPhone to use an existing Apple ID**   Select the Use My Apple ID To Register My iPad option button or the Use My Apple ID To Register My iPhone option button. Type your account details in the Apple ID text box and the Password text box, and then click the Continue button.

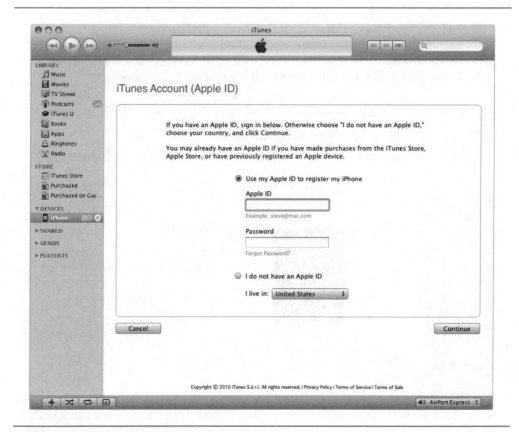

Figure 2-8.   On the iTunes Account (Apple ID) screen, you can start setting up the iPhone to use a particular iTunes account.

Figure 2-9.   This "iTunes Store request" error looks bad, but it's not a showstopper: It occurs when you cancel setting up an iTunes account for the iPad or iPhone. Click the OK button to restore normality.

- ■ **Create a new Apple ID**   Select the I Do Not Have An Apple ID option button. In the I Live In drop-down list or pop-up menu, choose your country (if in doubt, choose the country your credit card is registered in). Then click the Continue button, and follow through the process of creating an iTunes account.

6. Once you've dealt with the Apple ID question, iTunes displays the Set Up Your iPad screen (see Figure 2-10) or the Set Up Your iPhone screen.

Figure 2-10.   On the first Set Up Your iPad screen (shown here) or the first Set Up Your iPhone screen, you can choose to set up the iPad or iPhone as a new device or restore it from the backup of another device.

7. When you're setting up a new iPad or iPhone, select the Set Up As A New iPad option button or the Set Up As A New iPhone option button.

NOTE Instead of setting the iPad or iPhone up as a new device, you can select the Restore From The Backup Of option button and pick a backup from the drop-down list or pop-up menu. You can use this option either when you actually restore an iPad or iPhone to factory settings or when you're setting up a new iPad or iPhone and you want to load it with data backed up from another iPad or iPhone. See Chapter 10 for instructions on how to restore iPads and iPhones.

8. Click the Continue button to reach the next Set Up Your iPad screen or Set Up Your iPhone screen (see Figure 2-11).

9. In the Name text box, type the name for the iPad or iPhone. For devices you manage, you'll likely want to use a naming convention.

10. Select the Automatically Sync Songs To My iPad check box or the Automatically Sync Songs To My iPhone check box if you want iTunes to try to put all of the computer's iTunes music library on the iPad or iPhone. Normally, you'll want to clear this check box and have the user add music to the iPad or iPhone either manually or by synchronizing playlists.

11. Select the Automatically Add Photos To My iPad check box or the Automatically Add Photos To My iPhone check box if you want iTunes to add photos to the iPad or iPhone. On Windows, these photos come from folders you select; on the Mac, they come from your iPhoto library.

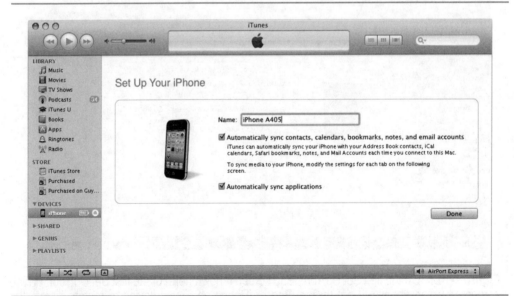

Figure 2-11. On the second Set Up Your iPhone screen (shown here) or Set Up Your iPad screen, name the iPhone or iPad and choose which items to sync automatically onto it.

12. Select the Automatically Sync Applications To My iPad check box or the Automatically Sync Applications To My iPhone check box if you want iTunes to automatically install each iPad or iPhone app you download using iTunes on the iPad or iPhone.

   ■ For an iPad or iPhone you're setting up on the computer with which it'll be used, it's a good idea to select this check box.

   ■ For an iPad or iPhone you're setting up on a different computer than the one with which it'll be used, clear this check box.

13. When you've made your choices on the Set Up Your iPad screen or the Set Up Your iPhone screen, click the Done button. iTunes synchronizes the data and apps you chose onto the device (see Figure 2-12).

Figure 2-12. Synchronizing the data and apps onto the iPad or iPhone for the first time may take a while, especially if you choose to sync songs and photos.

Updating the Carrier Settings on an iPad or iPhone

When you set up a 3G iPad or an iPhone, iTunes may display a message box telling you that an update to the device's carrier settings is available. Figure 2-13 shows an example for the iPad on the Mac.

Usually, you'll want to update the carrier settings to get the best performance from the cellular network. Click the Download And Update button in the dialog box to proceed with the installation.

The carrier settings typically involve only a small amount of data, so the update downloads and installs quickly. When the update is complete, iTunes displays a dialog box telling you that the settings have been updated successfully (see Figure 2-14).

By this point, the iPad or iPhone should be ready for use at the basic level—able to access the cellular network (unless it's a wireless-only iPad), and either ready to synchronize with iTunes or already synchronized.

So far, so good. But to make the iPad or iPhone a powerful work tool and a good citizen on your network, you'll usually want to configure it before putting it in the user's hands.

The next chapter shows you the fast and automated way of configuring the iPad and iPhone—by using iPhone Configuration Utility and configuration profiles. Turn the page when you're ready to get started.

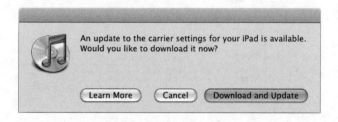

Figure 2-13.   If iTunes offers an update to the carrier settings on the iPad or iPhone, it's a good idea to apply them.

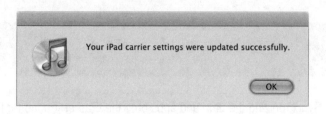

Figure 2-14.   iTunes confirms that the carrier settings have been updated successfully.

CHAPTER 3 | Configuring an iPad or iPhone Automatically

Whenation setting up a single iPad or iPhone in a home network, you can simply tap in the settings directly on the device. If your corporate network will have only a handful of iPads or iPhones, this approach may be practical (if not much fun). But if your network has many iPads and iPhones, you'll want to configure them automatically. To do so, you use the free iPhone Configuration Utility that Apple provides.

This chapter shows you how to get and install iPhone Configuration Utility and explains how you use it to configure iPads and iPhones automatically. You'll learn how to use iPhone Configuration Utility to create configuration profiles containing the settings you want to put on the devices. We'll look at some of the specific settings here, but we'll leave others until later chapters; for example, Chapter 4 discusses how to configure networking settings, Chapter 6 covers choosing e-mail settings and connecting to mail servers, and Chapter 9 talks you through setting up virtual private networking.

Toward the end of this chapter, I'll show you how to use iPhone Configuration Utility to apply configuration profiles directly to iPads and iPhones. This is the most straightforward way of getting the configuration profiles onto the devices, and you'll probably want to use it for at least some of the iPads and iPhones you manage. You can also apply configuration profiles to iPads and iPhones by distributing the profiles via e-mail or via web sites. This chapter looks briefly at these approaches, which you'll learn about in detail later in this book.

Let's start with getting and installing iPhone Configuration Utility.

Getting and Installing iPhone Configuration Utility

The first step is to get iPhone Configuration Utility from the Enterprise page on Apple's iPhone support site. Point your favorite browser at www.apple.com/support/iphone/enterprise/, and then download iPhone Configuration Utility for Windows or iPhone Configuration Utility for Mac OS X, as needed. The next section covers Windows, and the section after that covers Mac OS X.

Downloading and Installing iPhone Configuration Utility for Windows

iPhone Configuration Utility for Windows runs on Windows XP Service Pack 3, Windows Vista, Windows 7, Windows Server 2003, or Windows Server 2008. You can install iPhone Configuration Utility on either a workstation or a server, so you'll probably want to use the PC from which you normally administer the network—for example, your go-everywhere laptop.

After the download completes, run the file. Depending on the browser you're using, you'll normally have to go through a security warning before you can install the application. For example, in the Internet Explorer – Security Warning dialog box shown in Figure 3-1, you can check the application's digital signature before installing it.

Choosing Whether to Run iPhone Configuration Utility on a Windows Server or Workstation

Although iPhone Configuration Utility does install and run on Windows Server 2008 R2, you'll usually do better to run it on a workstation instead—for example, the PC you usually use for administering the network.

If you do choose to use iPhone Configuration Utility on Windows Server 2008 R2, make sure that the .NET Framework 3.5 Service Pack 1 is installed first. To check that .NET Framework 3.5 Service Pack 1 is installed, follow these steps:

1. Launch Server Manager. For example, choose Start | Administrative Tools | Server Manager.

2. In the left pane, click the Features item to display the Features pane.

3. Make sure that an item called .NET Framework 3.5.1 Features appears in the Features list.

If you find .NET Framework 3.5 Service Pack 1 is not installed, follow these steps to install it:

1. In the Features pane in Server Manager, click the Add Features link to launch the Add Features Wizard.

2. In the Features list box, click the + sign next to the .NET Framework 3.5.1 Features item to expand the entry. (Don't just select the check box next to this item—otherwise, the Add Features Wizard will spring to life, offering to install extra role services and features.)

3. Select the .NET Framework 3.5.1 check box.

4. Click the Next button, and then follow through the installation procedure.

Figure 3-1.   As with most applications you download from the Internet, check that you've got the right file before installing it. Click the Publisher link to display the digital signature for verifying the file.

The installation process is straightforward and unremarkable. To avoid conflicts and grumbles, it's best to close all the programs you're running before you start the installation. As usual, you must accept the license agreement if you want to proceed. On the Installation Options screen (see Figure 3-2), you can click the Change button if you want to choose a destination folder, but you shouldn't need to, as the default folder (an iPhone Configuration Utility in your Program Files folder) is usually a solid bet.

When the installation finishes, click the Finish button to close the installer, and then launch iPhone Configuration Utility from the Start menu—choose Start | iPhone Configuration Utility | iPhone Configuration Utility.

TIP   If you'll use iPhone Configuration Utility frequently, pin it to your Taskbar (in Windows 7) or to the Start menu (in any version of Windows that iPhone Configuration Utility will run on).

Move ahead to the next main section unless you're also interested in installing iPhone Configuration Utility on Mac OS X.

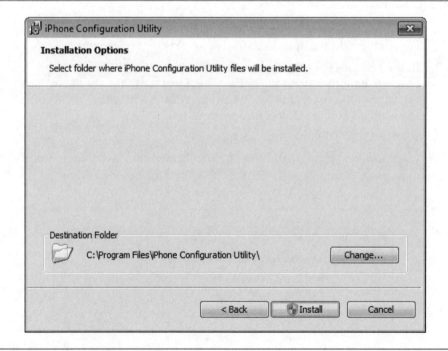

Figure 3-2.   You can change the installation folder for iPhone Configuration Utility, but that's the full extent of the excitement.

Downloading and Installing iPhone Configuration Utility for Mac OS X

IPhone Configuration Utility for Mac OS X runs on Mac OS X version 10.6 (Snow Leopard). You can install it on either the client version or the Server version of Mac OS X. Usually, installing iPhone Configuration Utility on the Mac you use to administer the network is the best bet.

When you download iPhone Configuration Utility for Mac OS X, you get a disk image (.dmg) file, as usual. Depending on how you've set up your Mac, your browser may open the disk image for you and launch Installer; if not, double-click the disk image to open it, and then double-click the iPhoneConfigurationUtility.pkg file to open Installer.

Follow through the Installer steps. After you accept the license agreement, your only decision (see Figure 3-3) is whether to install iPhone Configuration Utility on your Mac's hard drive or on another drive. Unless you need to install iPhone Configuration Utility on a disk that you carry with you, the Mac's hard drive should be fine.

On the screen called "The installation was completed successfully," click the Close button. You can then run iPhone Configuration Utility from the /Applications/ Utilities/ folder (or from Spotlight, if you find that more convenient).

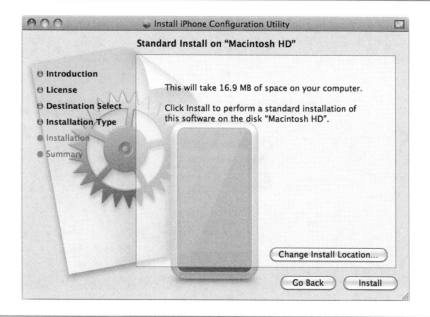

Figure 3-3. Click the Change Install Location button on the Standard Install screen if you need to install iPhone Configuration Utility on a different disk.

Meeting the iPhone Configuration Utility Interface

When you open iPhone Configuration Utility from the Start menu (on Windows) or the Applications folder (on the Mac), it looks pretty much the same on either operating system. Figure 3-4 shows iPhone Configuration Utility running on Windows and with an iPhone connected.

The iPhone Configuration Utility window contains a toolbar, the Source list, and the Details pane. The following sections introduce you to what these items do.

The Toolbar

The toolbar in the iPhone Configuration Utility contains buttons for adding items (devices, provisioning profiles, and apps) or creating new configuration profiles, sharing the current item, exporting the current item, and toggling between displaying and hiding the detail for the current item. There's also a Search box that you can use to search by various items—for example, by phone number, identifier, or e-mail address.

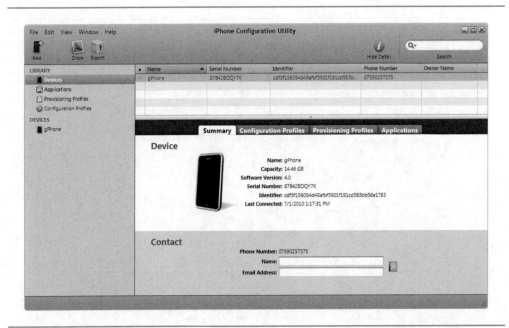

Figure 3-4. iPhone Configuration Utility automatically detects any iPads, iPhones, or iPod touches connected to your PC or Mac.

NOTE If you find you don't use the toolbar, you can hide it by choosing View | Hide Toolbar or pressing CTRL-ALT-T on Windows or ⌘-OPTION-T on the Mac. On the Mac, you can also click the jellybean button at the right end of the title bar to toggle the display of the toolbar. When you need the toolbar back, choose View | Show Toolbar, press the keyboard shortcut again, or (on the Mac) click the jellybean button once more.

The Source List

On the left side of the iPhone Configuration Utility window is the Source list, which works in a similar way to the Source list in other Apple applications—for example, iTunes or iPhoto.

At the top of the source list is the Library section. This section always appears, and it contains four items:

- **Devices** The Devices pane lists all the devices—iPads, iPhones, and iPod touches—that you've connected to your computer or added by using mobile configuration files. You can click a device in the list to display its configuration screens—a Summary tab that provides the device's essential information, a Configuration Profiles tab that you use to see which configuration profiles are installed on the device, a Provisioning Profiles tab that shows you which provisioning profiles are installed on it, and an Applications tab that lists the apps installed.

- **Applications** The Applications pane lists the custom apps that you have added to iPhone Configuration Utility so that you can install them on devices. These custom apps are ones you've developed, not ones you've hauled down from the App Store on the iTunes Store.

- **Provisioning Profiles** The Provisioning Profiles pane lists the provisioning profiles you've created for installing custom apps on the devices. If you don't need to install custom apps on the devices, you don't need to use provisioning profiles.

- **Configuration Profiles** The Configuration Profiles pane lists the configuration profiles you've created (as described later in this chapter) for configuring the devices.

Below the Library section, the Devices section appears when one or more devices is connected. This section shows an entry for each device.

The Detail Pane

The Detail pane (which you see in the lower part of Figure 3-4) shows the detail about the item that's currently selected. For example, if you click the Devices item in the Library category of the Source list, and then click a device in the main list, the Detail pane shows the details about that device.

You can toggle the display of the Detail pane by clicking the Show Detail button on the toolbar or the Hide Detail button that replaces it when the Detail pane is displayed. You can also choose View | Show Detail or View | Hide Detail, or press CTRL-I (on Windows) or ⌘-I (on the Mac).

Understanding Applications, Configuration Profiles, and Provisioning Profiles

You use iPhone Configuration Utility to work with applications, configuration profiles, and provisioning profiles. Here's what these three items are:

■ **Applications**   An *application*, usually referred to simply as an *app* in the context of iPhone OS (iOS), is a program you install on the iPad or iPhone—anything from a word-processor app to a utility app to a game. You can add either apps from Apple's App Store or apps your company develops.

■ **Configuration profile**   A *configuration profile* is a file that contains details of the device's configuration and what it's allowed to do—for example, connect to your wireless network and access your Exchange server. You use the configuration profile to set up the device automatically rather than needing to change its settings manually. This chapter shows you the essentials of creating configuration profiles and the easiest means of installing them.

■ **Provisioning profile**   A *provisioning profile* is a file that contains the information needed to install an app on an iPad or iPhone. The apps you buy (or get free) from Apple's App Store come with their own provisioning profiles, so you have to create a provisioning profile only if you need to install custom apps you've developed. To create a provisioning profile, you need to sign up with Apple's Developer program for iOS. This gives you a digital certificate that you use to sign the provisioning profile with a digital signature, so that the iPad or iPhone can tell it's from an approved developer rather than J. Random Hacker.

NOTE   Chapter 5 explains how to create provisioning profiles and install apps with them.

Creating a Configuration Profile

To configure an iPad or iPhone automatically, you create a *configuration profile*. This is an XML file that contains details of the settings and restrictions you want to apply to the device. The configuration profile contains *payloads*, groups of settings for different aspects of the configuration. For example, a configuration file can contain one payload of e-mail settings and another payload of settings for virtual private networking.

Planning Your Configuration Profiles

For most deployments, your first move should be to plan which configuration profiles you need to create and what their contents should be.

If you're deploying only one type of device (for example, the iPad), and all the users will have similar needs, you may be able to get away with a single configuration profile. But in most cases you'll want to create different configuration profiles for the different devices and the different groups of users who will use them. For example, users of your iPad Sales Roving configuration profile may get VPN access to the network, while users of your iPad Sales In-House configuration profile won't need to be able to access the network from outside.

 TIP In many cases, it's useful to create a base configuration profile that applies to all the devices (or to all iPads, or all iPhones), and then use further configuration profiles to add other features as needed.

Draw up a list of the groups who will use iPads and iPhones, both right now and in the future—if your deployment is successful, odds are that other groups will want to use iPhones and iPads in the future, so you may as well plan for it. List the features and apps that each group will need, and determine which payloads you'll use (see the table of payloads in the next section). Again, try to anticipate future demands as well as planning to meet current demands.

Unless your workplace is seriously informal (or even if it is), you'll probably want to use a naming convention for your configuration profiles so that you can instantly grasp which device and which group of users a profile is for.

Understanding the Types of Payloads You Can Create

Table 3-1 provides an overview of the types of payloads you can add to a configuration profile. We'll look at most of these payload types in detail later in this chapter, leaving some of the more complex ones (Wi-Fi, VPN, Email, and Exchange ActiveSync) to later chapters that dig into those topics in depth.

Starting a Configuration Profile and Setting Its General Information

Now that you've made your plan and you have a rough idea of the payloads you can create, start a new configuration profile and set its General information—the profile's name and identifier, your organization's name, the description of the profile, and the type of security you want it to have.

To start the profile and set the General information, follow these steps:

1. In the Library section of the Source list, click the Configuration Profiles item. iPhone Configuration Utility displays the list of configuration profiles. If you're just getting started, this list will be empty.

2. Click the New button on the toolbar or choose File | New Configuration Profile; you can also press CTRL-N on Windows or ⌘-N on the Mac. iPhone Configuration Utility creates a new configuration profile and displays the controls for editing it (see Figure 3-5).

Payload Type	What the Payload Contains
General	Essential information including the configuration profile's name, identifier, and whether the user is allowed to remove it. This payload identifies the configuration profile and is required; all the others are optional.
Passcode	Settings for requiring the user to create a passcode for protecting the iPad or iPhone against unauthorized access.
Restrictions	Settings for turning off some of the iPad's or iPhone's built-in features and preventing the user from accessing explicit content in the iTunes Store.
Wi-Fi	Settings for connecting to one or more wireless networks.
VPN	Settings for connecting to one or more virtual private networks.
Email	Settings for connecting to one or more POP or IMAP mail servers.
Exchange ActiveSync	Settings for connecting to one or more Exchange servers.
LDAP	Settings for connecting to one or more LDAP servers to access directory information.
CalDAV	Settings for connecting to one or more CalDAV servers to access calendar information.
CardDAV	Settings for connecting to one or more CardDAV servers to access address information.
Subscribed Calendars	Settings for subscribing to one or more calendars published on the network or Internet.
Web Clips	Web clips (shortcuts to web sites) to add to the iPad's or iPhone's Home screen.
Credentials	Digital certificates to install on the iPad or iPhone.
SCEP	Settings for connecting to a Simple Certificate Enrollment Protocol (SCEP) server to acquire certificates.
Mobile Device Management	Settings for connecting to Mobile Device Management servers that will manage the device remotely.
Advanced	Settings for specifying the carrier access point to which the iPhone connects.

Table 3-1.   Types of Payloads You Can Add to a Configuration Profile

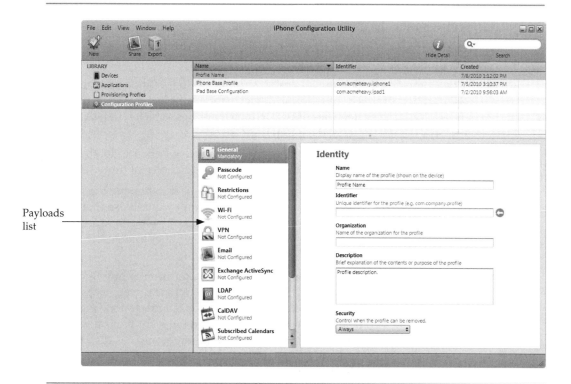

Figure 3-5. You're ready to edit a new configuration profile in iPhone Configuration Utility.

3. Make sure the General item is selected in the Payloads list.

4. In the Name text box, type the name you want to use for the profile.

   ■ This is the name that appears in the Name list in the upper pane.

   ■ As discussed in the previous section, you'll probably want to use a naming convention for your profiles so that you can easily distinguish them.

NOTE   The payload configuration panes display a red circle containing a white arrow next to each required field to help you avoid missing them.

5. In the Identifier text box, type the unique identifier you want to use for the profile—for example, **com.acmevirtualindustries.iphone1**. This identifier appears in the Identifier list in the upper pane.

6. In the Organization text box, type the name of your company or organization.

7. In the Description text box, type a description of this profile to help you distinguish it from the other profiles you create.

   ■ The description is optional, but it's useful to enter one even if you use a well-thought-out naming convention.

   ■ To make the description most helpful, summarize the settings that the configuration profile applies to the device—for example, whether it uses a passcode, which categories of restrictions it applies, which wireless networks the Wi-Fi payload contains, and so on.

8. In the Security drop-down list or pop-up menu, choose whether to let the user remove the profile from the iPad or iPhone. You have a choice of three settings:

   ■ **Always**   Choose the Always setting to allow the user to remove the profile without having to authenticate. Normally, you won't want to use this setting for managed devices, but it's useful in a campus-type environment in which the iPads and iPhones belong to the users rather than to the company or organization.

   ■ **Never**   Choose the Never setting to prevent the user from removing the profile from the iPad or iPhone. The user can still update the device with a newer version of the profile that overwrites the existing version. You can remove the profile by connecting the device to the computer on which you're running iPhone Configuration Utility and removing it as discussed in the section "Removing a Configuration Profile by Using iPhone Configuration Utility," later in this chapter.

   ■ **With Authentication**   Choose the With Authentication setting to allow the user to remove the profile from the iPad or iPhone provided that they can furnish suitable authentication. Type the password in the Authorization Password text box that iPhone Configuration Utility displays. This setting is useful when you need users to be able to remove the profile after contacting you for the password, or when support techs need to remove the profile directly from the device rather than using iPhone Configuration Utility.

 NOTE   iPhone Configuration Utility automatically saves the changes you make to a configuration profile. You don't need to save the changes manually.

After setting the General information like this, set the payloads by following the instructions in the following sections as needed. For example, if you want to create a configuration profile that contains only Wi-Fi, VPN, and Email payloads, follow the instructions in only those sections.

Until you set up a payload for an item, the words Not Configured appear under it; when you've created one or more payloads, iPhone Configuration Utility shows the details (for example, 2 Payloads Configured) under the item. If you need to remove a payload, click it in the Payloads pane, and then click the – (Remove) button in the upper-right corner

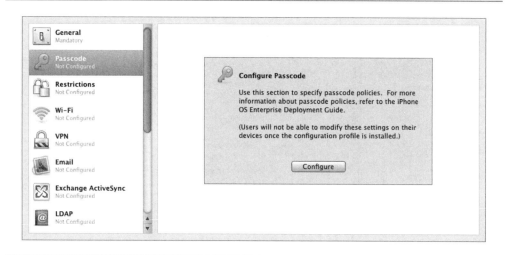

Figure 3-6. Click an item in the Payloads list to display the Configure pane, and then click the Configure button to access the settings.

of the configuration pane. You can't remove the General payload from a configuration profile, as this payload is required.

When you click an item you haven't yet configured, iPhone Configuration Utility displays a Configure pane for the item. This pane contains an explanation of the item and the Configure button. When you click the Configure button, iPhone Configuration Utility creates a payload with default settings, and then displays the payload configuration pane so that you can customize the settings. Figure 3-6 shows the Configure Passcode pane.

Creating a Passcode Payload

To keep your iPads and iPhones secure, always protect them with a passcode that the user must enter before using the device. To apply a passcode, you create a passcode payload in the configuration profile.

To create a passcode payload, follow these steps:

1. Click the Passcode item in the Payloads list. The right pane displays the Configure Passcode Policy box. Click the Configure button to display the screen shown in Figure 3-7.

2. Select the Require Passcode On Device check box to activate the other controls.

3. Select the Allow Simple Value check box if you want to allow users to use repeating sequences (such as 1111), ascending sequences (such as 1234), or descending sequences (such as 9876) as the passcode.

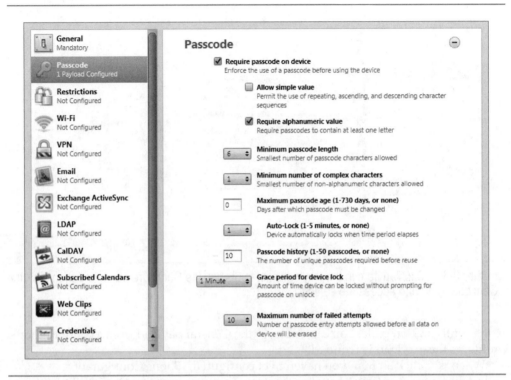

Figure 3-7. To protect the iPad or iPhone, you'll probably want to lock it with a passcode.

4. Select the Require Alphanumeric Value check box if you want to force the passcode to include one or more letters instead of just numbers. Including letters makes the passcode much stronger, so it's a good idea from a security viewpoint—but it does make the passcode harder to type in.

5. Open the Minimum Passcode Length drop-down list or pop-up menu and set the length for the shortest passcode you'll allow:

   ■ To use passcodes effectively, you need to balance security needs against what you can reasonably expect each user to type each time he or she needs to use the iPad or iPhone.

   ■ Four to six characters usually works reasonably well as a minimum, especially if you set a fairly low number for the Maximum Number Of Failed Attempts setting.

6. Open the Minimum Number Of Complex Characters drop-down list or pop-up menu and set the minimum number of symbols the passcode must contain.

   ■ Forcing the user to include a symbol creates a stronger passcode, which helps make it hard for a would-be intruder to break into an iPad or iPhone—but including a symbol makes the passcode that much harder to type in.

   ■ If you make the user include a symbol in the passcode, one symbol is usually enough.

7. In the Maximum Passcode Age text box, enter the number of days you will allow the passcode to last:

   ■ Enter 0 (zero) to let the passcode last forever, or until the user chooses to change it of her own volition. Unless you have a reason to force the user to change the passcode periodically (see the nearby sidebar), this is a good choice.

   ■ Enter a number between 1 and 730 to make the passcode last that number of days, and then force the user to change it.

8. Open the Auto-Lock drop-down list or pop-up menu and set the number of minutes after which the iPad or iPhone should lock itself automatically. You can set from 1 to 5 minutes. You can turn off Auto-Lock by choosing the 0 (zero) setting, but this is seldom a good idea except for special needs—for example, iPads you're using in a lab or demonstration environment.

9. In the Passcode History text box, enter the number of different passcodes the user must use before being allowed to repeat a passcode they've used before. You can set any number between 1 and 50. If you want users to be able to reuse passcodes freely, set 0 (zero).

Should You Force Users to Change Passwords and Passcodes Regularly?

Some security experts recommend forcing users to change their passwords and passcodes regularly—for example, every 30 days. Other security experts argue that there's no reason to change passwords and passcodes unless you suspect they may have been compromised; in this case, you must change the password or passcode immediately, rather than waiting until the end of whichever arbitrary time period you've chosen.

The main benefit to changing a password or passcode regularly is that it cuts out an attacker who has learned the password or passcode and is using it to snoop on the network without making changes.

10. Open the Grace Period For Device Lock drop-down list or pop-up menu and set the period during which the user can unlock the iPad or iPhone without having to enter the passcode.

■ Your choices are None, 1 Minute, 5 Minutes, 15 Minutes, 1 Hour, and 4 Hours.

■ Either 1 Minute or 5 Minutes is usually a good choice for typical users.

■ Use the None setting only if you need exceptionally tight security on the iPads and iPhones. Otherwise, having to enter the passcode each time may dissuade users from using the device to take quick notes or refer to materials. Usually, half the point of having an iPad or iPhone is that you can turn it on instantly and use it wherever you are.

11. Open the Maximum Number Of Failed Attempts drop-down list or pop-up menu and set the number of passcode failures you will accept before the iPad or iPhone automatically erases its contents.

■ You can set any number from 4 to 16 attempts. Choose the -- setting if you don't want to use the automatic erasure feature.

■ The stronger the passcode requirements you set, the higher the number of failed attempts you'll normally want to use to avoid having the devices erased because of the user's clumsy typing.

NOTE   After several failed attempts to enter the passcode, iOS locks the iPad or iPhone for several minutes. This delay both gives genuine users a pause to realize they've been using the wrong passcode and makes it harder for malefactors to break the passcode by using many attempts.

■ When the user enters the wrong passcode, he receives a Wrong Passcode: Try Again message, but no indication that an automatic wipe may be imminent. It's a good idea to explain to users about the automatic wipe so that they know what will happen if they keep hammering in the wrong passcode.

NOTE   To create stronger passcode requirements, select the Require Alphanumeric Value check box, set a longer minimum length in the Minimum Passcode Length download or pop-up menu, and require one or more complex characters in the Minimum Number Of Complex Characters drop-down list or pop-up menu.

Creating a Restrictions Payload

The next type of payload you can configure is a Restrictions payload to limit the use of specific features that may undermine the user's morals or productivity, or the security of your company or your data.

To create a Restrictions payload, follow these steps:

1. Click the Restrictions item in the Payloads list, and then click the Configure button in the Configure Restrictions box. iPhone Configuration Utility displays the Restrictions pane (see Figure 3-8).

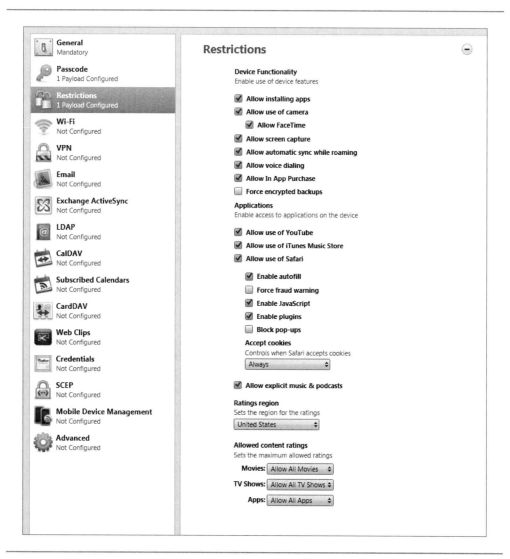

Figure 3-8.   Configure a Restrictions payload to turn off iPad and iPhone features that may cause problems for the user or for your company.

2. In the Device Functionality area, select or clear the check boxes to control which functions are available to the user:

    ■ **Allow Installing Apps**   Clear this check box if you need to prevent the user from installing apps. This is usually a good idea for iPads and iPhones you manage tightly.

    ■ **Allow Use Of Camera**   Clear this check box if you want to turn off the camera on an iPhone. Clearing this check box removes the Camera icon from the Home screen. If you leave the Allow Use Of Camera check box selected, you can choose whether to select or clear the Allow FaceTime check box, which controls whether the user can make video calls with the FaceTime feature.

    ■ **Allow Screen Capture**   Clear this check box if you want to turn off the device's built-in Screen Capture feature. Screen Capture is usually useful for capturing anything from sections of web pages to error messages that appear, but you may want to prevent the user from capturing screens of confidential data. (That said, you'll have a tough time preventing the user from writing down the data or memorizing it.)

TIP   If you allow the use of Screen Capture, make sure users know it's available and how to use it. To take a screen capture, hold down the power button, press the Home button so that the screen flashes, and then release the power button. To view the screen captures, open the Photos app, and then open the Camera Roll album (on an iPhone) or the Saved Photos album (on an iPad). From here, you can use or send the screen capture like any other photo.

    ■ **Allow Automatic Sync While Roaming**   Clear this check box if you want to prevent the iPhone or iPad 3G from synchronizing automatically while it is using Data Roaming. Shoveling data unnecessarily across the 3G connection can rack up charges, so you may want to clear this check box—especially for iPads and iPhones that travel abroad.

    ■ **Allow Voice Dialing**   Clear this check box if you want to prevent the user from using the Voice Dialing feature. Voice Dialing is pretty neat, but it can be indiscreet in public.

    ■ **Allow In App Purchase**   Clear this check box if you want to prevent the user from making purchases from inside apps.

    ■ **Force Encrypted Backups**   Select this check box if you want to make iTunes encrypt backups of the iPad or iPhone.

3. In the Applications area, clear the Allow Use Of YouTube check box if you want to prevent the user from conducting research on YouTube.

4. Also in the Applications area, clear the Allow Use Of iTunes Music Store check box if you want to prevent the user from browsing the iTunes Store and buying items.

5. Still in the Applications area, clear the Allow Use Of Safari check box if you want to prevent the user from using Safari. (The user can still use any other browser you have installed or that you allow them to install.) If you do allow the use of Safari, use the check boxes below it to control what the user can do with it:

   ■ **Enable Autofill**   Clear this check box if you want to prevent Safari from storing the user's entries in web forms and inserting them automatically when the user displays a form again. Autofill can save time and effort, but it can also reduce your security.

   ■ **Force Fraud Warning**   Select this check box to turn Safari's Fraud Warning feature on and prevent the user from turning it off. This is usually a good idea.

   ■ **Enable JavaScript**   Clear this check box if you want to prevent Safari from running JavaScript on web sites that use it. JavaScript can perform many useful functions, but it can also be used to attack computers, so you may want to disable JavaScript if you need tight security.

   ■ **Enable Plugins**   Clear this check box if you want to prevent Safari from using plug-ins to add extra functionality.

   ■ **Block Pop-Ups**   Select this check box if you want to prevent web pages from displaying pop-up messages. Pop-ups can be a headache, especially if the user wanders onto the wilder side of the Web; but many reputable sites use pop-ups to provide extra information. So it's tough to decide whether to block pop-ups. Consider allowing them until you find users running into trouble with them.

   ■ **Accept Cookies**   In this drop-down list or pop-up menu, choose which cookies Safari should accept from web sites trying to track what Safari is doing. You can choose Never to block all cookies, but this prevents many sites (including reputable ones such as Amazon.com) from working correctly. In most cases, the best choice is From Visited Sites, which allows first-party cookies (from the sites the user actually goes to) but not third-party cookies that advertisers and special marketing partners try to slip into the cookie jar. The third choice is Always, which makes Safari accept any cookie offered to it; this setting is too wide-eyed and trusting for safe use of the Web.

6. In the Ratings Region area, open the drop-down list or pop-up menu and choose the region to use for ratings. The default setting is United States.

7. In the Allowed Content Ratings area, open each of the three drop-down lists or pop-up menus—Movies, TV Shows, and Apps—in turn, and choose the upper level of content rating you're prepared to allow. The options available depend on the Ratings Region setting you choose. For example, if you choose United States, the Movies drop-down list or pop-up menu offers the choices Don't Allow Movies, G, PG, PG-13, R, NC-17, and Allow All Movies.

CAUTION   The Allowed Content Ratings settings affect only the iTunes Store. They have no effect on other apps. If you want to prevent the user wallowing in the mire of turpitude we call the Internet, turn off Safari and YouTube, as discussed earlier in this section.

Creating a Wi-Fi Payload

To set up the Wi-Fi network or networks the iPad or iPhone can connect to, click the Wi-Fi item in the Payloads list, and then click the Configure button in the Configure Wi-Fi pane that appears. iPhone Configuration Utility then displays the Wi-Fi pane (shown in Figure 3-9 with some settings chosen), and you can set up a network.

For a wireless network that uses WPA security (or WEP security, for those who like to live dangerously), the settings are straightforward: You type the SSID in the Service Set Identifier text box, select the Hidden Network check box if the network is hidden, choose the security type in the Security Type drop-down list or pop-up menu, and then type the password in the Password text box.

For the Enterprise security types, the settings are more involved. We'll look at them in detail in Chapter 4, which covers networking.

NOTE   After setting up the first network, you can click the + (Add) button in the upper-right corner of the Wi-Fi pane to add another network. To remove a network, display it in the Wi-Fi pane, and then click the – (Remove) button.

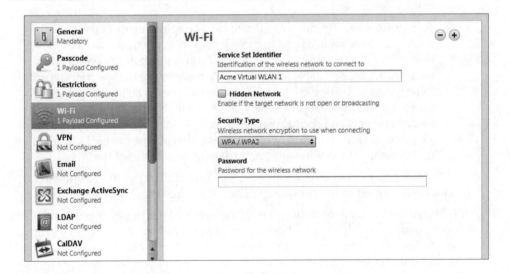

Figure 3-9.   Use the Wi-Fi pane to add the details for one or more wireless networks to the iPad or iPhone.

Creating a VPN Payload

If the iPads and iPhones will need to connect to your network via virtual private networking, you can add a VPN payload to the configuration profile. To do so, click the VPN item in the Payloads list, and then click the Configure button in the Configure VPN pane that appears. iPhone Configuration Utility displays the VPN pane (shown in Figure 3-10 with basic settings chosen), in which you can enter the details of the VPN connection.

We'll look at how to choose the right settings for your needs in Chapter 9. The iPad and iPhone support five connection types (L2TP, PPTP, Cisco IPSec, Cisco AnyConnect, and Juniper SSL) and various means of authentication, giving you a fair amount of flexibility in setting them up to suit your remote-access arrangements.

Creating an E-Mail Payload

For e-mail, the iPad and iPhone can connect to IMAP or POP e-mail servers or to Exchange servers. To set up e-mail on IMAP or POP servers, click the Email item in the Payloads list, and then click the Configure button in the Configure Email box that appears. iPhone Configuration Utility displays the Email pane (see Figure 3-11), in which you specify the details of the e-mail account.

Chapter 6 looks in detail at how to set up e-mail.

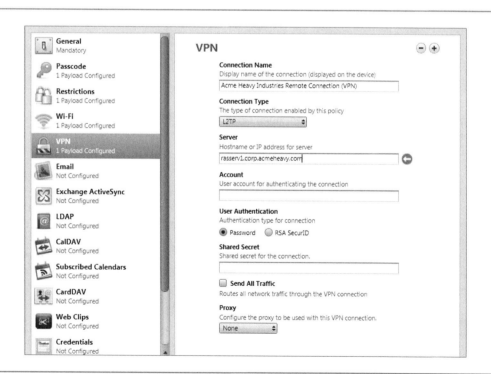

Figure 3-10.   In the VPN pane, set up one or more virtual private network connections for the iPad or iPhone.

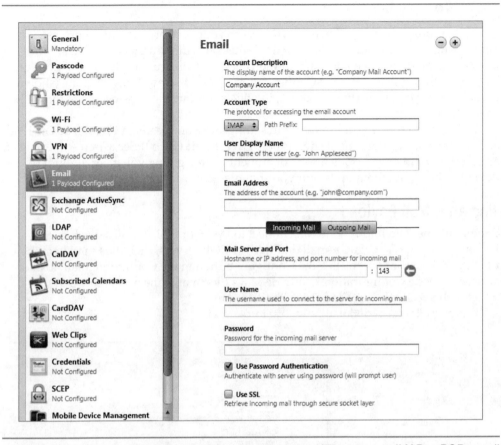

Figure 3-11. Use the Email pane in iPhone Configuration Utility to set up IMAP or POP e-mail accounts for the iPad or iPhone.

Setting Up an Exchange ActiveSync Payload

If your iPhones or iPads will need to connect to a server running Microsoft Exchange, you can include an Exchange ActiveSync payload for the configuration file. Click the Exchange ActiveSync item in the Payloads list, and then click the Configure button in the Configure Exchange ActiveSync box that appears. iPhone Configuration Utility displays the Exchange ActiveSync pane (see Figure 3-12), in which you choose settings for the account.

Chapter 6 discusses how to set up Exchange ActiveSync accounts and how to troubleshoot problems that occur with them.

Figure 3-12.   You can add an Exchange ActiveSync payload to a configuration profile.

Setting Up an LDAP Payload

If the iPad or iPhone will need to connect to an LDAP directory, configure an LDAP payload to set it up. Click the LDAP item in the Payloads list to display the Configure LDAP box, and then click the Configure button. In the LDAP pane (see Figure 3-13), choose settings like this:

1. Type a friendly name for the account in the Account Description text box—for example, **Company Directory**.

2. Optionally, type the username in the Account Username text box and the password in the Account Password text box.

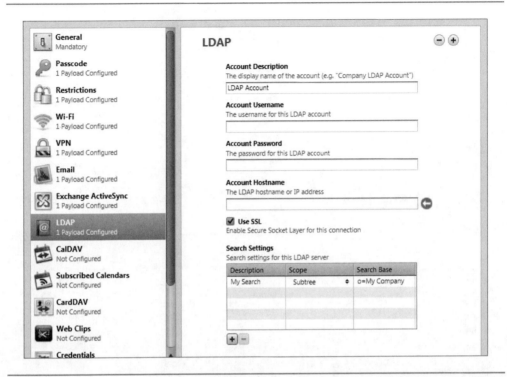

Figure 3-13. You can set up an LDAP payload to enable the iPad or iPhone to connect to an LDAP directory.

3. Type the hostname or IP address of the LDAP server in the Account Hostname text box.

4. Select the Use SSL check box if you want to secure the connection using Secure Sockets Layer, as is usually wise.

5. In the Search Settings list box, double-click the default name for the first entry, and then type the name you want to use. In the Scope column, use the drop-down list or pop-up menu to set the scope of the search by choosing the appropriate item (see Figure 3-14):

- **Base** Select Base to restrict the searches to the base object. This makes the searches run fastest, but users may not find the objects they're looking for.

- **One Level** Select One Level to search one level below the base object. This increases the search scope somewhat, but not all the way. Searches should still run pretty fast.

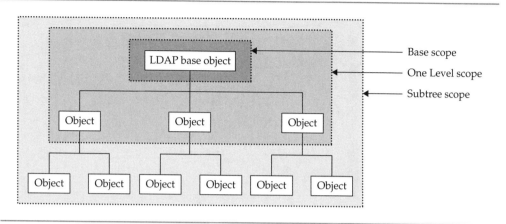

Figure 3-14.   You can choose whether the iPad and iPhone search only the Base object, One Level down, or the entire Subtree of an LDAP directory.

■ **Subtree**   Select Subtree to search the base object and all objects descended from it. This gives you the widest search, so it's the most likely to return the results users are looking for. The disadvantage is that searches will take longer.

 NOTE   You can click the + (Add) button below the Search Settings list box to add another search setting.

If necessary, click the + (Add) button in the upper-right corner of the LDAP pane to add another LDAP item, and then follow the preceding steps to choose settings for it. If you need to remove an LDAP item, display it in the LDAP pane, and then click the – (Remove) button.

Setting Up a CalDAV Payload

You can also set up the iPad or iPhone to connect to a calendaring server that uses the CalDAV protocol so that the device's Calendar app can exchange calendar data with the server.

Click the CalDAV item in the Payloads list to display the Configure CalDAV box, and then click the Configure button. Follow these steps to choose settings in the CalDAV pane (see Figure 3-15):

1. Type a descriptive name in the Account Description text box—for example, **Company Calendars** or **Shared Calendars Account**.

2. Type the CalDAV server's hostname or IP address in the left Account Hostname And Port text box, and change the port in the right text box if necessary.

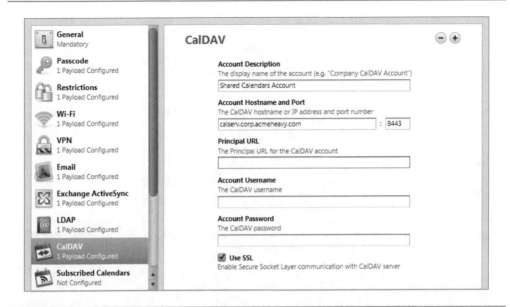

Figure 3-15. Use the CalDAV pane to set up an iPad or iPhone to connect to your CalDAV server.

3. To direct the iPad or iPhone to a particular URL, enter it in the Principal URL text box.

4. If you're creating this profile for a particular user, type the CalDAV user name in the Account Username text box and the corresponding password in the Account Password text box. Otherwise, leave these text boxes blank so that the device prompts the user for the name and password.

5. Select the Use SSL check box if you want to secure the connection with Secure Sockets Layer. This is usually a good idea.

If you want to add another CalDAV item, click the + (Add) button, and then repeat the preceding steps. To remove a CalDAV item, display it in the CalDAV pane, and then click the – (Remove) button.

Setting Up a Subscribed Calendars Payload

To subscribe the iPad or iPhone to one or more calendars that are published on the Internet or a local network, click the Subscribed Calendars item in the Payloads list to display the Configure Calendar Subscriptions Policy box, and then click the Configure button. iPhone Configuration Utility displays the Subscribed Calendar pane (see Figure 3-16).

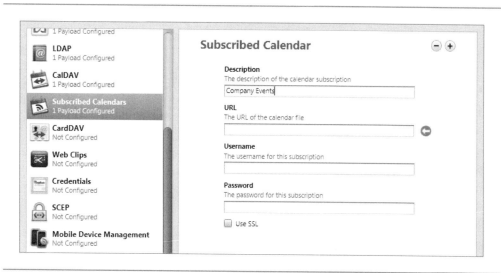

Figure 3-16.   You can also subscribe the iPad or iPhone to published calendars—for instance, a calendar of company events.

You can then choose settings like this:

1. Type a descriptive name in the Description text box.

2. Type the calendar's URL in the URL text box.

3. If this profile is for a single user, type the username in the Username text box, and the password in the Password text box. Otherwise, leave these text boxes blank, so that the device prompts the user to enter them.

4. Select the Use SSL check box if you want to secure the connection with Secure Sockets Layer. For a company calendar, you'll probably want to use SSL to make sure outsiders don't glom on; for a public calendar (for example, a calendar of public holidays), you probably won't.

If you want to add another subscribed calendar, click the + (Add) button, and then repeat the preceding steps. To remove a subscribed calendar, display it in the Subscribed Calendars pane, and then click the – (Remove) button.

Setting Up a CardDAV Payload

If your users will connect to a CardDAV server, create a CardDAV payload. Click the CardDAV item in the Payloads list to display the Configure CardDAV box, and then click the Configure button. iPhone Configuration Utility displays the CardDAV pane (see Figure 3-17).

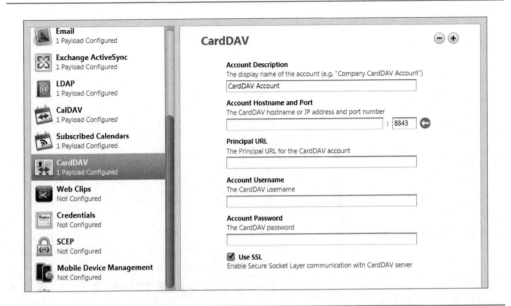

Figure 3-17. Create a CardDAV payload in the CardDAV pane if your users will connect to a CardDAV server.

You can then choose settings like this:

1. Type a descriptive name in the Account Description text box.

2. In the Account Hostname text box, type the IP address or hostname of the CardDAV server. In the Port text box, either accept the default port (8843) or type the port your server is using.

3. In the Principal URL text box, type the CardDAV account's principal URL.

4. If this profile is for a single user, type the username in the Username text box, and the password in the Password text box. Otherwise, leave these text boxes blank, so that the device prompts the user to enter them.

5. Select the Use SSL check box if you want to secure the connection with Secure Sockets Layer. This is usually a good idea.

If you want to add another CardDAV account, click the + (Add) button, and then repeat the preceding steps. To remove a CardDAV account, display it in the CardDAV pane, and then click the – (Remove) button.

Setting Up a Web Clips Payload

To give your iPad and iPhone users instant access to particular web pages, you can add a payload of Web clips to the configuration profile. This is a great way to make sure that the users can easily reach important URLs without having to type a single character on the soft keyboard. You may want to create a Web clip for a site on which you distribute configuration profiles.

 TIP If your users will receive updated configuration profiles by visiting a web site, add a Web clip for the appropriate page on the site so that they can get there directly from the home screen.

To set up a payload of Web clips, click the Web Clips item in the Payloads list. In the Configure Web Clips pane that appears, click the Configure button. iPhone Configuration Utility displays the Web Clip pane (see Figure 3-18). You can then quickly add as many clips as you need by following these steps:

1. In the Label text box, type the name to display on the home screen. Keep it succinct.

2. Type or paste the page's URL in the URL text box.

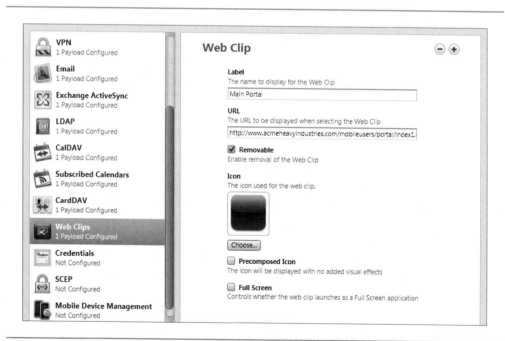

Figure 3-18.   Web clips let you add shortcuts to useful web pages directly to the iPad's or iPhone's home screen.

3. If you want the user to be able to remove the Web clip from the home screen, select the Removable check box. If you want the Web clip to remain on the iPad or iPhone (as is often best), make sure this check box is cleared.

4. Add an icon to the Icon text box by clicking the Choose button, picking the picture file in the dialog box that opens, and then clicking the Open button. The configuration file stores a text string representing the contents of the icon.

TIP On the Mac, you can drag a picture from a Finder window or from iPhoto to the Icon well in the Web Clip pane of iPhone Configuration Utility.

To add another Web clip, click the + (Add) button in the upper-right corner of the Web Clip pane, and then repeat these steps. To remove a Web clip, click it in the Web Clip pane, and then click the – (Remove) button.

Setting Up a Credentials Payload

For most networks, you'll need to use one or more digital certificates to authenticate the iPad or iPhone to the network. To install these certificates on the device, you create a Credentials payload in the configuration profile.

To create a Credentials payload, follow these steps:

1. Click the Credentials item in the Payloads list to display the Configure Credentials box.

2. Click the Configure button to display the dialog box for adding the credential:

   ■ **Windows**   Windows 7 displays the Windows Security: Personal Certificate Store dialog box shown in Figure 3-19. Windows XP displays the Personal Certificate Store dialog box.

   ■ **Mac OS X**   Mac OS X displays the Add Credential dialog box (see Figure 3-20).

3. Click the certificate you want to add, and then click the OK button (on Windows) or the Open button (on the Mac). The certificate then appears in the Credential pane in iPhone Configuration Utility (see Figure 3-21).

4. In the Credential Name text box, you can type a different name for the credential if necessary. For example, you may want to use a more descriptive name than the certificate has.

5. If you want to view the certificate, click the View Certificate button.

To add another credential, click the + (Add) button in the upper-right corner of the Credential pane, and then repeat these steps. To remove a credential, display it in the Credential pane, and then click the – (Remove) button.

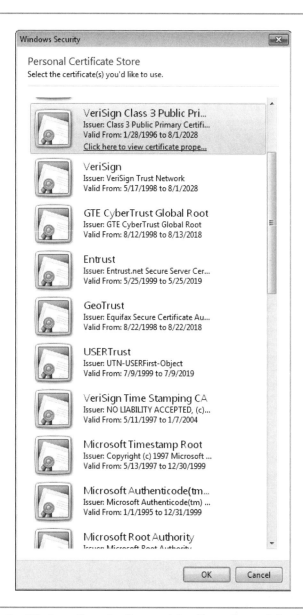

Figure 3-19.   In the Windows Security: Personal Certificate Store dialog box, click the certificate you want to add to the Credentials payload.

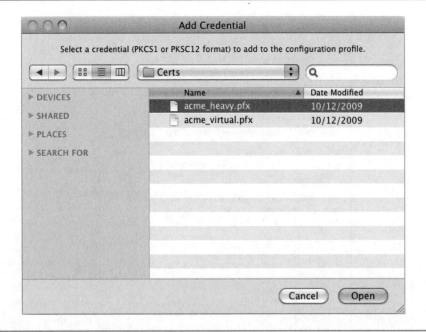

Figure 3-20.   In the Add Credential dialog box, navigate to the certificate you want to add, and then select it.

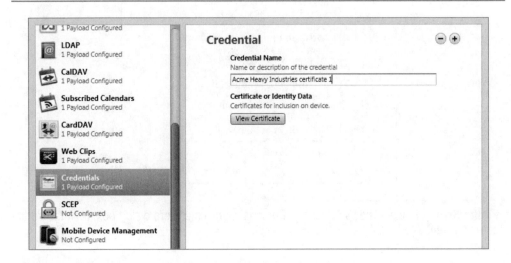

Figure 3-21.   The Credential pane appears only when you have added a credential to the Credentials payload.

Setting Up a SCEP Payload

If the iPads and iPhones need to obtain certificates from a CA, you can add a Simple Certificate Enrollment Protocol (SCEP) payload to the configuration profile. Using SCEP enables you to install certificates securely over the air rather than having to connect the devices to a PC or Mac.

To set up a SCEP payload, follow these steps:

1. Click the SCEP item in the Payloads list to display the Configure SCEP pane.

2. Click the Configure button to display the SCEP pane (see Figure 3-22).

3. In the URL text box, type the address of the SCEP server—for example, **http:// www.example.com/certsrv/mscep/mscep.dll**.

4. In the Name text box, type the string of text that the CA will use to identify the request.

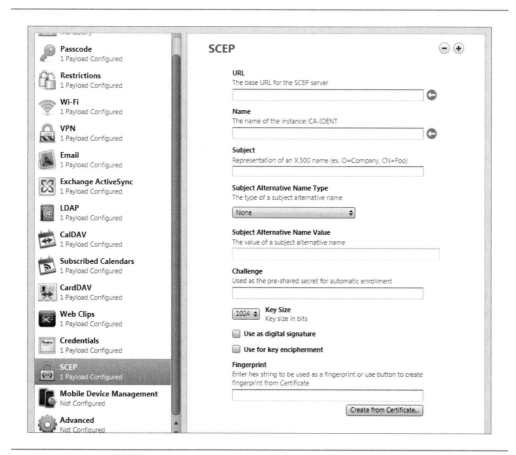

Figure 3-22.   In the SCEP pane, you can create a SCEP payload to enable an iPad or iPhone to acquire certificates securely over the air from a CA.

5. In the Subject text box, type the X.500 name represented as an array containing pairs of an object identifier (OID) and a value. Put each pair inside two brackets, separated from the next pair by commas, and put the whole address inside outer brackets. For example, the name /C=US/O=Acme Heavy Industries becomes [[["C","US"]],[["O","Acme Heavy Industries"]]].

6. If you need to use an alternative name type for the subject, open the Subject Alternative Name Type drop-down list or pop-up menu, and then choose the type: RFC 822 Name, DNS Name, or Uniform Resource Identifier. (The fourth choice is None, which disables the Subject Alternative Name Value text box.) Type the name in the Subject Alternative Name Value text box.

7. In the Challenge text box, type the pre-shared secret the device will provide to the SCEP server.

8. In the Key Size drop-down list or pop-up menu, choose the key size—either 1024 bits or 2048 bits.

9. Select the Use As Digital Signature check box if you want to use the key as a digital signature.

10. Select the Use For Key Encipherment check box if you want to use the key for enciphering items.

11. In the Fingerprint text box, enter the SHA1 or MD5 fingerprint to use when connecting to the CA via HTTP. You can type or paste in the fingerprint if you happen to have it to hand, but the normal way is to click the Create From Certificate button, select the certificate in the dialog box that opens, and then click the OK button.

To add another SCEP server, click the + (Add) button in the upper-right corner of the SCEP pane, and then repeat these steps. To delete a SCEP server, click it in the SCEP pane, and then click the – (Remove) button.

Setting Up a Mobile Device Management Payload

If you need to set up the iPad or iPhone for remote device management, create a Mobile Device Management payload. Click the Mobile Device Management item in the Payloads list to display the Configure Mobile Device Management box, and then click the Configure button. iPhone Configuration Utility displays the Mobile Device Management pane (see Figure 3-23).

To choose settings, follow these steps:

1. In the Server URL text box, type the URL at which the Mobile Device Management server is located.

2. In the Check In URL text box, type the URL the iPad or iPhone should use to check in during installation.

3. In the Topic text box, type the Push notification topic to use for Management messages.

Figure 3-23.   Create a Mobile Device Management payload when you need to manage the iPad or iPhone via remote device management.

4. Open the Identity drop-down list or pop-up menu and click the credential to use for authentication.

5. Select the Sign Messages check box if you want messages to be digitally signed.

6. In the Access Rights section, make sure the check box is selected for each item you want remote administrators to be able to query the device about, add and remove, and change. Clear the check box for any item you don't want remote administrators to be able to access.

   ■ **Query Device For**   Select the General Settings check box, the Security Settings check box, the Network Settings check box, the Restrictions check box, the Configuration Profiles check box, the Provisioning Profiles check box, and the Applications check box, as needed.

- **Add/Remove**   Select the Configuration Profiles check box if you want remote administrators to be able to remove configuration profiles from the device. Select the Provisioning Profiles check box if you want them to be able to remove provisioning profiles from the device.

- **Security**   Select the Change Device Password check box if you want remote administrators to be able to change the device's password (for example, to lock the user out). Select the Remote Wipe check box if remote administrators will need to be able to wipe the device from the comfort of their workstations.

7. If you want to use the Development Apple Push Notification Service instead of the regular Apple Push Notification Service, select the Use Development APNS Server check box.

To add another Mobile Device Management server, click the + (Add) button in the upper-right corner of the Mobile Device Management pane, and then repeat these steps. To delete a Mobile Device Management server, click it in the Mobile Device Management pane, and then click the – (Remove) button.

Setting Up an Advanced Payload

The Advanced item lets you change the way the iPhone or iPad 3G connects to the cellular network. For a typical deployment, you won't need to change these settings unless the carrier's network engineers tell you to do so. But if they do, you can create an Advanced payload in the configuration profile.

To set up an Advanced payload, follow these steps:

1. Click the Advanced item in the Payloads list to display the Configure Advanced Settings pane.

2. Click the Configure button to display the Advanced pane (see Figure 3-24).

3. In the Access Point Name (APN) text box, type the name of the carrier access point to use. You can use an APN up to 20 characters long.

4. In the Access Point User Name text box, type the user name for connecting to the access point.

5. In the Access Point Password text box, type the password for connecting to the access point. The password can be up to 32 characters long.

6. In the Proxy Server And Port text box, type the full address and port of the proxy server to use when connecting through this network.

 NOTE   You can configure only a single Advanced payload for a configuration profile.

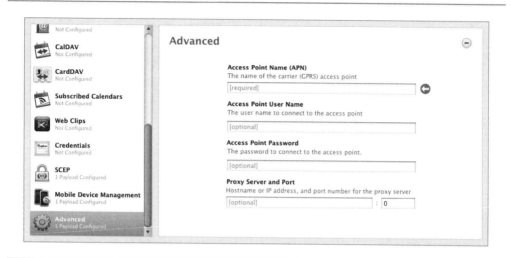

Figure 3-24.   Create an Advanced payload when you need to make the iPhone connect to a specific access point on the carrier's network.

Applying a Configuration Profile

You can apply a configuration profile to an iPad or iPhone in three ways:

- **Directly**   Connect the iPad or iPhone to the PC or Mac on which you're running iPhone Configuration Utility, and apply the profile to the device.

- **By download**   Post the profile to a web site, and have the user download it and apply it.

- **By e-mail**   Send the profile to the user's iPad or iPhone, and have the user apply it.

NOTE   For an iPhone, you must activate the device on a carrier network before you can install a configuration profile on it.

Applying a Configuration Profile Directly

The easiest way to apply a configuration profile is directly—by connecting the iPad or iPhone to the PC or Mac on which you're running iPhone Configuration Utility, and then using iPhone Configuration Utility to put the profile on the iPad or iPhone.

To apply a configuration profile directly to an iPad or iPhone, follow these steps:

1. Launch iPhone Configuration Utility if it's not already running.

2. Connect the iPad or iPhone to the PC or Mac with a USB cable. The computer detects the device and adds it to the Devices list in iPhone Configuration Utility.

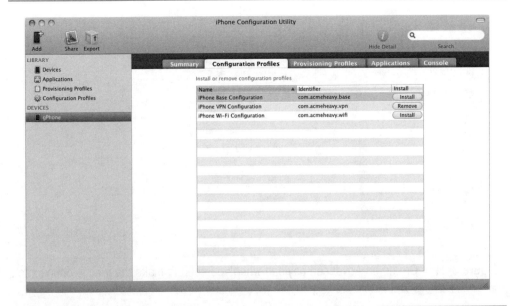

Figure 3-25.   Click the Install button in the Configuration Profiles pane of iPhone Configuration Utility to apply a profile to an iPad or iPhone.

3. Click the device in the Devices list to display its configuration screens.

4. Click the Configuration Profiles tab to display the Configuration Profiles pane (see Figure 3-25).

5. Click the Install button for the configuration profile you want to install.

6. The device displays the Install Profile screen (shown on the left in Figure 3-26), where you can click the More Details button to display details about the profile (as shown on the right in Figure 3-26).

7. To install the profile, touch the Install button on the Install Profile screen. The device then displays a confirmation dialog box:

   ■ **Install Profile dialog box**   If the profile is one the user is permitted to remove, the device displays the Install Profile dialog box, shown at the top of the left side of Figure 3-27. This dialog box simply makes sure you understand that installing the profile will change the device's settings.

   ■ **Locked Profile dialog box**   If the profile cannot be removed without authorization, or cannot be removed at all, the device displays the Locked Profile dialog box, shown in the middle and bottom sections of the left side of Figure 3-27. This dialog box warns the user that the profile cannot be removed without authorization or cannot be removed at all, as appropriate.

Figure 3-26.   To install the profile, click the Install button on the iPad or iPhone (left). To see the details of the profile (right), touch the More Details button.

8. Touch the Install Now button to continue. The iPad or iPhone then installs the profile and displays the Profile Installed screen (shown on the right in Figure 3-27).

NOTE Depending on the contents of the payloads in the profile you're installing, you may be prompted to enter user names, passwords, or other information at this point. We'll look at how to do this in later chapters.

From here, you can touch the Done button in the upper-right corner to go to the Profile screen, or simply press the Home button to go back to the Home screen as usual.

Applying a Configuration Profile from a Web Page

The second way of applying a configuration profile to an iPad or iPhone is by downloading the profile from a web page. The user opens Safari and goes to the web page, downloads the configuration profile, and then installs it.

Figure 3-27. Touch the Install Now button to confirm that you understand that installing the profile will change the iPad's or iPhone's configuration (left). When the installation finishes, the device shows the Profile Installed screen (right).

TIP For an iPhone, you can send the web page's URL via SMS. This ensures that the message reaches the right iPhone and allows you to customize the URL to that iPhone if necessary.

This approach is straightforward enough, but the devil is in the security details—how to make sure that only an authorized person (or device) downloads and installs a configuration profile. You can take care of security in several different ways, such as using certificates to authenticate the device, encrypting the configuration profile, and typing the configuration profile to a particular iPad or iPhone. We'll look at how to implement security later in this book.

NOTE If you're installing a base configuration profile on the device and then having the user download a further configuration profile, you can include a certificate on the device to identify it. You can also install a Web clip to give the user one-touch access to the web site that contains the other configuration profile.

When you need to put a configuration profile on a web site so that users can download and install it, export the configuration profile from iPhone Configuration Utility. To export a profile, follow these steps:

1. In iPhone Configuration Utility, click the Configuration Profiles item in the Library category in the Source list to display the list of configuration profiles.

NOTE   You can also use the Export command to put a configuration profile on another computer—for example, so that you can install it directly on an iPad or iPhone from there. But bear in mind that if you encrypt the profile when you export it, you need to create updated profiles using the same version of iPhone Configuration Utility so that the updated profiles are signed in a way the iPad and iPhone will accept.

2. Click the configuration profile you want to export.
3. Click the Export button on the toolbar to display the Export Configuration Profile dialog box (Figure 3-28 shows the Mac version of this dialog box).

NOTE   You can also give the Export command by choosing File | Export or by pressing CTRL-SHIFT-S (on Windows) or ⌘-SHIFT-S (on the Mac).

4. In the Security drop-down list or pop-up menu, choose the type of security you want to use for the exported profiles:

   ■ **None**   Select the None item if you don't need to secure the profile file. The result is a .mobileconfig file in plain text.

CAUTION   If you don't encrypt a configuration profile, anyone who gets the .mobileconfig file can read almost the whole thing just by opening it in a text editor. Some of the more sensitive information is obfuscated, but everything else is there in black and white. If you know which devices you're creating configuration profiles for, you will normally want to sign and encrypt your configuration profiles for security.

   ■ **Sign Configuration Profile**   Select the Sign Configuration Profile item if you want to apply a digital signature to ensure that the configuration profile hasn't been altered.

NOTE   Signing the configuration profile protects the iPad or iPhone in two ways. First, the device will install the configuration profile only if the file is in the same state as when it was signed; if the file has been changed, the device will refuse to install the configuration profile. Second, the iPad or iPhone will update the profile only with a newer version of the profile that has the same identifier (in the General payload) and that you've signed using the same copy of iPhone Configuration Utility.

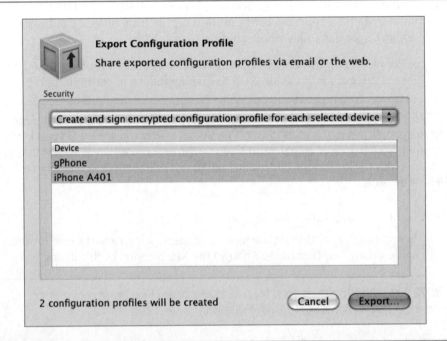

Figure 3-28. In the Export Configuration Profile dialog box, choose the type of security for the exported profile.

■ **Create And Sign Encrypted Configuration Profile For Each Selected Device**   Choose this item to sign each profile with a digital signature, to encrypt the contents of the profile, and to lock the profile to a particular device. Select the devices in the Device list in the lower part of the dialog box. The Device list shows devices you've added by connecting them to the computer on which you're running iPhone Configuration Utility and devices you've added by using the File | Add To Library command.

5. Click the Export button. iPhone Configuration Utility displays the Export Document To dialog box (on Windows) or the Select A Location To Export The Specified Configuration Profile dialog box (on the Mac).

6. Navigate to the folder in which you want to store the configuration profiles.

7. In the File Name text box (on Windows) or the Save As text box (on the Mac), type the name you want to give the file. When you're creating a separate configuration profile for each device, iPhone Configuration Utility uses this name as the base name and adds the device's name after it—for example, creating files such as Base Configuration-iPhone 401 and Base Configuration-iPhone 402.

8. Click the Save button. iPhone Configuration Utility closes the dialog box and exports the configuration profile or configuration profiles.

 NOTE   Applying a configuration profile from a web page usually works best for updates: Once the iPad or iPhone is securely connected to your company's internal network, it can pick up an updated profile securely from an intranet page. When the user touches the button to open the file, she sees the Install Profile screen.

Applying a Configuration Profile via E-Mail

The third way of applying a configuration profile to an iPad or iPhone is via e-mail. As long as the device already has an e-mail account set up, this is easy for both you (the administrator) and the user. So once you've set up your iPads and iPhones with e-mail (perhaps by applying a profile directly), you may want to use this method to apply other configuration profiles or updates.

You can attach a configuration profile file to an e-mail message in the same way as you can attach any other file, but you can also start creating a message directly from iPhone Configuration Utility, exporting the configuration profile and choosing whether to encrypt and sign it. To do so, follow these steps:

1. In iPhone Configuration Utility, click the Configuration Profiles item in the Library category in the Source list to display the list of configuration profiles.

2. Click the configuration profile you want to send.

3. Click the Share button on the toolbar to display the Share Configuration Profile dialog box (Figure 3-29 shows the Windows version).

4. In the Security drop-down list or pop-up menu, choose the type of security you want to use for the exported profiles: None, Sign Configuration Profile, or Create And Sign Encrypted Configuration Profile For Each Selected Device. See the preceding section for a full explanation of these items.

5. Click the Share button. iPhone Configuration Utility creates an e-mail message using your computer's default e-mail program (for example, Microsoft Outlook or Apple Mail), gives it a canned subject ("Configuration Profile"), and attaches the configuration profile.

6. Address the message, improve the subject line, type or paste in a suitable explanation, and then send the message.

The user receives a message with the configuration profile file attached. The user opens the message, touches the button for the attachment, and then sees the Install Profile screen you met earlier in this chapter.

Figure 3-29. In the Share Configuration Profile dialog box, choose whether to sign and encrypt the configuration profile.

Dealing with Errors When Installing Configuration Profiles

Usually, installing a configuration profile on an iPad or iPhone with iPhone Configuration Utility is straightforward—but as at any time software meets hardware, errors can occur. Here are three errors that pop up pretty frequently and that you may need to deal with.

"Unexpected Error from Your Mobile Device" Message

The message "iPhone Configuration Utility has encountered an unexpected error from your mobile device" with an error term such as kAMDMuxConnectError (see Figure 3-30) or a similar smashed-caps error term means that iPhone Configuration Utility has lost its grip of the USB port. Unplugging and replugging the device is worth a try, but normally you'll need to reboot the PC.

"Configuration Profile Installation Failed" Message

If iPhone Configuration Utility displays the Configuration Profile Installation Failed dialog box (see Figure 3-31) when you try to install a configuration profile on an iPad or iPhone, the problem is usually that the configuration profile contains no payload.

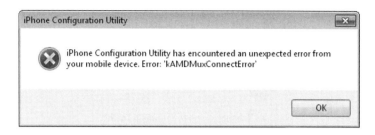

Figure 3-30.   You can usually clear this error by rebooting your PC.

"Invalid Profile: Profile Format Not Recognized" Error

The message "Invalid profile: Profile format not recognized" can occur at various times, but if you're getting it from the iPhone Configuration Utility, it usually means that the configuration profile's payload includes a self-signed certificate in a format the iPad or iPhone doesn't like.

In this case, remove the self-signed certificate from the payload, convert the certificate from the PEM (Privacy-Enhanced Mail) format to the DER (Distinguished Encoding Rules) format, and add it to the payload again. (To convert the certificate, use OpenSSL—www.openssl.org—or another tool.) Try installing the profile again, and it should work.

Seeing Which Profiles Are Installed on an iPad or iPhone

To find out which profiles are installed on an iPad or iPhone, you can either look directly on the device or hook it up to a computer and take a look in iPhone Configuration Utility.

To look on the iPad or iPhone, go to the Home screen, and then choose Settings | General | Profiles to display the Profiles screen (see Figure 3-32). This screen contains an entry for each profile that's installed. Touch the button for a profile to display the Profile screen showing the details of the profile.

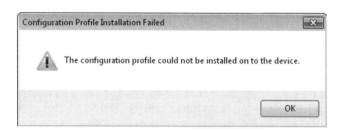

Figure 3-31.   The "Configuration Profile Installation Failed" dialog box typically means that the configuration profile has no payload.

Figure 3-32. The easiest way to see which profiles are installed on an iPad or iPhone is to open the Profiles screen on the device itself.

To use iPhone Configuration Utility to see which profiles are installed on an iPad or iPhone, follow these steps:

1. Connect the iPad or iPhone to your PC or Mac.

2. Run iPhone Configuration Utility.

3. Click the device in the Devices category to display its configuration screens.

4. Click the Configuration Profiles tab to display its contents. Each configuration profile you've installed has a Remove button, and each configuration profile you have yet to install has an Install button.

NOTE In iPhone Configuration Utility, you can also check which profiles you've installed on the device without connecting it to your computer. Open iPhone Configuration Utility, and then click the Devices item in the Library category to show the devices. Click the device in the list, click the Show Detail button on the toolbar if details are hidden, and then click the Configuration Profiles tab. But bear in mind that this shows only the profiles installed using iPhone Configuration Utility as of the time you last connected the device to your workstation. You won't be able to tell whether the user has removed one or more profiles (unless you've prevented that user from removing any of the profiles).

Removing a Configuration Profile from an iPad or iPhone

You can remove a configuration profile from an iPad or iPhone either by using iPhone Configuration Utility or directly from the device. Usually it's easiest to work on the device unless you've prevented the user from removing the profile.

Removing a Configuration Profile Directly

To remove a configuration profile directly from an iPad or iPhone, follow these steps:

1. On the iPad or iPhone, choose Settings | General | Profile to display the Profiles screen (if the device has two or more profiles installed) or the Profile screen (if it has only one profile installed).

2. If the device has multiple profiles installed, touch the profile you want to remove. The device displays the Profile screen.

3. Touch the Remove button on the profile. The device displays the Remove Profile dialog box (shown on the left in Figure 3-33).

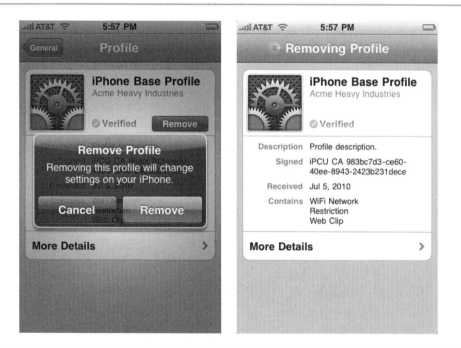

Figure 3-33.   Touch the Remove button in the Remove Profile dialog box (left) to start removing the profile. The iPad or iPhone then displays the Removing Profile screen while it removes the profile.

NOTE If the Remove button doesn't appear on the Profile screen, the administrator has set up the profile as one that can never be removed. The only way to remove it is by using iPhone Configuration Utility, as discussed in the next section.

 NOTE If the profile requires authorization to remove it, the device displays the Remove Protected Profile dialog box and the keyboard. Type the password for removing the profile, and then touch the Remove button.

4. Touch the Remove button to remove the profile.

5. The iPad or iPhone displays the Removing Profile screen (shown on the right in Figure 3-33) while it removes the profile.

Removing a Configuration Profile by Using iPhone Configuration Utility

To remove a configuration profile by using iPhone Configuration Utility, follow these steps:

1. Launch iPhone Configuration Utility if it's not already running.

2. Connect the iPad or iPhone to the PC or Mac with a USB cable. The computer detects the device and adds it to the Devices list in iPhone Configuration Utility.

3. Click the device in the Devices list to display its configuration screens.

4. Click the Configuration Profiles tab to display the Configuration Profiles pane.

5. Click the Remove button for the profile you want to remove. iPhone Configuration Utility displays the Configuration Profile Removal dialog box (Figure 3-34 shows the Mac version).

6. Click the Remove button.

Figure 3-34. When removing a profile from an iPad or iPhone using iPhone Configuration Utility, confirm in the Configuration Profile Removal dialog box that you want to get the profile off the device.

NOTE   If you get the error message "Profile Removal Failed: The profile could not be removed from the device" when removing a configuration profile, the problem is most likely that you're trying to remove the profile with a different computer than you used to apply it. You can remove a profile only by using iPhone Configuration Utility on the same computer you used to install the profile. This is to prevent users installing iPhone Configuration Profile and uninstalling those carefully crafted profiles you've installed.

Duplicating, Backing Up, and Deleting Your Configuration Profiles

To save time and effort and keep your configuration profiles in good order, you'll need to manage them. In this section, we'll look at how to create a new profile quickly by duplicating an existing profile, how to back up all the information you're storing in iPhone Configuration Utility, and how to delete a configuration profile.

Duplicating a Configuration Profile

When you need to base one configuration profile on an existing configuration profile, duplicate the existing profile and then modify the settings in the duplicate.

To duplicate a configuration profile, follow these steps:

1. In iPhone Configuration Utility, click the Configuration Profiles item in the Library category in the Source list to display the list of configuration profiles.

2. Click the configuration profile you want to duplicate.

3. Choose File | Duplicate or press CTRL-D (on Windows) or ⌘-D (on the Mac). iPhone Configuration Utility duplicates the profile, giving it the same name but the next ordinal number. For example, if you duplicate a configuration profile named iPhone Base Profile, iPhone Configuration Utility names the duplicate iPhone Base Profile 2; if you duplicate iPhone Base Profile 2, you get iPhone Base Profile 3, and so on.

4. Click the new profile in the list, and then click the General category in the Detail pane. (If the Detail pane is hidden, display it by clicking the Show Detail button on the toolbar.)

5. In the Name box, type the new name for the configuration profile.

You can now set up the configuration profile's payloads by changing the settings in the configuration profile you copied and adding other payloads as needed.

Backing Up Your iPhone Configuration Utility Data

You can share and export configuration profiles as described earlier in this chapter, but it's also a good idea to back up your iPhone Configuration Utility data in case your PC or Mac disagrees with itself, with the basic principles of electricity, or with gravity.

To back up your iPhone Configuration Utility data, add the appropriate folder to your regular backups, or copy the folder to a backup medium every time you see a portent of impending doom. These are the folders:

- **Windows**   The *%userprofile%*\Local Settings\Application Data\Apple Computer\ folder (where *%userprofile%* is your user profile folder) contains an iPhone Configuration Utility folder containing the log for the iPhone Configuration Utility and a MobileDevice folder that contains a Configuration Profiles folder and a Devices folder.

- **Mac OS X**   The ~/Library/MobileDevice folder (where ~ represents your home folder) contains a Configuration Profiles folder and a Devices folder.

Deleting a Configuration Profile

Normally, you'll probably keep most of the configuration profiles you create in iPhone Configuration Utility so that you can update them and apply them to further devices as needed. But when you do need to delete a configuration profile, follow these steps:

1. Click the Configuration Profiles item in the Library section of the Source pane to display the list of configuration profiles.

2. In the list, click the profile you want to delete.

3. Choose Edit | Delete or press DELETE. iPhone Configuration Utility displays the Delete The Selected Configuration Profile? dialog box (shown in Figure 3-35).

4. Click the Yes button (on Windows) or the Delete Configuration Profile button (on the Mac).

In the next chapter, we'll dig into the details of setting up networking on your iPads and iPhones.

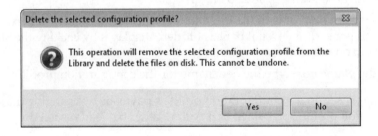

Figure 3-35.   iPhone Configuration Utility prompts you to confirm the deletion of a configuration profile.

CHAPTER 4 | Setting Up Wireless Networks on the iPad and iPhone

In this chapter, we'll look at how to connect your iPads and iPhones to your wireless network. Unless you're content to have the iPads and iPhones live their online life through the cell network, this is a vital step to getting the most out of the devices—and it's often the first step to applying policy to them.

We'll start by discussing how to plan your wireless network connections. If you already have a wireless network that has plenty of bandwidth looking for business, you may be all set. Otherwise, you may need to reinforce the wireless network to provide extra bandwidth (and perhaps coverage) for the iPads and iPhones. If you don't have a wireless network, we'll look briefly at the decisions you'll need to make in order to set up a suitable network.

After that, we'll move on to setting up the wireless network connections. First, we'll look at the simplest type of connection—connecting to a wireless network by entering the appropriate settings directly on the iPad or iPhone. This takes a minute or three, so it's not something you'd want to do yourself for hundreds of devices—but you could have the users do it for you. We'll also look at how to configure the iPad or iPhone to use a specific IP address and other network settings if necessary—again, by manipulating the settings on the device itself with your trusty forefinger.

But in most cases you'll want to automate the process of setting up networking. That means creating a Wi-Fi payload in a configuration profile that you install on the device. Unless you've set up a wireless network manually, you'll need to install the profile without using a wireless network—for example, by connecting the device to a computer and installing the profile via iPhone Configuration Utility. Otherwise, you're facing the chicken-and-egg problem of needing to establish a network connection in order to install the information needed for a network connection. Chapter 3 showed you how to create configuration profiles and add payloads to them, and in this chapter, we'll dig into the settings you can use in a Wi-Fi payload.

On the way, we'll discuss the different means of authentication you can use for the iPads and iPhones—good old passwords, the users' existing directory credentials, and digital certificates.

Planning Your Wireless Network

If your company or organization already has a wireless network—as most do these days—you may simply be able to snap the iPads and iPhones into it by giving them the appropriate Wi-Fi settings and credentials. For example, if you use a RADIUS server to authenticate wireless clients with login information from your directory, you can have the iPad and iPhone users log in with their existing information.

 NOTE RADIUS is the acronym for Remote Authentication Dial-In User Service, a networking protocol for authenticating users connecting to a network from outside. ("Dial in" doesn't have to involve literal dialing, thank progress.)

But if you're adding many iPads and iPhones to the network, you may need to beef up its bandwidth to accommodate them by adding extra access points. You may also need to add repeaters or high-gain antennas to boost the signal in areas where the signal is patchy or simply too weak for the devices' puny antennas to pick it up adequately.

NOTE   Rather than adding the iPads and iPhones to the main network, you may need to set up a guest wireless network that gives iPad and iPhone users access to the Internet but not to the internal network. Some wireless access points include built-in features for running a guest wireless network alongside the main network; if your access points don't have such a feature, create a separate network with the access point in the DMZ rather than inside the network. (The DMZ—demilitarized zone—is a scorched-earth subnet you use to expose your network's external services to the wilds of the Internet.)

If you don't already have a wireless network, you'll face all the existential questions of how to create a suitable one:

- **Who will use the network?**   Are you setting up the wireless network for just iPad and iPhone users, or will you support other wireless clients as well?

- **What will they use the network for?**   E-mail and Internet access are pretty much givens these days. But you'll also need to determine which other services wireless users will need and estimate how much bandwidth you'll have to provide. For example, if you'll allow iPad and iPhone users to use video conferencing, you should expect your bandwidth to vanish faster than pizza at a pajama party. If you allow VoIP, the bandwidth hit will be less, but perhaps more constant.

- **Which wireless standard and equipment will you use?**   A few years ago, choosing among 802.11g, 802.11a, and 802.11b was tough. But at this writing, 802.11n wireless networking is so far ahead of earlier standards that it's barely worth considering 802.11g, 802.11b, or 802.11a unless you have stacks of existing equipment you need to reuse rather than buying new equipment.

- **Where will you place your access points?**   To enable users to get the most use out of the iPads and iPhones, plan your wireless network so that it provides a strong enough signal throughout those parts of your premises where users will use the devices. Position the access points and repeaters so as to spread out the coverage across the iPad- and iPhone-enabled area—but not to throw it too far beyond the boundaries of the premises.

- **Which form of security will you use?**   Barring exceptional circumstances, you'll need to use strong authentication and encryption to protect your wireless network and the devices that connect to it. For most deployments, the best choice is WPA2 with Extensible Authentication Protocol with Transport Layer Security (EAP-TLS) or Protected Extensible Authentication Protocol

(PEAP, an encapsulated form of Extensible Authentication Protocol sometimes referred to as EAP-PEAP). But your hardware and software setup (or your managers) may dictate another choice.

NOTE Choosing between using certificates and using passwords for authentication can be tricky. Generally speaking, certificates provide stronger security than passwords, but with the certificate, you're trusting the device rather than the user—after all, you can't embed a certificate in the user (now, now—banish that unworthy thought from your mind!). If you want the user to control the credential, use a password instead. Passwords are usually easier to administer than certificates, and you can provide them quickly when needed (for example, over the phone).

Setting Up a Wireless Network Connection Manually

Sometimes the easiest way to get an iPad or iPhone connected securely to the wireless network is to set it up manually. In this section, we'll go quickly through the basics of connecting to a wireless network, and then dig into the settings you can choose manually if needed. Lastly, I'll show you how to make the iPad or iPhone forget a wireless network after their relationship is over.

Establishing a Wireless Network Connection Manually

To establish a wireless network connection manually on the iPad or iPhone, go to the Home screen and choose Settings | Wi-Fi to display the Wi-Fi Networks screen (shown on the left in Figure 4-1). Make sure the Wi-Fi switch at the top is in the On position; if it's in the Off position, touch the left part of the switch to move it to the On position.

Joining an Open Wireless Network

If the wireless network is *open* (that is, it's broadcasting its SSID) and is within range, it appears in the Choose A Network list on the Wi-Fi Networks screen. To join the network, touch it.

If the network uses a password, the iPad or iPhone prompt displays the Enter Password screen (shown on the right in Figure 4-1). Type in the password, and then touch the Join button.

The iPad or iPhone then tries to join the wireless network. If it succeeds, it displays the Wi-Fi Networks screen with a check mark next to the network to which the device is connected.

Joining a Closed Wireless Network

If the wireless network is *closed* (it's configured not to broadcast its SSID), the network doesn't appear in the Choose A Network list on the Wi-Fi Networks screen. The iPad or iPhone can't see the network, so you need to tell it which network to look for and how to get in touch with it. To do this, touch the Other button to display the Other Network screen (shown on the left in Figure 4-2).

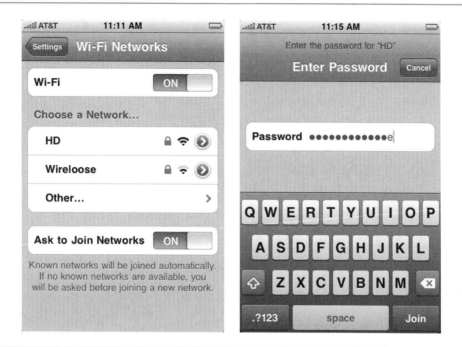

Figure 4-1.   On the Wi-Fi Networks screen (left), you can turn wireless networking on and off and (when it's on) select which network to join. On the Enter Password screen (right), type in the password, and then touch the Join button.

Type the network's name in the Name box, and then touch the Security button to reach the Security screen (shown on the right in Figure 4-2). Touch the button for the security type the wireless network uses, putting a check mark next to it. Then touch the Other Network button to return to the Other Network screen, which now shows the fields required for the security type you chose.

Type the required information—for example, your username and password—and then click the Join button to join the network.

If you need to change the security mode the iPad or iPhone is using to access the wireless network, follow these steps:

1. Touch the Mode button to display the Mode screen (shown on the left in Figure 4-3).

2. Touch the appropriate mode—for example, touch EAP-TLS instead of Automatic—to place a check mark next to it.

3. Touch the Enter Password button to return to the Enter Password screen, on which the Password field will have been replaced by the Identity button.

4. If you need to select the identity to use, touch the Identity button to display the Identity screen (shown on the right in Figure 4-3).

Figure 4-2.   Use the Other Network screen (left) to enter the name of a closed network you want to connect to. On the Security screen, touch the security type the closed network uses.

Deciding Whether to Use the "Ask to Join Networks" Feature

The Ask To Join Networks switch at the bottom of the Wi-Fi Networks screen controls whether the iPad or iPhone offers to connect to available wireless networks when none of its known networks is available.

The Join Networks feature is useful if you want the iPad or iPhone to alert the user to a wireless network he or she may need to join—for example, for connecting at an airport or coffee shop. If the user will need this functionality, leave the Ask To Join Networks switch set in the On position.

For managed iPads and iPhones that should connect only to the approved networks you've set up, you'll probably want to turn the Ask To Join Networks feature off. You (or the user) may also want to turn it off temporarily when the iPad or iPhone is somewhere with many wireless networks around—in this case, the device is wasting battery power keeping track of all the networks around.

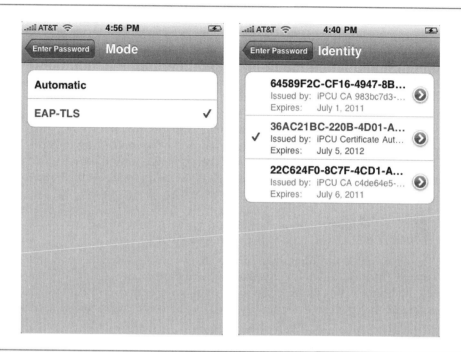

Figure 4-3.   Use the Mode screen (left) if you need to change security modes. You can then touch the Identity button on the Enter Password screen to display the Identity screen (right), on which you touch the identity you want to use.

5.   Touch the identity you want to use, placing a check mark next to it.

6.   Touch the Enter Password button to return to the Enter Password screen.

7.   Touch the Join button to join the network.

Configuring the Network Connection Manually

If you need to change the settings for the network connection, choose Settings | Wi-Fi to display the Wi-Fi Networks screen, and then touch the > button on the right side of the network's listing. The device displays the configuration screen for the wireless network, which shows the network's name at the top. You can then choose settings on this screen's three tabs as described in the following subsections.

NOTE   At the bottom of each tab on the screen for a wireless network is the HTTP Proxy area. See the section "Setting Up an HTTP Proxy Server," later in this chapter, for coverage of the options this area contains.

Setting DHCP Information

Dynamic Host Configuration Protocol (DHCP) is a great way of allocating IP addresses to network clients, and in many networks, it's easiest to use DHCP to provide IP addresses to the iPads, iPhones, and other devices on the network. When the device connects to the network, it picks up the IP address, subnet mask, router information, and so on from the DHCP server.

If the DHCP server gives the device all the information it needs, you won't need to make any changes. But if you do need to make changes, touch the DHCP tab on the wireless network's screen to display its contents (shown on the left in Figure 4-4). Then touch the field you need to change, and then type the information using the soft keyboard the device displays. You can't change the IP address, the subnet mask, or the router, but you can change these three settings:

- **DNS** If you need to point the iPad or iPhone at a different Domain Name Service (DNS) server, type in the server's address.

- **Search Domains** Enter any domains that you want the iPad or iPhone to search automatically when the user enters a partial address in a Web browser or other Internet client. For example, if you enter **acmeheavy.com** as a search domain, the user can enter simply **corp** to connect to **corp.acmeheavy.com**.

- **Client ID** If you need to be able to identify the iPad or iPhone by client ID, enter the name in this field. By default, the iPad or iPhone uses the name you apply or the user applies during setup.

The change you're perhaps most likely to need to make here is renewing the DHCP lease to sort out network problems. To renew the lease, touch the Renew Lease button at the bottom of the DHCP tab of the screen for the wireless network. (Depending on the device, you may need to scroll down to reach this button.)

Setting BootP Information

If your network uses BootP rather than DHCP to provide network configuration information, touch the BootP tab on the screen for the wireless network to display the BootP settings (shown on the right in Figure 4-4). Then fill in the DNS setting or the Search Domains setting as needed. You can't change the IP address, the subnet mask, or the router.

Setting a Static IP Address

DHCP and BootP are great for many purposes, but sometimes it's useful to set up an iPad or iPhone with a static IP address—for example, when you need to be able to always easily identify the device by its IP address rather than needing to dig through logs.

Figure 4-4.   On the DHCP tab of the screen for the wireless network (left), you can change the DNS setting, the Search Domains setting, and the Client ID setting. On the BootP tab (right), you can change the DNS setting or the Search Domains setting.

To set up a static IP address, touch the Static tab to display its contents (see Figure 4-5). Then touch the IP address field and fill in the address on the soft keyboard (which the device displays automatically). When you're done, touch the Return button on the keyboard to move to the next field, and continue filling in the information.

Setting Up an HTTP Proxy Server

At the bottom of each of the three tabs on the screen for the wireless network, you can set up an HTTP proxy to tell Safari and other Web apps where to direct their HTTP requests.

To control HTTP proxying, you touch the appropriate one of the three buttons under the HTTP Proxy heading: Off, Manual, or Auto. Normally, you'll find the Off button active until you make a change here.

To set up an HTTP proxy manually, touch the Manual button, and then enter the details in the Server field and the Port field (shown on the left in Figure 4-6). If the proxy server requires authentication, touch the left side of the Authentication switch to

Figure 4-5. If you need the iPad or iPhone to have a static IP address, fill in the details on the Static tab of the screen for the wireless network.

move it from Off to On (as in the figure), and then fill in the username and password in the fields that the device displays.

To set up an HTTP proxy automatically, touch the Auto button, and then enter the server's address in the URL field (shown on the right in Figure 4-6).

Making the iPod or iPhone Forget a Wireless Network

When you no longer want to use a particular wireless network, tell the iPad or iPhone to forget it. To do so, open the wireless network's configuration screen, and then touch the Forget This Network button at the top. Touch the Forget Network button on the confirmation screen that the device displays.

If you find you need to join the wireless network again, join it as described earlier in this chapter. You will need to type the password for the network again.

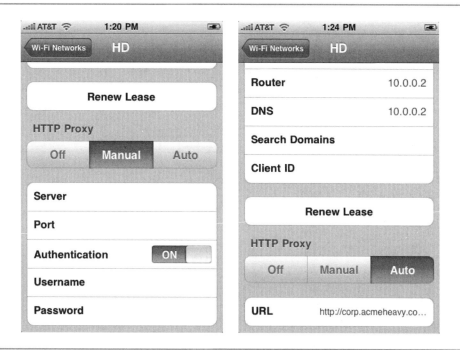

Figure 4-6.   To set the iPad or iPhone to use an HTTP proxy server, fill in the details on the Manual tab (left) or the Auto tab of the HTTP Proxy area of the screen for the wireless network.

Setting Up a Network Connection Using a Wi-Fi Payload

For most of your network's iPads or iPhones, you'll probably want to use a Wi-Fi payload in a configuration profile to set up the network connections automatically.

To create a Wi-Fi payload, open iPhone Configuration Utility and follow these steps:

1. Click the Configuration Profiles item in the Source list to display the list of configuration profiles.

2. Click the configuration profile to which you want to add the Wi-Fi payload.

3. Click the Wi-Fi item in the Payloads list to display the Configure Wi-Fi pane.

4. Click the Configure button to display the Wi-Fi pane (shown in Figure 4-7 with settings for a WPA/WPA2 Enterprise network underway).

5. In the Service Set Identifier (SSID) text box, type the SSID or network name.

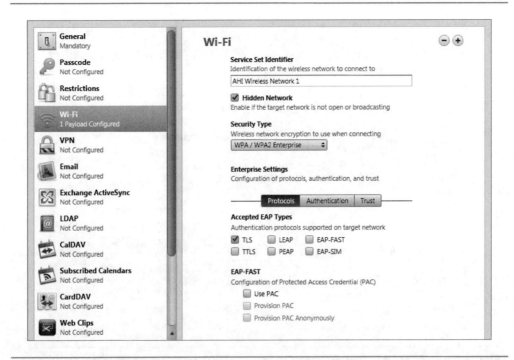

Figure 4-7.   Use the Wi-Fi pane in iPhone Configuration Utility to create a payload for setting up one or more wireless networks automatically.

6. Select the Hidden Network check box if you've set the access point to suppress broadcasts of the network's SSID. This setting tells the iPad or iPhone to go looking for the network by name rather than trying to pick it from a list of networks that are broadcasting their SSIDs.

7. Open the Security Type drop-down list or pop-up menu and choose the wireless security type the network uses. You have seven choices:

    ■ **None**   Use this setting for networks that don't use authentication. Normally, such networks are a security risk, but you may sometimes need to set up the iPad or iPhone to use them.

    ■ **WEP**   Use this setting for networks that use the personal level of Wired Equivalent Privacy (WEP). WEP has widely known weaknesses in its encryption algorithm, so it's best not to use it—but many wireless networks still do.

    ■ **WPA/WPA2**   Use this setting for networks that use Wi-Fi Protected Access (WPA) or Wi-Fi Protected Access 2 (WPA2).

- **Any (Personal)** Use this setting for networks that use either WEP, WPA, or WPA2. The iPad or iPhone won't connect to networks that don't use authentication.

- **WEP Enterprise** Use this setting for networks that use WEP with enterprise security.

- **WPA/WPA2 Enterprise** Use this setting for networks that use WPA or WPA2 with enterprise security.

- **Any (Enterprise)** Use this setting for networks that use WEP, WPA, or WPA2 with enterprise security.

You now need to provide the means of authentication for the wireless network. This depends on which type of security the wireless network uses. See the following sections for details.

Providing the Password for a Personal Wireless Network

A "personal" wireless network—one secured with WEP, WPA, or WPA2—uses only a password for authentication. For such a wireless network, simply type the password in the Password text box that appears in the Wi-Fi pane in iPhone Configuration Utility when you choose WEP, WPA/WPA2, or Any (Personal) in the Security Type drop-down list or pop-up menu.

Providing the Authentication for an Enterprise Wireless Network

When you choose one of the Enterprise types of wireless network authentication—WEP Enterprise, WPA Enterprise, or WPA2 Enterprise—the Wi-Fi pane displays the Enterprise Settings section below the Password text box. This section has three tabs: the Protocols tab (shown in Figure 4-8), the Authentication tab, and the Trust tab.

If the wireless network uses a password, type that password in the Password text box. Beyond that, choose the appropriate settings on the three tabs, as discussed next.

Choosing Protocols Settings

On the Protocols tab of the Enterprise Settings section, specify which protocols your network uses for authentication and set up EAP-FAST if you're using it.

In the Accepted EAP Types area, select the check box for each authentication protocol your network uses:

- **TLS** Extensible Authentication Protocol with Transport Layer Security. This protocol is an IEEE standard.

- **TTLS** Extensible Authentication Protocol with Tunneled Transport Layer Security. This is a proprietary protocol developed by Certicom and Funk Software.

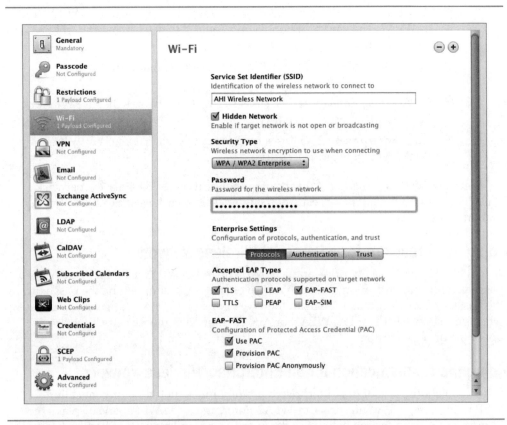

Figure 4-8.   When you choose an Enterprise type in the Security Type drop-down list in iPhone Configuration Utility, the Wi-Fi pane displays the Enterprise Settings section.

- **LEAP**   Lightweight Extensible Authentication Protocol. Cisco, which developed this proprietary authentication protocol, now recommends PEAP instead of LEAP.

- **PEAP**   Protected Extensible Authentication Protocol. Cisco, Microsoft, and RSA Security developed this proprietary protocol together. PEAP is widely used because it's not only compatible with most vendor hardware but provides machine-level authentication and integrates with Active Directory.

- **EAP-FAST**   Extensible Authentication Protocol–Flexible Authentication via Secure Tunneling. This Cisco protocol is intended to provide better security than LEAP but can be difficult to deploy securely.

- **EAP-SIM** Extensible Authentication Protocol for Subscriber Identity Module. EAP-SIM uses the SIM card in the iPhone or iPad (3G models only) to authenticate the client.

If your network uses EAP-FAST, use the controls in the EAP-FAST area to set up the Protected Access Credential (PAC). There are three check boxes here:

- **Use PAC** Select this check box to turn on the use of PAC and make the Provision PAC check box available.

- **Provision PAC** Select this check box if you want to provide the PAC. Selecting this check box makes the Provision PAC Automatically check box available.

- **Provision PAC Anonymously** Select this check box if you want to provide the PAC automatically.

Choosing Authentication Settings

Click the Authentication tab in the Enterprise Settings area to display the Authentication controls (see Figure 4-9), and then choose the appropriate settings for your network.
   These are the controls you can set:

- **Username** In this text box, you can type the username for connecting to the wireless network. Add the username only if you're tying this configuration profile to a particular user. Otherwise, leave the Username text box blank so that each user can enter his or her own username.

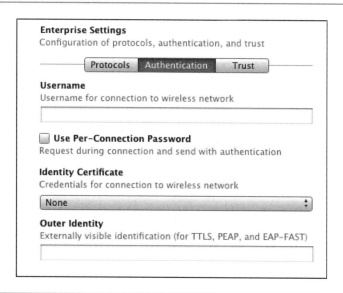

Figure 4-9. Use the controls on the Authentication tab of the Enterprise Settings area to add any authentication information the Wi-Fi payload requires.

■ **Use Per-Connection Password** Select this check box if you want the user to be challenged for a password on each connection. Usually, you'd use this only in a very high-security network.

■ **Identity Certificate** If you've installed a credential, you can open the Identity Certificate drop-down list or pop-up menu and choose the certificate to use.

NOTE You can install a certificate on the iPad or iPhone either by creating a Credentials payload in iPhone Configuration Utility (as discussed in Chapter 3) or by sending the certificate attached to a e-mail message and installing it from the Mail app.

■ **Outer Identity** To use a different outer identity with TTLS, PEAP, or EAP-FAST, type it in this text box. Otherwise, leave this text box blank.

Choosing Trust Settings

Click the Trust tab in the Enterprise Settings area to display the Trust controls (see Figure 4-10), and then choose the appropriate settings for your network.

The Trusted Certificates list box shows the certificates you've added to the Credentials payload in the configuration profile. For each certificate, you can select the check box (or leave it selected) to designate the certificate as one expected for authentication.

Enterprise Settings
Configuration of protocols, authentication, and trust

| Protocols | Authentication | Trust |

Trusted Certificates
Certificates trusted/expected for authentication

☑ Acme Heavy Industries access certificate

Trusted Server Certificate Names
Certificate names expected from authentication server

+ −

☑ **Allow Trust Exceptions**
Allow trust decisions (via dialog) to be made by the user

Figure 4-10. On the Trust tab in the Enterprise Settings area, specify the certificates required for authentication.

In the Trusted Server Certificate Names list box, you can set up a list of the certificate names the iPad or iPhone expects to receive from the authentication server. To add a certificate name, click the + button, and then type the server's certificate name over the default entry that iPhone Configuration Utility displays ("Trusted Server Common Name"). To remove a certificate name, click it in the list, and then click the – button.

Select the Allow Trust Exceptions check box if you want the iPad or iPhone to prompt the user to decide how to handle situations when it can't establish the chain of trust. The iPad or iPhone displays a dialog box asking the user whether to trust the server in question.

 NOTE   Allowing trust exceptions is useful for users who have the smarts to figure out whether it's a good idea to connect to the untrusted server or not. For example, you and your tech staff will be able to determine whether the server is a trustworthy one that has suffered a certificate problem or whether it lives on the wrong side of the street. Regular users may not be able to tell (and may not care)—in which case, you'll probably choose not to allow trust exceptions. To split the difference, create one configuration profile for techs and power users that allows trust exceptions, and another configuration profile for everyone else that removes this temptation.

Applying the Wi-Fi Payload to the iPad or iPhone

After setting up the Wi-Fi payload in the configuration profile, you can apply the configuration profile to the iPad or iPhone using the techniques discussed in Chapter 3.

For the wireless-only (3G-free) iPad, the wireless network is the only means of communicating with the rest of the world, so the first wireless network is vital to getting the device configured at all. For the 3G iPad and the iPhone, which can reach web sites via the cell network, the first wireless network is less vital—but you probably still won't want to mess about unnecessarily.

The easiest way of getting the first Wi-Fi network payload onto the iPad or iPhone is to apply the configuration profile directly using iPhone Configuration Utility. This method enables you to sidestep the chicken-and-egg problem of needing to have a wireless network connection already established in order to get the network connection's settings onto the iPad or iPhone. The only problem is that you need direct access to the iPad or iPhone; if you don't have that, you'll need to take a different approach.

If you need users rather than you to add the first wireless network, you can take other approaches. For example, you can provide users with the wireless network name and credentials they need to connect to the wireless network. For instance if you use a RADIUS server, you can let users connect to the wireless network using the same username and password they use for connecting a computer to the network.

Troubleshooting Network and Access Problems

In this section, we'll look at how to troubleshoot several network problems that can occur when you connect iPads and iPhones to wireless networks.

iPad Fails to Renew DHCP Lease and Continues to Use Current Address

When running iPhone OS 3.2, the iPad may fail to renew its DHCP lease and simply continue to use the latest IP address the DHCP server gave it. This problem occurs when several things happen in just the right sequence. First, the iPad is not connected to a power source. Second, you lock the iPad's screen (or the iPad automatically locks it) before the time for renewing the DHCP lease arrives, and you don't unlock the iPad until after the lease has expired. Third, the iPad maintains its network connection to fetch push mail or other notifications; if the iPad isn't set up to get updates like this, the problem doesn't occur.

So, assuming all those stars align themselves, the iPad keeps its grip on the IP address and clings on for dear life. That's when problems occur.

If the DHCP server has assigned that same IP address to a different device or computer in the meantime, you'll get IP errors—either on the iPad or on the other device or computer. In many cases, the iPad will retain control of the IP address, so the network connection will work fine, and the user won't see anything wrong—but the other device or computer will be unable to use the network.

The errors you'll get from the IP address conflict vary depending on the operating system. If the system suffering the conflict is a Windows PC or a Mac, it'll give an error that Goldilocks would be proud of—"someone's been using my IP address, and *they're still there*." Figure 4-11 shows the error you'll see from Mac OS X.

If the iPad or iPhone is affected, the operating system tends not to identify the problem, so it usually shows up as problems with individual apps being unable to connect. Here are three examples:

- **Mail** "Cannot Get Mail: The connection to the server 'mail.acmeheavy.com' failed."

- **Safari** "Cannot Open Page: Safari cannot open the page. The error was 'Operation could not be completed. Invalid argument.'"

- **Maps** "No results found"

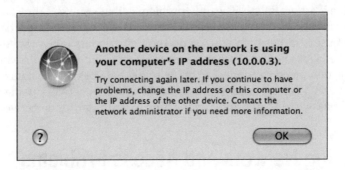

Figure 4-11. Windows and Mac OS X give you a clear indication when another device is using the same IP address. With iOS, the error messages are confusing.

As you can see, these errors seem to indicate a problem with the individual apps rather than with the network connection. Try using another network-happy app to see if it can connect. For example, if Mail is unhappy, open Safari and point it at a site you know is up. If Safari gives an error as well, check the network connection.

To sort out this problem, choose Settings | Wi-Fi from the Home screen, and then touch the > button for the wireless network. Touch the Renew Lease button for the network, and the device should be back in business.

Safari Gives "Cannot Open Page" Error

If Safari gives the message "Cannot Open Page: Safari cannot open the page because the server cannot be found," first check that the web site's address appears valid. If you're not sure, try to open a major site such as Google or Yahoo. If you still get this error (see Figure 4-12), check the HTTP proxy server set for the wireless network.

NOTE   If the HTTP proxy server is set incorrectly, Safari and other web-based apps won't work correctly. But Internet apps that use other protocols, such as Mail, will work just fine.

Troubleshooting SSL Connections to Web Sites on the iPad

Early versions of the iPad firmware sometimes have problems establishing an SSL connection to a web site even though you've installed the appropriate SSL certificate on the iPad.

NOTE   You may see the message "localized string not found" in the certificate dialog box when the iPad runs into this problem.

If this happens, grab an iPhone that has the same set of certificates installed, and see if you can access the site. If so, you know it's the iPad causing the problem.

To fix this problem, make sure the iPad's software is up to date. If not, install all available updates. If you still can't connect, try reinstalling the certificates on the iPad.

Figure 4-12.   The "Cannot Open Page" error in Safari may indicate that the iPad or iPhone has the wrong HTTP proxy server set.

TIP   For some sites, you may need to use a different browser than Safari. If you find that Safari won't access a web site correctly even though you've installed the SSL certificate required, try a different browser instead. For example, Opera Mini can sometimes access SSL web sites that Safari can't access.

Safari on iPad and iPhone Can't Access me.com Directly

If your network's users use Apple's MobileMe service with their iPads and iPhones, you may find they complain that the iPads and iPhones can't access the MobileMe site (me.com) directly.

To borrow a line out of Microsoft's playbook, this isn't actually a problem—it's a feature. Apple has set up Safari on the iPad and iPhone so that it can't connect to the me.com web site. Instead, you see the MobileMe page (see Figure 4-13), which provides shortcuts for setting up your Mail, Contacts, and Calendar; installing the Find My iPhone feature; installing the Gallery app; and installing the iDisk app.

You can't get to the other parts of me.com by using Safari. To reach them, use a different browser, such as Opera Mini or iCab.

In the next chapter, we'll look at how to equip the iPad and iPhone with the apps that users need to get their jobs done. It's a big topic, so take a break and gird your loins.

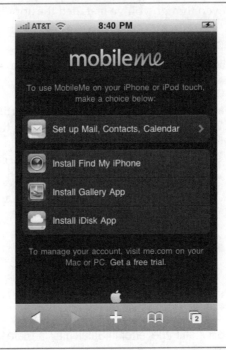

Figure 4-13.   Safari on the iPad or iPhone displays this MobileMe page when you ask to go to the me.com site.

CHAPTER 5

Equipping the iPad and iPhone with the Apps That Users Need

Both the iPad and the iPhone come with a good amount of system software—everything from the Safari browser and the full-fledged Mail client to the Calendar app and the Notes app. But for your network's users to get the maximum business mileage out of the iPad and iPhone, you'll almost certainly need to add further apps to them.

In this chapter, we'll look at how you can add apps to the iPad and iPhone and keep those apps under control and up to date. The first order of business is to decide which apps you're going to get and install for the users—productivity apps, utility apps, or whatever will help them get their work done. I mention a couple dozen apps that are widely useful, but beyond this, you'll need to dig on your own.

After that, we'll examine the different ways of installing the apps on the iPad and iPhone—by working directly on the device, by using iPhone Configuration Utility, and by creating provisioning profiles to install custom apps. We'll also go through how to rearrange the apps on the iPad or iPhone, a skill you'll probably want to make sure users know. We'll look at how to keep iOS and the apps up to date. And finally I'll show you how to uninstall apps that the devices no longer need.

Choosing Apps for Your Network's iPad and iPhone Users

Before you install any apps on the iPads and iPhones your network's users will wield, spend a while figuring out which apps the users will need to get their jobs done. The iPad and iPhone come with enough software installed to tranquilize many consumers, but for most business purposes, you'll want to add other apps—and most likely best-of-breed apps at that.

 CAUTION   The App Store offers a ferocious number of apps, with scores or hundreds more being added every day. Many of the apps have little worth—some clearly have none, and some arguably a negative worth—so be prepared to spend time identifying quality apps. Read the user reviews as well as the promotional material; most of the reviews seem honest, and many are helpful in evaluating how well the apps live up to their promises.

From a business perspective, the iPad and iPhone's app bucket is at best half full. When you ignore the apps for enjoying most forms of digital entertainment known to mankind (up till this point in our glorious history), the iPad and iPhone come with apps for browsing the Web (Safari), communicating via e-mail (Mail), keeping track of appointments (Calendar), and taking text-based notes (Notes).

This is great up to a point—but you'll almost certainly want to add other apps so that users can get other tasks done. So this section gives you a quick introduction to some of the most widely useful apps at this writing.

Understanding the Three Main Sources of iPad and iPhone Apps

Apart from the apps that come preinstalled, there are three main sources of apps for the iPad and iPhone:

- **App Store on iTunes Store**   The App Store is the central location where Apple sells the apps that it and third-party developers have created for the iPad and iPhone and have submitted for testing and approval. The App Store is a firmly walled garden, and these apps are all guaranteed to run and to behave well. Occasionally a developer sneaks in a surprise—for example, in July 2010, the developer of the Handy Light flashlight app included a hidden tethering proxy—but in general, Apple polices the App Store pretty tightly. Which of the tested and approved apps are actually useful is another question—and this question is for you.

- **Apps for jailbroken devices**   Anyone who wants to take their iPad or iPhone past the boundaries of Apple's comfort zone can *jailbreak* the device—changing the software so that the device will act in different ways than Apple permits (for example, installing unapproved software). Jailbreaking an iPad or iPhone enables you to install a wide range of software that doesn't qualify for inclusion in the App Store. Jailbreaking generally suits power users rather than companies; those sets admittedly often overlap, but this book doesn't discuss jailbreaking further.

- **Custom apps**   To meet your company's or organization's business needs, you may require a custom app—an app developed to do exactly what you want it to. You or your colleagues can create a custom app by using Apple's Xcode smithy or third-party tools. If you don't have the expertise in-house, you can also pay a third-party developer to create a custom app for you. We'll discuss how to install custom apps later in this chapter.

Productivity Apps

The Notes app that comes with the iPad and iPhone is fine for creating short documents, but for most business use, you'll need to create and edit documents, spreadsheets, and presentations. For most Windows users and many Mac users, that means using the Microsoft Office formats: Word documents, Excel workbooks, and PowerPoint presentations. For some Mac users, it means using the iWork apps and their file formats: Pages documents, Numbers spreadsheets, and Keynote presentations.

NOTE   For productivity apps, one of the biggest challenges is transferring and synchronizing documents between the iPad or iPhone and a computer or online storage. Chapter 7 explains your options for transferring documents back and forth.

iWork Apps: Pages, Numbers, and Keynote

If you need to create Mac-compatible documents, spreadsheets, and presentations on the iPad, you'll probably want to get the iWork apps. Unlike for the Mac version of iWork, you can buy each of the iWork for iPad apps separately.

- **Pages** Pages for iPad (see Figure 5-1) is a word processor and layout app. You can either create a blank document and work from scratch or base a document on one of Pages' slickly designed templates, then replace the placeholder text with your own content. Pages provides essential styles, such as different heading levels and body text, and makes it easy to insert and position photos, tables, charts, and shapes. Pages can import Microsoft Word documents, but it saves them in the Pages format rather than keeping them in Word format.

NOTE Pages can export documents in the widely used Microsoft Word format; Numbers can export spreadsheets in the similarly ubiquitous Microsoft Excel format; and Keynote can export presentations in the market-leading Microsoft PowerPoint format.

- **Numbers** Numbers for iPad (see Figure 5-2) is a spreadsheet and charting app. You can either import existing spreadsheets in Microsoft Excel format or Numbers for Mac format, or create new spreadsheets on the iPad (using either a blank template or a template from the selection that Numbers provides). Numbers makes it easy to create and edit spreadsheets, build formulas, and add graphical items (such as photos, charts, and shapes) where needed.

- **Keynote** Keynote for iPad (see Figure 5-3) is an app for creating, editing, and delivering presentations using the iPad. You can either import existing presentations in Microsoft PowerPoint or Keynote for Mac format, or create new presentations on the iPad using either a plain template (with white, black, or gradient background) or one of Keynote's colorful design templates. Keynote for iPad supports standard presentation features such as animations (for example, making an object appear on a slide or disappear from it) and transitions between slides.

Documents To Go

If you need to work with Microsoft Office documents on the iPad or iPhone without converting them to iWork formats, look at apps such as Documents To Go (discussed here) and Quickoffice (discussed in the next section). These apps can transfer Word documents, Excel workbooks, and PowerPoint presentations to the iPad and iPhone, edit them there, and transfer them back.

Documents To Go (shown in Figure 5-4 editing a Word document on the iPad in landscape mode) enables you to create and edit Word documents, Excel workbooks, and PowerPoint presentations either on the iPad or on the iPhone.

Figure 5-1.   Pages provides impressive word-processing and layout features on the iPad.

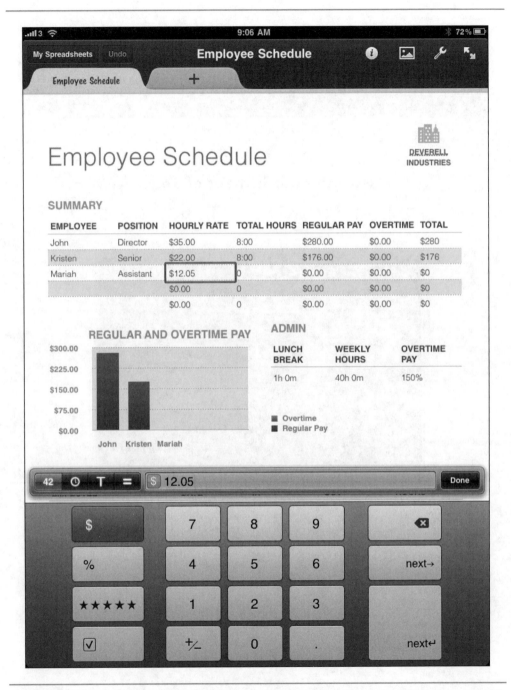

Figure 5-2. Numbers is great for creating spreadsheets on the iPad or working on spreadsheets you've imported. You can export a spreadsheet from Numbers to the widely used Microsoft Excel format.

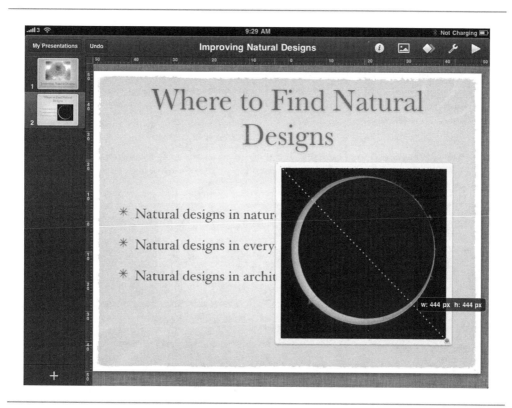

Figure 5-3.   Keynote lets you create, edit, and give presentations using the iPad. You can export the presentation files in Microsoft PowerPoint format for wide compatibility.

Documents To Go supports most of the essential features for each document type, but not the most advanced features. For example, while Documents To Go provides direct formatting (such as boldface, italics, and alignment), it doesn't let you apply styles; and widely used advanced features, such as Track Changes (for marking revisions), are off the menu.

Generally speaking, anything Documents To Go doesn't let you modify on the iPad or iPhone, it leaves in the document, so it is still there when you return the document to the PC or Mac. So if you transfer a Word document containing revision marks to the iPhone and open it in Documents To Go, you won't see the revision marks; but when you transfer the document back to your PC, the revision marks will still be there.

NOTE   At this writing, the basic version of Documents To Go can open PowerPoint presentations but cannot edit them. To edit a presentation, you need to buy Documents To Go Premium Edition.

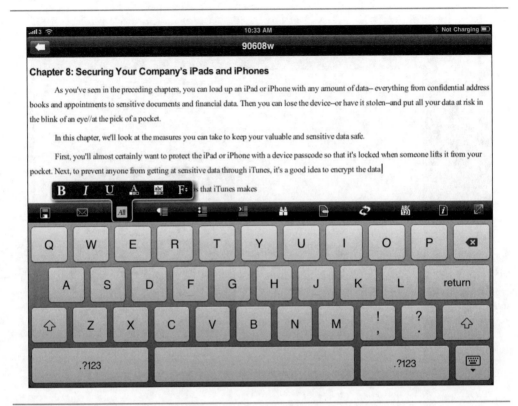

Figure 5-4. In Documents To Go, you open Word documents (as shown here), Excel workbooks, and PowerPoint presentations and edit the main parts.

Quickoffice Connect and Quickoffice Mobile Suite

Like Documents To Go, Quickoffice is an app for creating and editing Microsoft Office documents. Quickoffice comes in two main versions:

- **Quickoffice Connect**   Quickoffice Connect comes in versions for both the iPad and the iPhone. Quickoffice Connect can create and edit Office documents on the iPad or iPhone, and it can access major online storage sites such as Google Docs, Box.net, and Apple's MobileMe. Figure 5-5 shows the file-management screen in the iPad version of Quickoffice Connect.

- **Quickoffice Mobile Suite**   Quickoffice Mobile Suite runs on both the iPad and the iPhone, but at this writing it doesn't have a version that's optimized for the iPad—you're just running the iPhone version at double size. Quickoffice Mobile Suite can create, open, and edit Word documents, Excel workbooks, and PowerPoint presentations, but it cannot access online storage sites.

Figure 5-5.   Use Quickoffice to create and edit Word documents, Excel workbooks, and Power-Point presentations.

Note-Taking Apps

For taking basic notes, the iOS Notes app gets the job done. But if you're using the iPad or iPhone to capture serious amounts of information, or anything other than text, you'll need a different app. This section introduces you to four apps you can use to capture different types of data.

Evernote

Evernote (see Figure 5-6) is an app for capturing audio notes, photo notes, or text notes on the iPad or iPhone. You can set Evernote to synchronize the notes automatically to your PC or Mac and to the Evernote online service, making it easy to keep your notes synchronized across the devices you use.

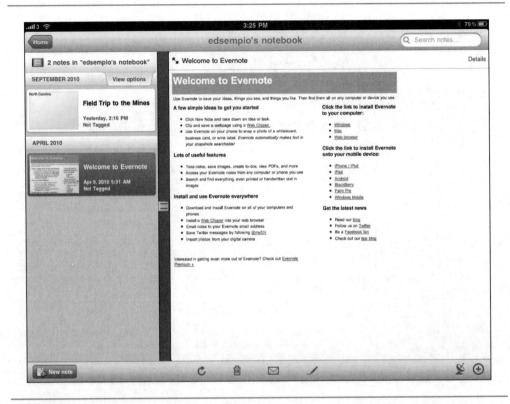

Figure 5-6.   Evernote can capture text, audio, or photo notes—and synchronize them to your computer or to the Web.

Simplenote

Simplenote is an app for taking text notes and synchronizing them with the PC or Mac. Once you've created an account via the Simplenote app, you can access your notes via a browser on the Simplenote web site (http://simplenoteapp.com).

Adobe Ideas

Adobe Ideas is an app for making sketches and drawings. Adobe provides a version of Ideas for the iPad and another for the iPhone.

Ideas (see Figure 5-7) lets you draw on the screen with your finger, much as you would on a whiteboard. Even if you're as clumsy as I am, Ideas is great for jotting down ideas visually; if you're more skilful, you can let your artistry flow.

FiRe (Field Recorder)

FiRe (short for Field Recorder) is an audio-recording app for the iPhone and iPad. FiRe is designed to give you control when recording high-quality audio with an external

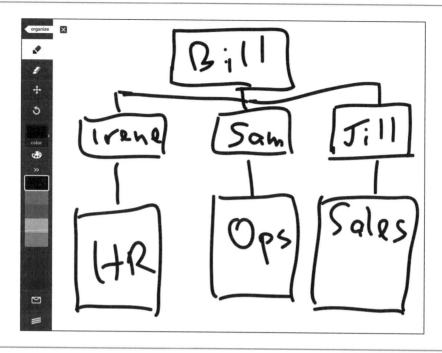

Figure 5-7. You can use Adobe Ideas to capture ideas, create illustrations, and get your point across visually.

microphone, but you can also use it with the built-in microphone on the iPhone and iPad. The left screen in Figure 5-8 shows FiRe on the iPhone recording audio through a microphone and displaying the waveform of the audio recorded, while the right screen in Figure 5-8 shows the FiRe screen for playing back and managing your recordings.

Social Networking

Even if you view social networks such as Facebook as the biggest blight on the landscape since bubonic plague, you'll probably find yourself dealing with users who consider social networks the greatest thing since chocolate-chip pancakes on a stick—or possibly to accompany them.

If your iPad and iPhone users need to keep up with social networks as part of their work, you'll need to provide suitable apps for them. This section provokes you with a glimpse of the iPad and iPhone clients for the business-oriented LinkedIn social network and for Facebook itself.

Figure 5-8.   The FiRe recording app shows you the waveform as it records (left). From the Recordings screen (right), you can play back and manage your recordings.

LinkedIn

LinkedIn (shown on the left in Figure 5-9) is an app for keeping up with your contacts on the LinkedIn social network.

Facebook

As you'd guess, the Facebook app is the iPad and iPhone's way of staying up to speed with your contacts on the Facebook social network and unearthing their latest phone numbers. The right screen in Figure 5-9 shows the main screen of the Facebook app.

Readers and Newsreaders

Entering text on the iPad or iPhone via the onscreen keyboard may be heavy going, but both devices are great for displaying information. Chances are that both you and your network's users will need to read books, PDF files, and other information on the iPad and iPhone—and maybe news as well.

For reading e-books, iOS comes with the iBooks reader software. But you may also want to get other reader apps that enable you to easily download content or transfer

Figure 5-9.   Use the LinkedIn app (left) to keep up with contacts on the LinkedIn social network. Use the Facebook app (right) to stay in touch on Facebook.

it from your computer. This section shows you some of the main contenders for your attention.

If you enjoy (or must endure) reading news online, you can also find newsreader apps for the iPad and iPhone that will let you pursue your reading habits wherever you happen to be. This section also shows you a newsreader app you may want to investigate.

Stanza

Stanza is an e-book reader app that's great for reading and downloading e-books on either the iPad or the iPhone. Stanza can open books in several widely used formats, including ePub, eReader, PDF, and Comic Book Archive. If you have e-books on your computer, you can add them to Stanza by using iTunes' File Sharing feature (discussed in Chapter 7). Stanza also hooks into online book archives and bookstores, including the many free books in Project Gutenberg and Feedbooks.

Figure 5-10 shows the Books screen of the Library area in Stanza.

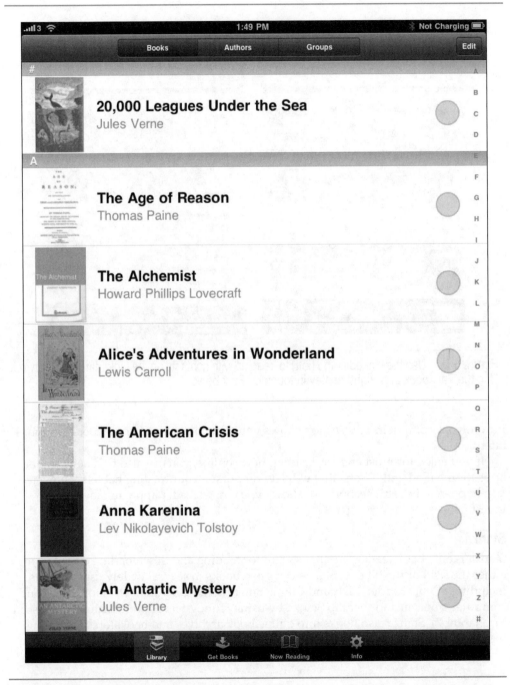

Figure 5-10.   Stanza is a popular e-book reader app that can open books in widely used formats, including ePub and PDF.

Kindle

Kindle, Amazon.com's e-book reader app, enables you to access Amazon's bookstore and download e-books. Kindle is free, but you need to register it with your Amazon account in order to use it. Amazon provides a free sample of each book, but the usual cautions about purchasing e-books apply: You can't share them with others, and you can't resell them. With Kindle, Amazon can also delete books from your iPad if it discovers legal reasons it shouldn't have sold you the books (for example, copyright issues).

PDF Reader

If you need to read many PDF files on the iPad or iPhone, you may want to use a dedicated PDF reader rather than iOS' iBooks app.

The App Store offers various PDF reader apps with similar names. It can be tough to distinguish between the app named PDF Reader Pro and the app named PDF Reader Pro Edition, let alone the three apps that have the name PDF Reader.

Figure 5-11 shows PDF Reader Pro (no "Edition" there), which works well for me.

Aji Annotate PDF

Aji Annotate PDF is a PDF reader app for the iPhone that includes features for annotating PDFs. If you read PDFs widely, you may find it helpful to highlight the sections you need to focus on, or scribble notes in the margins.

 NOTE   At this writing, there's no iPad version of Aji Annotate PDF. Instead, try iAnnotate PDF.

Reeder

Reeder is an offline newsreader that can synchronize with Google Reader and cache your newsfeeds offline so that you can read them anywhere. You can browse your items by feeds or by folders, share items with friends, and open items in Safari or other apps. Figure 5-12 shows Reeder for iPad.

Utility Applications

iOS comes with some utility apps, but third-party developers have created huge numbers of other apps to fill unmet needs—some apparently imagined, but most of them real. This section suggests a calculator app you may want to add to the iPad, a means of making essential files available to the iPad and iPhone wherever you are, and a utility for locating open Wi-Fi networks.

Calculator for iPad

In a strange move, Apple has chosen not to include a calculator app on the iPad. Many users feel the lack of a calculator app almost immediately.

Figure 5-11. PDF Reader Pro has straightforward features for transferring PDF files to the iPad and iPhone and reading them there.

Figure 5-12.   Reeder is an offline newsreader that synchronizes with your Google Reader account.

There's a free app called simply Calculator that has a quirky style but meets basic needs. For serious users, a straightforward paid app such as Calculator HD or Big Calculator is a better choice.

Dropbox

If you need to store files online so that you can get at them quickly from any computer or device that has Internet access, Dropbox can be a great tool. You can upload files from a computer, using either a web browser or the Dropbox program, to your account on the Dropbox service, and then use the Dropbox app to access and view them on your iPad and iPhone. Figure 5-13 shows the Dropbox app running on an iPad.

Wi-Fi Finder Apps

To get the most out of the iPad and iPhone, you and your colleagues will probably want to connect to wireless networks rather than the cellular network as much as possible. In the office and at home, connecting should be easy enough; on the road, rather less so. The App Store offers a variety of apps for locating open Wi-Fi networks that you should be able to connect to. Figure 5-14 shows a Wi-Fi finder app, Open WiFi Spots HD, running on the iPad.

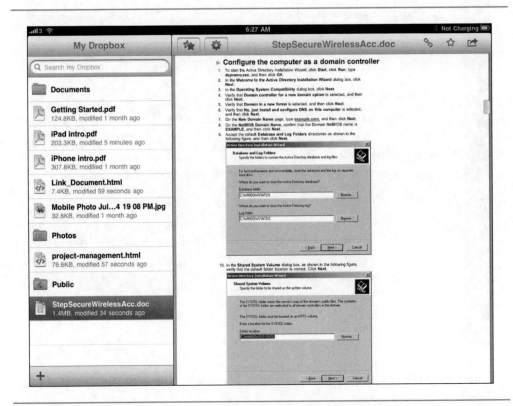

Figure 5-13.   Dropbox lets you access your online file storage easily from the iPad or iPhone.

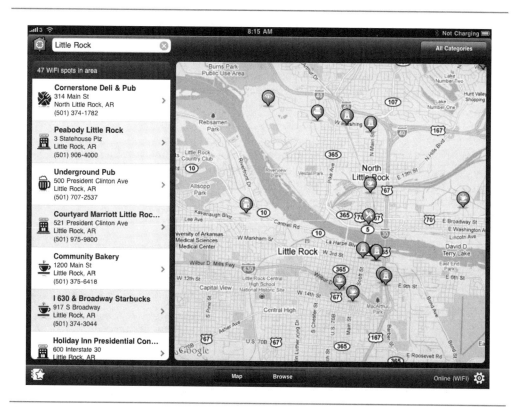

Figure 5-14. Wi-Fi finder apps such as Open WiFi Spots HD (shown here) can help you locate open wireless networks when you're off home territory.

CAUTION   Before choosing a Wi-Fi finder utility, read the App Store blurb carefully—and be sure to read the product reviews too to see whether the app lives up to its promises. Being able to pinpoint every Wi-Fi-enabled McDonalds in Los Angeles won't help much when you're on the road and find Bogotá is a blank.

Network and Remote-Access Apps

For network and systems administrators, the iPad and iPhone can be great tools for checking network and server status, connecting remotely, and troubleshooting problems. This section introduces you to a handful of network and remote-access apps you may find useful for keeping your network up and in good order.

NOTE   To connect across the Internet using most remote-access apps, either the target computer must have a public IP address (rather than a private IP address inside the network) or your router must be configured to direct the appropriate packets to the target computer. For example, if you use the standard port for VNC (port 5900), you can configure your router to set incoming traffic on port 5900 to the target computer.

Mocha VNC

Mocha VNC is a Virtual Network Computing (VNC) client that provides remote access to any computer running a VNC server. Mac OS X and most Linux distributions include a built-in VNC server, and you can add one to Windows easily enough. Figure 5-15 shows Mocha VNC (running on an iPad) remotely accessing a Mac via VNC.

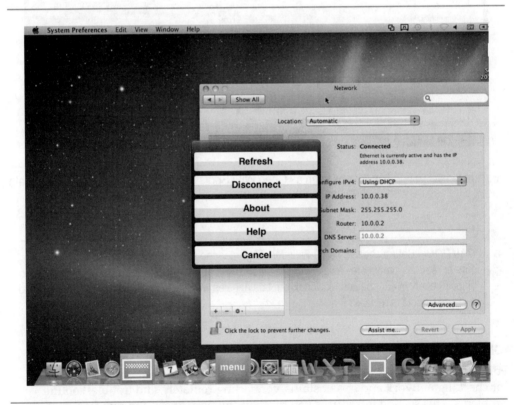

Figure 5-15.   Mocha VNC lets you easily connect remotely to a PC, Mac (shown here), or Linux box across the network or Internet. To display the menu shown here, you touch the Menu button at the bottom of the screen.

LogMeIn Ignition

LogMeIn Ignition is a remote-access app that enables you to connect to a remote PC or Mac either across the network or across the Internet. To avoid problems with firewalls, you create an account at the LogMeIn web site (https://secure.logmein.com/) and run the LogMeIn program on your PC or Mac. After the computer establishes a connection to the LogMeIn service, LogMeIn Ignition on the iPad or iPhone can discover the computer and connect to it via the LogMeIn service.

WinAdmin

WinAdmin is a Remote Desktop Protocol (RDP) client for the iPad and iPhone. You can use WinAdmin to remotely control Windows servers or any version of Windows that includes the Remote Desktop feature—for example, Windows 7 Professional or Ultimate, Windows Vista Business or Ultimate, or Windows XP Professional. (The Home versions of Windows don't include Remote Desktop, because Microsoft positions it as a business feature.)

Figure 5-16 shows WinAdmin on the iPad connecting to a PC running Windows Server 2008.

NOTE   Before you can use WinAdmin, you must turn on the Remote Desktop feature on the Remote tab of the System Properties dialog box. On Windows Server 2008, Windows 7, or Windows Vista, you need to select the Allow Connections From Computers Running Any Version Of Remote Desktop option button rather than the Allow Connections Only From Computers Running Remote Desktop With Network Level Authentication option button.

Network Ping

Network Ping is a utility for running ping, subnet ping, traceroute, and telnet on your LAN. The first three features are useful for troubleshooting network problems, while telnet is still useful for connecting to remote servers (albeit with minimal security).

The left screen in Figure 5-17 shows the Ping feature in Network Ping pinging a device on the local network. The right screen in Figure 5-17 shows the Traceroute feature in Network Ping tracing the route to an Internet site.

NOTE   If you need only telnet capability for connecting remotely to a telnet server, look for a telnet client such as Telnet or pTerm.

Network Utility Pro

Network Utility Pro is an iPhone utility for running pings, port scans, and whois queries. You can use it to check network status and troubleshoot network problems

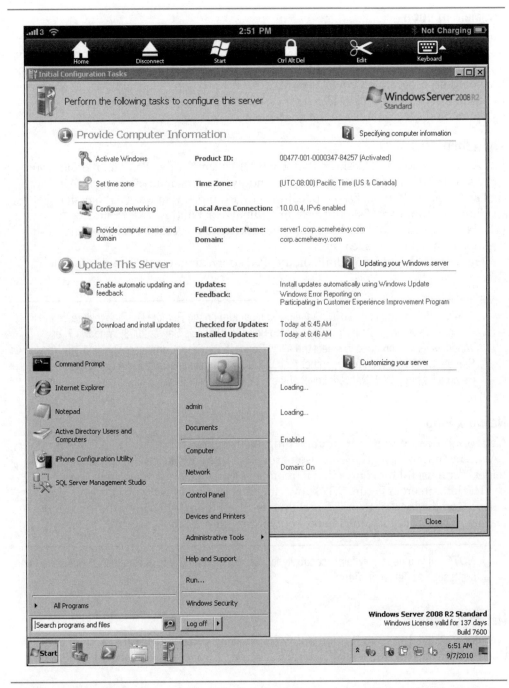

Figure 5-16. WinAdmin is an RDP client that can connect to any Windows PC that's running the Remote Desktop feature.

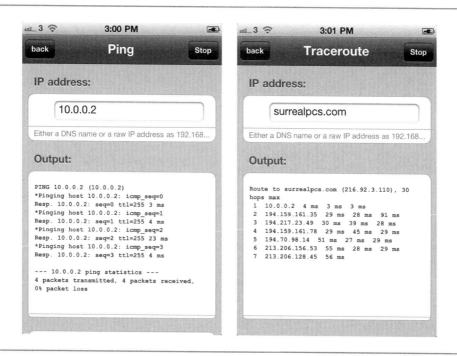

Figure 5-17.   Network Ping includes a Ping feature (left) and a Traceroute feature (right) as well as a Subnet Ping feature and a Telnet feature.

from your iPhone. Figure 5-18 shows Network Utility Pro's main screen (on the left) and Network Utility Pro pinging the Yahoo! web site (on the right).

Snap

Snap (Simple Network Area Prober) is an iPhone app that'll run on the iPad as well. Snap scans your network and produces a list of the devices on it, as shown in the left screen in Figure 5-19. You can drill down to see the details of a device, as shown in the right screen in Figure 5-19.

Citrix Receiver

Citrix Receiver (made—as you'd guess—by remote-access specialists Citrix Systems, Inc.) is a utility for connecting to virtual desktops and apps running Citrix XenApp or XenDesktop. Citrix Receiver lets you run programs remotely from your iPad or iPhone. This is useful both when you need to get work done from a distance and when you need to run programs that won't run directly on the iPad and iPhone.

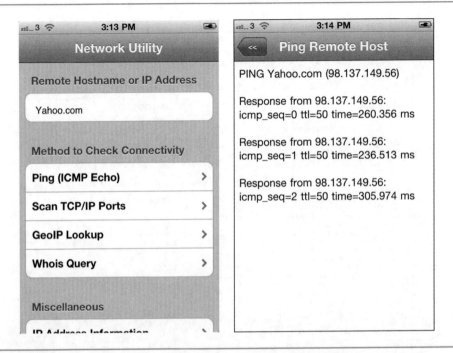

Figure 5-18. Network Utility Pro (left) includes Ping, TCP/IP Port Scan, GeoIP Lookup, and Whois Query features. Use Ping (right) to check connectivity to a remote computer.

GoToMeeting

GoToMeeting (also from Citrix Systems, Inc.) is a utility for participating in online meetings.

To set up and run an online meeting, you need the free GoToMeeting desktop program (for PC or Mac, from www.gotomeeting.com) and a GoToMeeting account (for which you have to pay; you can start with a 30-day trial, also at www.gotomeeting.com).

To join a meeting, all you need is GoToMeeting on your iPad and either an invitation to a meeting (for example, in an e-mail message) or the Meeting ID that you enter directly into the GoToMeeting app (see Figure 5-20).

Web-Ex

Web-Ex (made by Cisco) is a utility for taking part in online meetings. The upper screen in Figure 5-21 shows a Web-Ex meeting with nothing yet being shared. The lower screen in Figure 5-21 shows Web-Ex sharing a document with an area marked up.

To set up and run an online meeting, you need to create a Web-Ex account at the Web-Ex web site (www.webex.com; you can start with a 14-day free trial). To join in a meeting, you follow a link in an e-mail or a calendar item, or run Web-Ex and enter the meeting number.

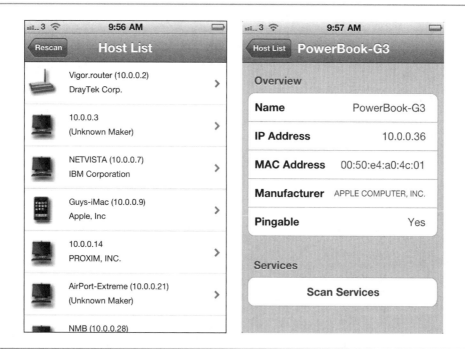

Figure 5-19.   Use Snap to discover which devices are on your network (left) and their details (right).

NOTE   On the iPhone, the Web-Ex icon is named Meet for reasons known only to Cisco. Searching for "Web-Ex" or "Cisco" doesn't find it.

Installing the Apps on the iPad or iPhone

In this section, we'll look at the different ways in which you can install apps on the iPad or iPhone. There are three ways of installing apps:

- **Install an app directly from the App Store**   This is the normal way for consumers to install apps on their iPads and iPhones.

- **Download an app using iTunes, then install it**   This is the other normal way for consumers to install apps on their iPads and iPhones.

- **Install an app using iPhone Configuration Utility**   When you're setting up the iPad or iPhone, you can quickly load all the apps it needs.

Figure 5-20. You can join a meeting by entering its Meeting ID directly in the Join A Meeting dialog box in GoToMeeting.

Preventing the User from Installing Apps on the iPad or iPhone

Depending on what users do, you may want to prevent them from installing any apps on the iPad or iPhone.

To do so, create a Restrictions payload in a configuration profile, and clear the Allow Installing Apps check box. In the General options, set the Security drop-down list or pop-up menu to Never or With Authorization (as appropriate) to prevent the user from removing the configuration profile. Then apply the configuration profile to the iPad or iPhone.

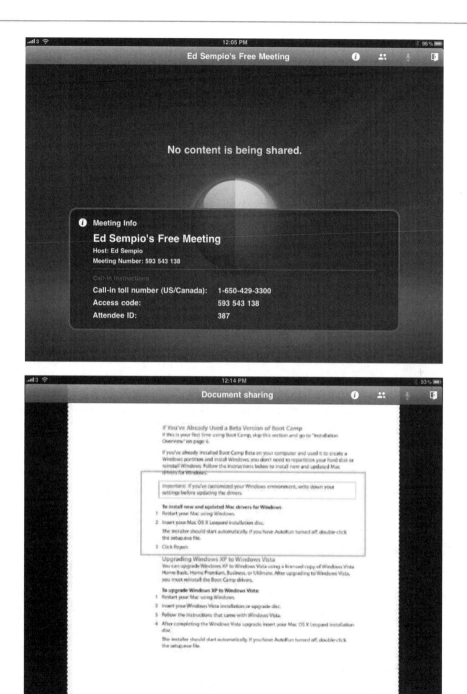

Figure 5-21.   With Web-Ex, you can join a meeting (top), chat, and share documents (bottom) and applications.

Installing an App from the App Store

You can install an app from the App Store either by downloading it to the iPad or iPhone (and then synchronizing it to the PC or Mac) or by downloading it using iTunes and then installing it on the iPad or iPhone.

 NOTE   At this writing, the App Store has a Volume Purchase Program for educational institutions (see www.apple.com/itunes/education/), but it doesn't yet have one for enterprises and other organizations. Given how widely iPads and iPhones are used in business, this seems likely to change soon.

To use the App Store, you need to have an iTunes Store account. To create one, follow these steps:

1. Open iTunes.

2. Click the iTunes Store item under the Store category in the Source list to display the iTunes Store. You can also double-click the iTunes Store item to open a new window showing the iTunes Store.

3. Click the Sign In button in the upper-right corner of the iTunes window. iTunes displays the Sign In To Download From the iTunes Store dialog box.

4. Click the Create New Account button, and then follow the instructions.

 NOTE   If you want to prevent users from creating iTunes Store accounts on their work computers, configure Parental Controls in iTunes to disable the iTunes Store. When working on the computer, choose Edit | Preferences to display the iTunes dialog box on Windows or choose iTunes | Preferences to display the Preferences dialog box on the Mac. Click the Parental Control tab, and then select the iTunes Store check box in the Disable area. If you want to permit users access to iTunes U, select the Allow Access To iTunes U check box. Then click the lock icon to apply the parental controls. You can also apply these parental controls through policy in Active Directory or Open Directory.

Downloading an App to the iPad or iPhone

If you allow users to install apps from the App Store, they (or you) can do so like this:

1. From the Home screen, touch the App Store button to open the App Store app.

2. Touch one of the buttons at the bottom of the screen to see the appropriate screen of apps:

    ■ **Featured**   This screen contains a New list (of the latest apps), a What's Hot list (showing the apps that are currently most popular), and a Genius list (which scans the apps you've already installed and tries to suggest other apps that'll interest you). The left screen in Figure 5-22 shows an example of the Featured screen.

Figure 5-22.   On the iPad or iPhone, you can browse the App Store using the Featured list (left) or the Categories list (right). You can also visit the Top 25 screen, search for apps, or update your existing apps.

- **Categories**   This screen lets you browse the apps by different categories: Games, Entertainment, Utilities, Social Networking, Music, Productivity, and so on. The right screen in Figure 5-22 shows the Productivity screen you can reach from the Categories screen.

- **Top 25**   This screen contains lists of the top 25 paid apps, the top 25 free apps, and the top 25 grossing apps (those that have made the most money over their lifetime). The masses aren't always right, but they'll often point you to the most useful or most amusing apps. If you're looking for paid apps, the Top Grossing list is worth a look, as it gives a better idea of sustained popularity than the Top Paid list (which gives a snapshot of what's currently popular).

- **Search**   This screen lets you search by using keywords. If you have a good idea of what you're looking for, this can be a good way to find it.

- **Updates**   This screen lets you quickly find updates for apps that are already installed on the device. The iPad and iPhone check automatically for new versions of apps.

3. If an app looks interesting, touch its icon to display the Info screen. The left screen in Figure 5-23 shows an example of the Info screen for a free app.

4. To get the app, touch the price button (for a pay app) or the Free button (for a free app), and then touch the Install button that replaces this button.

5. Enter the password when the iPad or iPhone prompts you for it. The device then displays the Home screen, which shows you a progress bar on the app's icon as the app loads and installs (see the last icon in the right screen in Figure 5-23).

6. Once the app has finished installing, touch the icon to launch it.

7. The next time you connect the iPad or iPhone to your computer and synchronize, iTunes copies the app from the device to the computer.

TIP   Most apps are licensed per computer rather than per device. So if a user uses both an iPad and an iPhone, they can load the same app on both.

Figure 5-23.   Check the Info screen (left) for details and reviews before buying or download-ing an app. As the app installs and downloads, the Home screen shows you what's happening (right).

Downloading an App Using iTunes

Browsing the apps on the App Store using the iPad works pretty well, but many people find the iPhone's screen is small enough to make browsing awkward. In this case, iTunes is a better bet.

To browse the App Store with iTunes, follow these steps:

1. Open iTunes.

2. Open the iTunes Store in the main iTunes window or a separate window:

   ■ **Main iTunes window**   Click the iTunes Store item under the Store category in the Source list.

   ■ **Separate window**   Double-click the iTunes Store item to open a new window showing the iTunes Store.

3. Click the App Store button in the navigation bar at the top of the window to go to the App Store's home page, or click the App Store drop-down button (on the right of the App Store button) to display a menu from which you can choose the category of apps you want. Figure 5-24 shows this menu open and the mouse making a Stakhanovite choice, the Productivity category.

Figure 5-24.   You can either go to the App Store's home page or use this menu to go directly to the category of apps you want.

4. Once you've reached the App Store, you can browse by category or by the lists of apps (for example, the Top Grossing list), or use the Search Store box in the upper-right corner to search by keywords. When you find an app you want to get, click the price button (for a paid app) or the Free App button (for a priceless app, as in Figure 5-25). Follow the prompts for confirming that you want to pay (or get the app for free). iTunes then starts downloading the app.

NOTE At the top of the App Store is an iPhone/iPad button that you can click to switch between viewing iPhone apps and iPad-only apps. Any app that runs on the iPhone runs on the iPad as well, though the display may be scaled up and so appear blocky. Any iPad-only app runs only on the iPad—for example, because it requires acres of screen real-estate.

5. When the download has finished, connect the iPad or iPhone to the computer and wait for iTunes to recognize it.

Figure 5-25. Click the price button or the Free App button (as shown here on the left side, under the icon) to start the download process.

6. Click the iPad's or iPhone's item in the Devices category of the Source list.
7. Click the Apps tab to display its contents.

NOTE If the Automatically Sync New Apps check box on the Apps tab is selected, iTunes automatically installs each new app when you sync the iPad or iPhone.

8. Make sure the app's check box is selected in the list of apps.
9. Click the Apply button (if you selected the app's check box or made another change) or the Sync button. iTunes installs the app on the device.

Installing Custom Apps by Using Provisioning Profiles

If you develop custom apps for your company's or organization's iPads or iPhones, you need to use provisioning profiles to install the apps. The provisioning profile contains the information required to make the iPads or iPhones install the app.

To install a custom enterprise app, you need three things: a valid Enterprise Developer Account, a provisioning profile, and an app distribution bundle. Make sure you have all three before trying to install an app.

NOTE You can start creating iOS apps by signing up for the iPhone Developer program, which is free, and downloading the iOS Software Development Kit (SDK), which includes the Xcode integrated development environment (IDE) and the iPhone Simulator (which includes an iPad simulator). To sign up, go to the iPhone Dev Center (http://developer.apple.com/iphone/index. action), click one of the Log In links, and then click the Join Now link on the Sign In screen.

You create the provisioning profile in iPhone Configuration Utility, and then install it on the iPad or iPhone. We'll look at each step in turn.

NOTE In order to install your custom apps on the iPad and iPhone, you must sign the apps with a digital certificate provided by Apple. To get such a certificate, you sign up for the iPhone Developer Enterprise Program. This costs $299; to qualify, your company or organization must have at least 500 employees and a Dun & Bradstreet listing. To sign up for the iPhone Developer Enterprise Program, steer your web browser to the iPhone Developer Enterprise Program home page (https://developer.apple.com/programs/iphone/enterprise/), and then click the Apply Now button.

Getting a Provisioning Profile for One or More Custom Apps

After you create one or more custom apps, you have your Team Agent at Apple's Enterprise Program Portal create a provisioning profile for you. The provisioning profile can cover a single app or multiple apps, depending on your needs. For example, if you will install the same set of apps on every iPad and iPhone your network uses, you may prefer a single provisioning profile. If you need to be able to install the apps separately, as is often the case, get a separate provisioning profile for each.

The Team Agent provides you with the provisioning profile in a .mobileprovision file. You then add it to the Provisioning Profiles item in the Library category in iPhone Configuration Utility like this:

1. Open iPhone Configuration Utility.

2. In the Source list, click the Provisioning Profiles item to display the list of provisioning profiles.

3. Click the Add button, or choose File | Add To Library from the menu bar, or press CTRL-O (on Windows) or ⌘-O (on the Mac). iPhone Configuration Utility displays an Open dialog box.

4. Navigate to the folder that contains the provisioning profile, and then click the file.

5. Click the Open button. iPhone Configuration Utility adds the provisioning profile to the list.

Installing a Provisioning Profile on an iPad or iPhone

Next, you need to put the provisioning profile on the iPad or iPhone. You can do this either by using iPhone Configuration Utility or by using iTunes.

Installing a Provisioning Profile Using iPhone Configuration Utility

The most direct way of installing a provisioning profile on an iPad or iPhone is by using iPhone Configuration Utility. Use this method when you have the device at your workstation—for example, when you're setting it up straight out of the box.

To install a provisioning profile using iPhone Configuration Utility, follow these steps:

1. Connect the iPad or iPhone to your computer.

2. Launch iPhone Configuration Utility.

3. In the Devices category in the source list, click the iPad or iPhone to display its configuration screens.

4. Click the Provisioning Profiles tab to display its contents.

5. Click the Install button for the provisioning profile you want to install.

Installing a Provisioning Profile Using iTunes

The other way of installing a provisioning profile on an iPad or iPhone is by using iTunes. Use this method when you've put the devices in the hands of the users, you've given the users the authorization and authentication required to install apps, and you need the users to install the provisioning profile without your help.

Supply the provisioning profile to the users in your preferred manner—for example, by sending the .mobileprovision file as an e-mail attachment, or having the user copy it from a folder or download it from a web site.

Making iTunes Install Provisioning Profiles Automatically

You can make iTunes automatically install provisioning profiles on iPads and iPhones by putting the .mobileprovision files in the appropriate folders (listed next). If the folder you need isn't already there, create it.

These are the folders to use on Mac OS X:

- ■ **User Profiles Folder**   ~/Library/MobileDevice/Provisioning Profiles/
- ■ **Mac Profiles Folder**   /Library/MobileDevice/Provisioning Profiles/

Because these folders are typically both on the Mac itself, you may not have a way of getting the .mobileprovision files directly into them. If the user's home folder is in a network share, you may be able to access that more easily. But there's also another approach you can use: Set the ProvisioningProfilesPath key in ~/Library/Preferences/ to the folder in which you want to place the provisioning profile files. iTunes checks all three of these folders automatically and installs the provisioning profiles it finds.

These are the folders to use on Windows 7 or Windows Vista, where *bootdrive* is the PC's boot drive (for example, C:) and *username* is the user's name (for example, sally):

- ■ **User Profiles Folder**   *bootdrive*:\Users*username*\AppData\Roaming\ Apple Computer\MobileDevice\Provisioning Profiles
- ■ **Computer Profiles Folder**   *bootdrive*:\ProgramData\Apple Computer\ MobileDevice\Provisioning Profiles

Because these folders are on the PC's boot drive, it can be difficult to put the .mobileprovision files directly into them. Instead, you can go into the Registry and set the ProvisioningProfilesPath key in either HKEY_CURRENT_USER\ Software\Apple Computer, Inc. (for the current user) or HKEY_LOCAL_ MACHINE\SOFTWARE\Apple Computer, Inc. (for the PC as a whole) in the Registry to specify the path on which iTunes should look for the provisioning profiles. For example, you can point these keys to a network folder.

These are the folders to use on Windows XP, where *bootdrive* is the PC's boot drive (for example, C:) and *username* is the user's name (for example, pwilson):

- ■ **User Profiles Folder**   *bootdrive*:\Documents and Settings*username*\ Application Data\Apple Computer\ MobileDevice\Provisioning Profiles
- ■ **Computer Profiles Folder**   *bootdrive*: \Documents and Settings\All Users\Application Data\Apple Computer\MobileDevice\Provisioning Profiles

For Windows XP, you can use the same Registry keys just given for Windows 7 and Windows Vista.

Then have the user install it by taking the following steps:

1. Drag the .mobileprovision file to the iTunes icon. iTunes automatically copies the provisioning profile to the appropriate folder (see the nearby sidebar for a list).

2. Connect the iPad or iPhone to the computer.

3. Synchronize the iPad or iPhone as usual.

Installing a Custom App

Once you've put the provisioning profile for a custom app in place, you can install the app itself on the iPad or iPhone by using either iPhone Configuration Utility or iTunes.

Installing an App Using iPhone Configuration Utility

If you will install the app yourself, use iPhone Configuration Utility. This approach is useful for when you're first setting up the iPad or iPhone for the first time or when a user brings it to you for troubleshooting.

NOTE   Chapter 3 contains detailed coverage of iPhone Configuration Utility.

First, add the app to the Apps list in iPhone Configuration Utility. Follow these steps:

1. Open iPhone Configuration Utility.

2. Click the Apps item under the Library category in the Source list to display the Apps list.

3. Click the Add button on the toolbar, or choose File | Add To Library, or press CTRL-O (on Windows) or ⌘-O (on the Mac). iPhone Configuration Utility displays the Browse For Folder dialog box (on Windows) or an unnamed dialog box (on the Mac).

4. Browse to the appropriate folder, and then click the app.

5. Click the OK button to close the dialog box and add the app to the Apps list.

After you've added the app to the Apps list, you can install it on an iPad or iPhone. Follow these steps:

1. Open iPhone Configuration Utility.

2. Connect the iPad or iPhone.

3. Click the iPad or iPhone in the Devices category in the Source list.

4. Click the Apps tab to display its contents.

5. Click the Install button for the app.

Installing an App Using iTunes

If you will have users install the apps on their iPads or iPhones, have them use iTunes. This is normally the best approach once you've loosed the iPads and iPhones into the wild of your network.

First, provide the app to the user. For example, make the app available on a network drive the user can access, or send the app via e-mail (if it's small enough not to upset delicate mail servers).

Whichever way the user receives the app, he or she can add it to iTunes by simply dragging it to the iTunes icon and dropping it there.

 NOTE   You (or the user) can also add the app by choosing File | Add File To Library or pressing CTRL-O (on Windows) or choosing File | Add To Library or pressing ⌘-O (on the Mac), selecting the app in the Add To Library dialog box that opens, and then clicking the Open button (on Windows) or the Choose button (on the Mac).

After adding the app to iTunes, the user follows these steps to install the app on the iPad or iPhone:

1. Connect the iPad or iPhone to the computer. Normally, iTunes launches automatically (if it wasn't running already); if not, the user can launch iTunes from the Start menu or the Dock.

2. Click the iPad's or iPhone's entry in the Devices list in the Source pane in iTunes to display the device's configuration screens.

3. Click the Apps tab to display the list of apps.

4. Make sure the Sync Apps check box is selected.

5. In the list of apps, select the check box for the app to install.

6. Click the Apply button to make the change. iTunes synchronizes the iPad or iPhone.

Rearranging the Apps on the iPad or iPhone

When you install a new app on the iPad or iPhone, iOS automatically puts the icon in the first available space on one of the Home screens. For example, if the first Home screen is full, and the second is only partly full, iOS puts the app's icon in the first empty space on the second screen. If there are several screens of apps, but there's an empty space on the first Home screen, iOS puts the app's icon in that space.

This automatic placement works fine and is easy enough to grasp, but your users will often get better use out of the iPad and iPhone by rearranging the apps on the Home screens. They can do this either in iTunes or on the iPad or iPhone itself. You'll probably want to make sure they know both ways of rearranging the apps and putting them into folders so that they can instantly launch or switch to the apps they need.

Rearranging the Apps Using iTunes

To use iTunes to rearrange the apps on the iPad or iPhone, first display the Home screen containing the icons to rearrange. Follow these steps:

1. Connect the iPad or iPhone to the computer.

2. If iTunes doesn't launch or activate automatically when the computer detects the iPad or iPhone, launch or switch to iTunes manually.

3. In the Devices list in the Source list, click the entry for the iPad or iPhone to display its control screens.

4. Click the Apps tab to display its contents.

5. In the scrolling list of Home screens, click the Home screen that contains the icons you want to rearrange.

6. Make the changes as discussed in the following sections, and then click the Apply button to apply them to the device.

Moving an App to a New Position on the Same Home Screen

To move an app to a new position on the same Home screen, click the app and drag it to where you want it to appear. The other apps move out of the way to make room for the app you're moving.

Moving an App to a Different Home Screen

To move an app to a different Home screen, follow these steps:

1. Click the app and drag it to the list of Home screens and hold it over the Home screen to which you want to move it. iTunes displays that Home screen.

2. Drag the app to where you want it to appear, and then drop it. The other apps move out of the way to make space for the app. If the Home screen is full, the last app gets bumped off it. If the next Home screen has a free space, the app lands on that Home screen; if the next Home screen is full, iOS creates a new Home screen and puts the app there all on its lonesome (until you rearrange the apps further).

NOTE You can customize the main apps at the bottom of the Home screens. Click one of the main apps and drag it off the bar at the bottom of the screen. Then click and drag there the app or folder you want instead.

Adding an App to a Folder

Even if you maintain rigorous quality control on apps and delete any unworthy ones with which you inadvertently sully your iPad or iPhone, the Home screens can easily become busy with too many apps. To save you from having to wade through many different Home screens, you can create folders and put apps into them. For example, you could put all your reference-related apps into a single folder.

To create a folder, follow these steps:

1. Identify the apps you want to put in a folder. You may prefer to put all the apps on the same Home screen as a preliminary move to make things easier.

2. Drag one of the apps that you want to put into a folder to the app in whose position you want to create a folder. iOS creates a folder, puts both apps into it, and displays a text box with a suggested name, as shown in Figure 5-26. iTunes darkens the other icons to make it clear that you're working with the folder.

3. To change the suggested name, edit it as needed, or click the × button to delete the suggested name, and then type the name you want.

4. Click the folder's icon to display the rest of the icons again.

You can now drag other apps to the folder and drop them there.

NOTE You can't nest one folder inside another. If you try to drag one folder to another folder, iOS moves the other folder smartly out of the way.

Figure 5-26. When you create a new folder, iTunes darkens the other apps and displays a box for naming the folder.

Removing an App from a Folder

To remove an app from a folder, double-click the folder to open it, then click the app and drag it up to the top of the screen. When the remaining icons appear, drag the app to where you want it.

Changing the Order of the Home Screens

In iTunes, you can quickly change the order of the Home screens by dragging them up and down the list of Home screens. You can't change the order on the iPad or iPhone itself.

Rearranging the Apps Directly on the iPad or iPhone

Instead of using iTunes to rearrange the apps on the iPad or iPhone, you can work directly on the iPad or iPhone. The following sections give you the details.

Moving an App to a New Position on the Same Home Screen

To move an app to a new position on the same Home screen, follow these steps:

1. Display the Home screen that contains the app.

2. Touch any app and keep touching it until the app icons start to jiggle (see Figure 5-27).

Figure 5-27.   To move apps, touch an app until the app icons start to jiggle. The × marks indicate apps you can delete.

3. Touch the app you want to move, and drag it to where you want it to appear. The other apps make room for it.

4. Move other apps as needed, and then press the Home button when you're ready to stop customizing.

Moving an App to a Different Home Screen

To move an app to a different Home screen, follow these steps:

1. Display the Home screen that contains the app.

2. Touch any app and keep touching it until the app icons start to jiggle.

3. Touch the app you want to move, then drag it off the left side of the screen (to get to the previous Home screen) or the right side of the screen (to get to the next Home screen). You can then drag to the left or right again if necessary.

4. Drag the app to where you want it to appear, and then drop it. The other apps move out of the way to make space for the app. If the Home screen is full, the last app gets bumped off it. If the next Home screen is full, its last icon gets bumped to the following home screen, and so on until you hit a Home screen that has a free parking space.

NOTE You can customize the main apps at the bottom of the Home screens. Touch and hold an app until the icons start jiggling, then drag one of the main apps off the bar at the bottom of the screen. Then drag there the app or folder you want instead.

Adding an App to a Folder

To reduce the number of icons on your Home screens, you can create folders containing related apps. (Or unrelated apps if you prefer—for example, you could create a Seldom Useful folder for the apps you rarely use but can't yet bring yourself to part with.)

To create a folder, follow these steps:

1. Decide which apps you'll put in the folder. To make the process easier, first put them on the same Home screen.

2. Touch any app and keep touching it until the app icons start to jiggle.

3. Drag one of the apps that you want to put into a folder to the app in whose position you want to create a folder. iOS creates a folder, puts both apps into it, and displays a text box with a suggested name (see Figure 5-28). iOS darkens the other icons to make it clear that you're working with the folder.

4. To change the suggested name, edit it as needed, or click the × button to delete the suggested name, and then use the soft keyboard to type the name you want.

5. Click the folder's icon to display the rest of the icons again.

You can now drag other apps to the folder and drop them there.

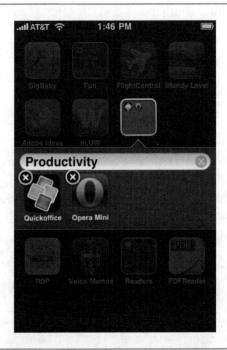

Figure 5-28.   You can create a new folder on the iPhone by dragging one app on top of another.

   NOTE   You can't nest one folder inside another. If you try to drag one folder to another folder, iOS moves the other folder, as it assumes you're rearranging the icons.

Opening an App in a Folder

To open an app that you've stored in a folder, touch the folder to open it, and then touch the app.

Removing an App from a Folder

To remove an app from a folder, touch the folder to open it, then touch the app and drag it up to the top of the screen. When the remaining icons appear, drag the app to where you want it, and then set it free.

Keeping iOS and the Apps on the iPad or iPhone Up to Date

To keep the iPad and iPhone running smoothly, it's a good idea to update them to the latest versions of iOS soon after Apple releases them. New versions can contain bug fixes, new features, or both. To update the iPad and iPhone, you use iTunes.

CAUTION   As you'll know from the excitement about iPhone 4 prototypes that escaped into the wild, Apple likes to keep its secrets tightly under wraps. This secrecy extends to software changes, and one result is that updates and fixes sometimes receive less real-world testing than they need. Unless your iPads and iPhone are suffering disastrously from a problem the latest update promises to fix, it's best to wait a few days—or weeks—before installing an update and let the early adopters discover any problems for you. As you know, fools rush in where angels fear to tread (and I'm guessing you're nearer the angelic end of the spectrum).

You'll also likely want to keep the apps on the iPad or iPhone up to date so that users have the most stable versions (in theory, anyway—practice may disagree) and all the latest features. Users can update the apps either on the devices or by using iTunes.

Updating iOS

To update iOS, you use iTunes rather than working on the iPad or iPhone itself.

The first step is to learn that a new version of iOS is available. If you need to find out right this moment, follow these steps:

1. Connect the iPad or iPhone to the computer.

2. If iTunes doesn't launch or activate automatically, launch it or switch to it manually.

3. Click the iPad's or iPhone's entry in the Devices category in the Source list to display the device's control screens.

4. On the Summary tab, look at the Version box.

   ■ If the Update button is available, you can update to the new version listed in the readout next to it.

   ■ If the Check For Update button appears, click it to make iTunes check whether a new version of the software is available.

 TIP   You can also force iTunes to check for updates (to itself, QuickTime, and iOS) by choosing Help | Check For Updates (on Windows) or iTunes | Check For Updates (on the Mac).

If you're in less of a hurry, you may prefer to let iTunes handle the checking. By default, iTunes checks automatically for updates to iTunes, QuickTime, and iOS once a week. When iTunes finds an update, it prompts you to download and install the update. Figure 5-29 shows the prompt on Windows for an update to iOS.

 NOTE   To prevent iTunes from checking automatically for updates, choose Edit | Preferences to display the iTunes dialog box (on Windows) or iTunes | Preferences to display the Preferences dialog box on the Mac. On the General tab, clear the Check For Updates Automatically check box (on Windows) or the Check For New Software Updates Automatically check box (on the Mac), and then click the OK button.

Figure 5-29.   iTunes checks automatically for updates to iOS and alerts you to any that are available.

Click the Download And Install button if you want to proceed with the installation as soon as the download completes. Click the Download Only button if you want to download the update now and install it later. When you're ready to install the update, connect the iPad or iPhone, click its entry in the Devices category in the Source list in iTunes, and then click the Update button on the Summary screen.

When iTunes prompts you to update the iPad or iPhone (see Figure 5-30), click the Update button.

The Updater then extracts the software, verifies the update, prepares the device for the update, and then installs the update. This takes a while; you'll see a progress bar on the iPad or iPhone as the update installs, but you may find it more entertaining to go to a meeting or watch paint dry.

If you're still there when the update finishes, you'll see iTunes display a dialog box (see Figure 5-31) telling you what's going on. After 15 seconds, iTunes dismisses the dialog box, restarts the iPad or iPhone, and then synchronizes it. After this, on the Summary tab of the iPad's or iPhone's configuration screens, the Software Version readout shows the new version number (for example, 4.0.1) and the Version box tells you that the device's software is up to date.

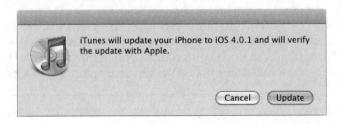

Figure 5-30.   Click the Update button in this dialog box to start updating the operating system on the iPad or iPhone.

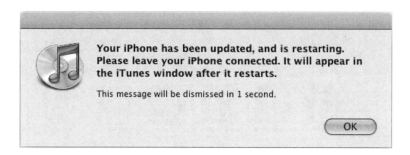

Figure 5-31.   When the update is complete, iTunes warns you that it's about to restart the iPad or iPhone, then goes ahead and does so.

Updating the Apps on the iPad or iPhone Using iTunes

In many cases, the easiest way to update the apps on the iPad or iPhone is by using iTunes. You can download all the available updates to a computer running iTunes before you connect the iPad or iPhone, so you can line up your ducks ahead of time. This is helpful when you need to install many updates, large updates, or both.

NOTE   To download and install updates from the iTunes Store, you must have an account with the iTunes Store.

To update the apps on the iPad or iPhone using iTunes, follow these steps:

1. Open iTunes (or switch to it if it's already running).

2. In the Library category in the Source list, click the Apps entry to display the list of apps (see Figure 5-32).

3. If the readout on the gray bar at the bottom shows that updates are available, click the arrow button next to the readout. (If not, click the Check For Updates button to check for available updates.) iTunes displays the My App Updates screen (see Figure 5-33).

4. Download the updates you want:

    ■ **Download a single update**   Click the Get Update button for the app.

    ■ **Download all free updates**   Click the Download All Free Updates button in the upper-right corner. Unless there are particular updates you don't want (for example, because they include huge data files), this is usually the best choice.

Figure 5-32. In the Apps list, click the Updates Available link to start getting updates to the apps installed on the iPad or iPhone.

5. Sign in to the iTunes Store when iTunes prompts you to. iTunes then confirms that you want to download all the free updates (see Figure 5-34).

6. Select the Don't Ask Me About Downloading Free Updates Again check box if you don't want to see this prompt in the future.

7. Click the Update All button. iTunes downloads the files, showing information about what it's doing in the display if you're not playing media files. If you want to see the details of the progress, click the Downloads entry in the Store category in the Source list.

8. When iTunes has downloaded all the updates, the My App Updates screen shows a message saying that no updates are available. Click the Done button if you want to go to the App Store, or click another entry in the Source list to display that instead.

Figure 5-33.   From the My App Updates screen, you can install the updates singly, or click the Download All Free Updates button to get all the free updates at once.

Figure 5-34.   Confirm that you want to download all the free updates. Select the Don't Ask Me About Downloading Free Updates Again check box if you want to suppress this prompt in the future.

When the downloads are complete, you can install the updates by synchronizing the apps on the iPad or iPhone. Follow these steps:

1. Connect the iPad or iPhone to the computer.

2. If iTunes doesn't launch or activate automatically when the computer detects the iPad or iPhone, launch or switch to iTunes manually.

3. In the Devices list in the Source list, click the entry for the iPad or iPhone to display its control screens.

4. Click the Apps tab to display its contents.

5. Click the Sync button. iTunes updates the apps.

Updating the Apps Directly on the iPad or iPhone

You can also update the apps directly on the iPad or iPhone. To do this, you must have an iTunes Store account, even if the updates to the apps are free, as many are.

NOTE Updating the apps directly on the iPad or iPhone usually works fine, but you'll usually want to make sure that users download the updates via Wi-Fi rather than via the 3G network. While many updates are modest (a mere handful of megabytes), others can be chunky—and the overall amount can take a hefty bite out of a data allowance.

Display the Home screen that contains the App Store app, and see whether the icon bears a red circle in the upper-right corner. If the red circle appears, as in the left screen in Figure 5-35, the number it contains shows how many updates for apps are available.

NOTE Displaying the Updates screen in the App Store app forces the iPad or iPhone to check for app updates. As a result, you'll often find that the Updates screen shows more updates than the App Store icon on the Home screen did.

If updates are available, touch the App Store icon to display the Updates screen (shown on the right in Figure 5-35). From here, you can touch an app's listing to see the details of the update, and whether it's free or it comes at a price; touch the Free button or the price button to install the update. Alternatively, from the Updates screen, simply touch the Update All button to get all the updates.

After you sign in to your iTunes Store account, the iPad or iPhone downloads the updates and then installs them.

Figure 5-35. The App Store icon (left) shows how many updates are available. The Updates screen (right) shows you the list of apps.

Uninstalling Apps

When you no longer need an app on the iPad or iPhone, you can uninstall it. You can do this either from the device itself, by using iTunes, or by using iPhone Configuration Utility.

 NOTE You can uninstall only those apps you've installed on the iPad or iPhone. The built-in apps are there to stay.

Uninstalling Apps Directly from the iPad or iPhone

In many cases, the easiest way to uninstall an app is directly on the iPad or iPhone. Follow these steps:

1. Press the Home button to display the Home screen.

2. Navigate to the Home screen that contains the app.

3. Touch an app and keep touching until the app icons start to jiggle. iOS displays a circle containing a × on each app that you can delete.

4. Touch the × circle to delete the app. iOS displays a confirmation dialog box to make sure (see Figure 5-36).

5. Touch the Delete button to delete the app.

6. Delete other apps as necessary, and then press the Home button to stop the apps jiggling.

Figure 5-36.   Confirm that you want to remove an app from the iPad or iPhone.

Figure 5-37.   Use iTunes when you need to remove several apps at once.

Uninstalling Apps Using iTunes

When you need to uninstall several apps at once, you may find it easier to use iTunes than to work directly on the iPad or iPhone. Follow these steps:

1. Connect the iPad or iPhone to the computer.

2. If iTunes doesn't launch or activate automatically, launch it or switch to it manually.

3. Click the iPad's or iPhone's entry in the Devices category in the Source list to display the device's control screens.

4. Click the Apps tab to display its contents (see Figure 5-37).

5. In the list of apps, clear the check box for each app you want to remove.

6. Click the Apply button. iTunes synchronizes with the iPad or iPhone and uninstalls the apps you marked for removal.

Uninstalling Apps Using iPhone Configuration Utility

You can also uninstall apps using iPhone Configuration Utility. To do so, follow these steps:

1. Open iPhone Configuration Utility.

2. Connect the iPad or iPhone.

3. Click the iPad or iPhone in the Devices category in the Source list.

4. Click the Applications tab to display its contents (see Figure 5-38).

5. Click the Uninstall button for the app.

By now, your network's iPads and iPhones should be fully loaded with the apps they need. In the next chapter, I'll show you how to connect the iPads and iPhones to your mail servers so that users can send and receive e-mail to their hearts' content.

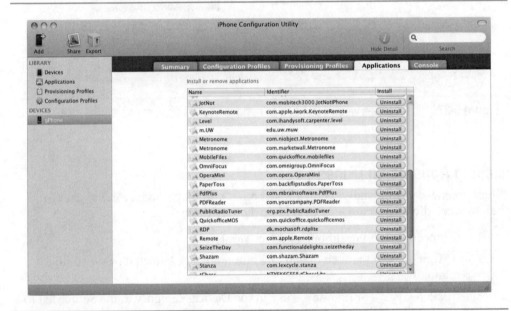

Figure 5-38. In iPhone Configuration Utility, use the Applications tab to uninstall apps from a connected iPad or iPhone.

CHAPTER 6 | Connecting the iPad and iPhone to Your Mail Servers

I n this chapter, I'll show you how to connect the iPad and iPhone to your mail servers so that users can send, receive, and mismanage their e-mail. We'll start with Microsoft Exchange, because it's the most widely used e-mail solution overall, but we'll also cover how to set up e-mail with other mail servers.

As with much iPad and iPhone configuration, you can set up Exchange or e-mail either by using a configuration profile or by working directly on the device. You'll probably use configuration profiles for most of the iOS devices you manage, but it's likely you'll also need to configure some of them manually, either from the word *go* or to troubleshoot particular problems.

Speaking of troubleshooting—toward the end of the chapter, you'll find information on curing common problems that occur with Exchange and with other mail servers. And right at the end of the chapter, you'll learn how to delete e-mail accounts from the iPad and iPhone.

Connecting the iPad and iPhone to Microsoft Exchange

If your company or organization runs Microsoft Exchange, you'll almost certainly want to connect the iPad and iPhone to Exchange. You can do so either by creating an Exchange ActiveSync payload in a configuration profile or by setting up the Exchange account on the iPad or iPhone manually. Chances are that you'll want to use configuration profiles for as many of your iPads and iPhones as possible, so we'll start there.

 NOTE You should be able to use the same Exchange configuration for the iPad as for the iPhone. So if you have users already set up to use the iPhone, you can migrate them to the iPad quickly if necessary.

Adding an Exchange Account by Using a Configuration Profile

In most cases, the easiest way to set up Exchange ActiveSync on the iPad or iPhone is to create an Exchange ActiveSync payload in a configuration profile that you then load on the iPad or iPhone. You can then apply the configuration profile either across a USB cable using iPhone Configuration Utility or by distributing it to the user—for example, via a web site or an e-mail account that's already configured on the iPad or iPhone.

Creating an Exchange ActiveSync Payload for a Configuration Profile

To create an Exchange ActiveSync payload, follow these steps:

1. Open iPhone Configuration Utility as usual from the Start menu (on Windows) or the Dock or the Utilities folder (on the Mac).

2. Click the Configuration Profiles item in the Source list to display the list of configuration profiles.

3. Click the configuration profile to which you want to add the Exchange ActiveSync payload.

NOTE   Rather than using an existing configuration profile, you may want to create a separate configuration profile for Exchange ActiveSync. If so, click the Configuration Profiles item in the Source list, click the New button, and then enter the essential details of the configuration profile in the General pane.

4. Click the Exchange ActiveSync item in the Payloads list to display the Configure Exchange ActiveSync pane.

5. Click the Configure button in the Configure Exchange ActiveSync pane to display the Exchange ActiveSync pane (shown in Figure 6-1 with settings underway).

6. In the Account Name text box, type the descriptive name the user will see for the account.

7. In the Exchange ActiveSync Host text box, type the hostname or IP address of the Exchange server.

8. Select the Use SSL check box if you want to secure the communications with Secure Sockets Layer. You'll normally want to do this.

9. Next, choose whether to enter anything in the Domain text box and the User text box. The choice is straightforward:

   ■ If you're setting up a specific account in this configuration profile, enter the domain in the Domain text box and the username in the User text box. Odds are you'll want to do this only occasionally, when you're creating a configuration profile for a single special user. The iPad or iPhone stores this information, so the account is set up in moments.

   ■ Leave both the Domain text box and the User text box blank. When you do this, the iPad or iPhone prompts the user to enter his or her information when installing the profile on the device. This is normally the best way to proceed. When the user enters her information, the iPad or iPhone stores it in the account.

10. If you're setting up a single account, type the e-mail address in the Email Address text box. Otherwise, leave it blank so that each user will need to enter her address.

11. Similarly, you'll usually want to leave the Password text box blank so that each user will need to enter his password.

12. In the Past Days Of Mail To Sync drop-down list or pop-up menu, choose how many days' worth of mail to synchronize with the iPad or iPhone:

   ■ Your choices are No Limit, 1 Day, 3 Days, 1 Week, 2 Weeks, or 1 Month.

   ■ The default setting, No Limit, can be useful for heavy users of e-mail who need to be able to refer back to older messages easily. But you probably won't want to use this setting for all users, because it can result in huge numbers of messages being synchronized with little benefit gained.

   ■ For most users, a setting such as 1 Week or 2 Weeks usually works pretty well—but this will depend on your workplace.

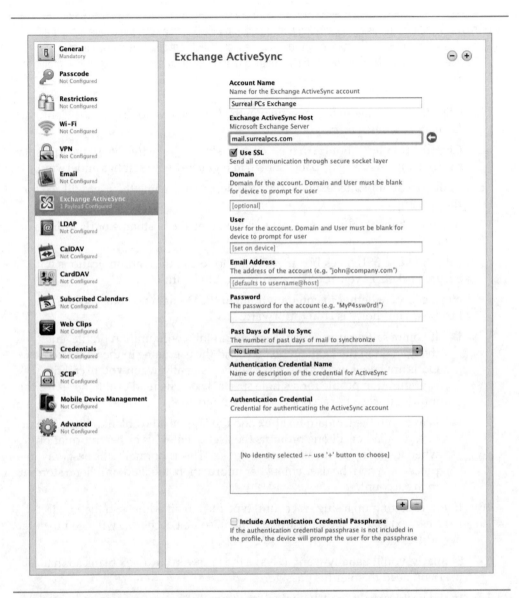

Figure 6-1. In the Exchange ActiveSync pane of iPhone Configuration Utility, enter the settings for Exchange accounts.

13.   To add to the payload a certificate for identifying the user, follow these steps:

    a.   Click the + button below the Authentication Credential text box to display the Windows Security dialog box (on Windows; see Figure 6-2) or the Select An Identity To Use With Exchange ActiveSync dialog box (on the Mac; see Figure 6-3).

    b.   Select the certificate you want to use.

NOTE   If needed, you can view the details of the certificate. On Windows, click the certificate, and then click the Click Here To View Certificate Properties link that appears. On the Mac, click the certificate in the list, and then click the Show Certificate button.

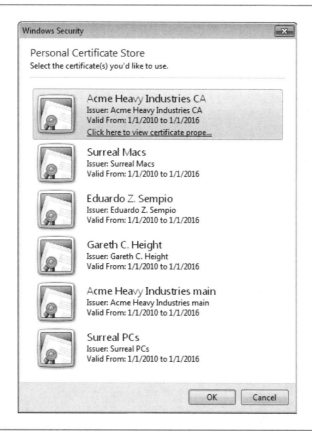

Figure 6-2.   In the Windows Security dialog box, click the certificate you want to add to the Exchange ActiveSync payload.

Figure 6-3. In the Select An Identity To Use With Exchange ActiveSync dialog box on the Mac, choose the certificate you want to add to the Exchange ActiveSync payload.

    c.   Click the OK button (on Windows) or the Choose button (on the Mac) to close the dialog box and apply the certificate. iPhone Configuration Utility displays the dialog box shown in the upper part of Figure 6-4 (on Windows) or the dialog box shown in the lower part of Figure 6-4 (on the Mac).

Figure 6-4. Secure the certificate with a passphrase. The upper dialog box is for Windows; the lower dialog box is for the Mac.

d. Type a passphrase in the Password text box and the Verify text box, and then click the OK button. The certificate then appears in the Authentication Credential box, and its name appears in the Authentication Credential Name text box.

e. If you want to include the passphrase rather than have the iPad or iPhone prompt the user for it, select the Include Authentication Credential Passphrase check box in the Exchange ActiveSync pane of iPhone Configuration Utility.

Configuring an Exchange Account Added Using a Configuration Profile

After creating the configuration profile that contains the Exchange ActiveSync payload, distribute it to the iPads and iPhones that need it by using one of the methods explained in Chapter 3. For example, if you're setting up the iPad or iPhone and have it under your control, connect it to your computer and use iPhone Configuration Utility to put the configuration profile on it directly. You can then have the user enter his or her details while installing the account.

To set up an Exchange account added to an iPad or iPhone using a configuration profile, touch the Install button on the Install Profile screen (see Figure 6-5). iOS then walks you through the process of adding the Exchange account to the device—for example, entering your e-mail address and password, and then choosing which items to synchronize.

At the end of the configuration process, iOS displays the Exchange Account screen, on which you decide which items to synchronize with the iPad or iPhone. See the section "Choosing Which Exchange Items to Synchronize to the iPad or iPhone," later in this chapter, for details.

Setting Up a Connection to an Exchange Server Manually

You'll probably want to set up most of your Exchange connections by using configuration profiles, as discussed in the preceding section. But sometimes it's useful to set up a connection to an Exchange Server manually on the iPad or iPhone. You may also need to manipulate the settings directly when troubleshooting Exchange problems that a particular iPad or iPhone is having.

To set up a connection to an Exchange Server manually, follow these steps:

1. From the Home screen, choose Settings | Mail, Contacts, Calendars to display the Mail, Contacts, Calendars screen.

2. In the Accounts area, touch the Add Account button to display the Add Account screen (see Figure 6-6).

3. Touch the Microsoft Exchange item to display the Exchange screen (see Figure 6-7).

4. Type the e-mail address in the Email field.

5. If you log in to an Active Directory domain, type the domain in the Domain field. If you're not sure whether you log in to a domain, and you can't find an administrator to tell you, leave the Domain field blank.

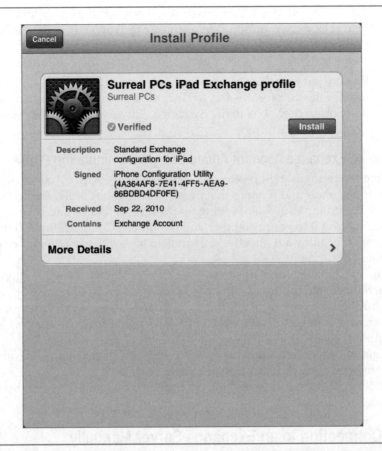

Figure 6-5. On the Install Profile screen, touch the Install button for the Exchange profile to start the installation process. iOS prompts you for each piece of information needed to set up the account.

 NOTE In Exchange Server 2007 and Exchange Server 2010, the Autodiscovery service normally enables you to locate the Exchange ActiveSync server without entering the domain name.

6. Type your username in the Username field.

7. Type your password in the Password field.

8. In the Description field, type the descriptive text you'd like the iPad or iPhone to display for the account. iOS enters your e-mail address by default, but you can usually improve on this.

Figure 6-6.   To start setting up an Exchange account manually, touch the Microsoft Exchange button on the Add Account screen.

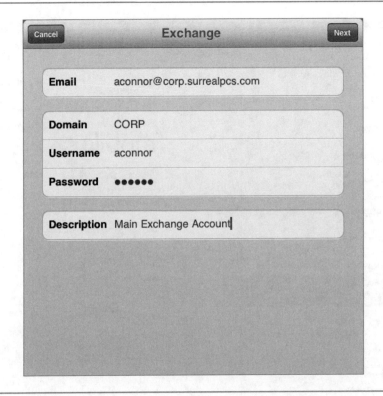

Figure 6-7. On the Exchange screen, enter the details of the Exchange account.

9. Touch the Next button. The iPad or iPhone displays the Verifying screen while it connects to the server and verifies the details of the account.

 NOTE Two things: First, finding the server and verifying the account may take several minutes. Second, if iOS can't locate the Exchange server, it displays the Exchange screen again, this time with the Server field added but blank. Type in the server's address, and then touch the Next button. Armed with this vital information, iOS then tries the verification again.

10. When iOS has finished verifying the account, it displays the Exchange screen with the server name in the Server field (see Figure 6-8).

11. Touch the Save button to save the account. iOS then displays the Exchange Account screen, discussed in the next section.

Figure 6-8.   After setting up the Exchange account, touch the Save button to save it.

Choosing Which Exchange Items to Synchronize to the iPad or iPhone

After you set up an Exchange account (either from a configuration profile or manually), iOS displays the Exchange Account screen (see Figure 6-9).

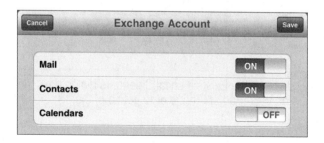

Figure 6-9.   On the Exchange Account screen, choose which of Mail, Contacts, and Calendars to synchronize with the iPad or iPhone.

Use the Mail switch, Contacts switch, and Calendars switch to choose which items to synchronize with the iPad or iPhone. In most cases, you'll want to synchronize all of them.

If the iPad or iPhone already contains contacts or calendars, iOS sets the Contacts switch or the Calendars switch to the Off position. When you move the switch to the On position, iOS displays the Existing Local Contacts dialog box or the Existing Local Calendars dialog box to warn you of the problem. Figure 6-10 shows the Existing Local Calendars dialog box; the Existing Local Contacts dialog box works in the same way.

Touch the Keep On My iPad button or Keep On My iPhone button if you want to keep the contacts. Otherwise, touch the Delete button to delete them, and then touch the Delete button in the Delete Local Contacts dialog box or Delete Local Calendars dialog box that appears. Figure 6-11 shows the Delete Local Calendars dialog box.

When you've finished choosing settings on the Exchange Account screen, touch the Save button to save the account. iOS saves the account and then displays the Mail, Contacts, Calendars screen.

Figure 6-10.   If iOS displays the Existing Local Calendars dialog box, choose whether to keep the existing calendars on your iPad or iPhone or to get rid of them.

Figure 6-11.   iOS makes sure you want to delete your local calendars.

Connecting the iPad and iPhone to Other Mail Servers

In this section, we'll look at how to connect the iPad and iPhone to mail servers other than Microsoft Exchange.

The first step is to set up the mail server so that the iPad and iPhone can connect to it. You can then either add an e-mail account, by creating and installing a configuration profile, or set up an e-mail account manually on the device. Either way, you may need to configure advanced settings and SMTP settings to make the account work the way you want it to.

Setting Up the Mail Server So That the iPad and iPhone Can Connect to It

To set up a mail server so that the iPad and iPhone can connect to it from outside the network, you need to implement three settings:

- **Open port 993 on the firewall**   Open port 993 for IMAP SSL e-mail so that e-mail can pass through the firewall.

NOTE   You can also use these settings for Exchange Server if you're planning to have clients connect through IMAP rather than natively to Exchange.

- **Install a digital certificate on the proxy server**   Get a digital certificate from a certification authority (CA) that you trust, and install it on your proxy server. The CA can be either a commercial CA (such as VeriSign or Comodo) or your company's or organization's own CA.

- **Open a port on the server to allow the iPad and iPhone to send e-mail**   If possible, open port 587 on your server, as this is the port that iOS tries first. If port 587 isn't available, use port 465; failing that, use port 25.

CAUTION   Avoid using port 25 if possible. Spammers and hackers frequently target this standard mail port.

Adding an E-Mail Account by Using a Configuration Profile

The quick and easy way of setting up an iPad or iPhone to connect to a mail server other than Microsoft Exchange is to create an Email payload in a configuration profile you load on the device. You can create a payload for either an IMAP account or a POP account, and you can create as many Email payloads as needed to load up all the users' e-mail accounts.

You can set up the Email payload either to configure a single person's e-mail account or to configure e-mail accounts for multiple users. When setting up a single user's account, you include all the details in the Email payload—the user name, account name, e-mail address, password, and so on. When setting up accounts for multiple users, you specify the common settings (such as the mail server and the ports), and then each person fills in her specifics on the iPad or iPhone.

We'll look first at creating an Email payload in a configuration profile. Then we'll go through how the user enters the details of her e-mail account in a profile that sets up accounts for multiple users.

Creating an Email Payload for a Configuration Profile

To create an Email payload, follow these steps:

1. Open iPhone Configuration Utility as usual from the Start menu (on Windows) or the Dock or the Utilities folder (on the Mac).

2. Click the Configuration Profiles item in the Source list to display the list of configuration profiles.

3. Click the configuration profile to which you want to add the Email payload.

4. Click the Email item in the Payloads list to display the Configure Email pane.

5. Click the Configure button in the Configure Email pane to display the Email pane. Figure 6-12 shows the Email pane with settings chosen for setting up a specific user's account on an IMAP server.

6. In the Account Description text box, type the descriptive name by which the user will identify the account.

7. Open the Account Type pop-up menu and choose IMAP or POP, as appropriate.

8. For an IMAP account, optionally type the path prefix in the Path Prefix text box. This is a text string that tells the iPad or iPhone where to locate the folders on the mail server.

 NOTE   You don't normally need to enter the path prefix for an IMAP account. But if you find that all the account's folders appear under the Inbox on the iPad or iPhone, you may need to enter the path prefix.

Figure 6-12.   You can set up one or more IMAP or POP e-mail accounts for the iPad or iPhone in the Email pane in iPhone Configuration Utility.

9. If you're setting up a profile for a single user, enter its details (as discussed here) in the upper part of the Email pane, on the Incoming Mail tab at the bottom, and on the Outgoing Mail tab. If you're setting up a profile for multiple users, leave each of these text boxes set to the default setting, which is called "[set on device]".

   ■ **User Display Name**   Type the user's name as you want it to appear on e-mail messages—for example, Bill P. Smith.

   ■ **Email Address**   Type the user's full e-mail address—for example, bpsmith@surrealpcs.com.

- **User Name (Incoming Mail pane)**   Type the user's account name for connecting to the incoming mail server—for example, bpsmith.

- **Password (Incoming Mail pane)**   Type the user's password for connecting to the incoming mail server.

- **User Name (Outgoing Mail pane)**   Type the user's account name for connecting to the outgoing mail server. This account name may be the same as that for the incoming mail server, but it may be different.

- **Password (Outgoing Mail pane)**   If the user's account uses a different password for connecting to the outgoing mail server, type that password in this field.

10.   Make sure the Incoming Mail tab is displayed (if not, click it).

11.   In the Mail Server And Port text box, enter the server name and the port to use.

NOTE   To retrieve IMAP mail over SSL, the iPad and iPhone use port 993, so make sure this port is open on your firewall. To send mail, you need to open one or more of ports 587, 465, and 25. The iPad and iPhone use port 587 first, so use this port unless you have a compelling reason not to.

12.   Leave the User Name text box set to "[set on device]" if you need to have each user enter his user name on the iPad or iPhone.

13.   In the Authentication Type drop-down list or pop-up menu, choose the type of authentication the mail server uses: None, Password, MD5 Challenge-Response, NTLM, or HTTP MD5 Digest.

14.   In the Password text box, type the password for the incoming mail server if you're setting up a complete Email payload for one user. Otherwise, leave the Password text box blank.

15.   Select the Use SSL check box if you want to use a secure connection for retrieving incoming mail. This is usually a good idea.

NOTE   When you select the Use SSL check box, iPhone Configuration Utility automatically changes the Port setting to 993 (the port used for SSL-encrypted mail) if it is currently set to 143, the default port setting for nonencrypted mail. Similarly, if you clear the Use SSL check box, iPhone Configuration Utility changes the default port setting back from 993 to 143. If you've entered a custom port number, iPhone Configuration Utility doesn't change it.

16.   Click the Outgoing Mail tab to display its contents. Figure 6-13 shows the Outgoing Mail tab of the Email pane, with settings chosen for a payload of a POP account whose details will be filled in by the users after the profile is installed on the iPads or iPhones.

17.   Type the mail server's hostname or IP address in the Mail Server text box.

Figure 6-13.   In the Outgoing Mail tab of the Email pane (shown at the bottom here), enter the mail server and port, choose the authentication type, and decide whether to secure the connection with SSL.

18. If your mail server uses a custom port, type it in the Port text box. Otherwise, leave iPhone Configuration Utility to set the default port—port 25 for unencrypted e-mail, port 465 for encrypted e-mail.

19. In the User Name text box, enter the user name only if you're setting up an Email payload for a single account. Otherwise, leave this text box blank so that each user will enter her user name manually.

20. In the Authentication Type drop-down list or pop-up menu, choose the type of authentication: None, Password, MD5 Challenge-Response, NTLM, or HTTP MD5 Digest.

21. If you're creating a payload for a particular user, you can enter the password in the Password text box. Otherwise, leave this text box blank to have iOS prompt each user for his password.

22. If the outgoing mail server uses the same password as the incoming mail server, select the Outgoing Password Same As Incoming check box. When you do this, iPhone Configuration Utility makes the Password text box unavailable, as you do not need to enter a password in it.

23. Select the Use SSL check box if you want to use encrypted connections for sending outgoing mail. This is generally a good idea if your e-mail architecture supports encryption. When you select this check box, iPhone Configuration Utility changes the default port number (25) to 465; if you've set a custom port for outgoing mail, iPhone Configuration Utility doesn't change it.

At this point, you've finished setting up the e-mail account. If you need to add another e-mail account, click the + button in the upper-right corner of the Email pane, and then follow the preceding steps again.

Configuring an E-Mail Account Added via a Configuration Profile

Now that you've created the configuration profile that contains the Email payload, distribute it to the appropriate iPads and iPhones using one of the methods explained in Chapter 3. For example, haul the user into your office, use iPhone Configuration Utility to put the configuration profile onto the iPad or iPhone directly via the USB cable, and then have the user enter her details. Or distribute the configuration profile via a web site.

When the configuration profile hits the iPad or iPhone, iOS displays the Install Profile screen (see Figure 6-14). The user can then set up the account like this:

1. On the Install Profile screen, check the details of the profile:
   - Make sure the Verified readout and check mark appears.
   - If you want to see the details of the profile, touch the More Details button to display the profile's screen. For example, Figure 6-15 shows the e-mail account the sample profile contains. Touch the Install Profile button when you're ready to return to the Install Profile screen.

2. Touch the Install button to start installing the profile. iOS displays the Install Profile dialog box to make sure you want to proceed.

3. Touch the Install Now button. iOS displays the Enter Description screen (see Figure 6-16), which suggests the name set in the Email payload's account description as the account name.

4. Touch the × button at the right end of the text box to wipe out the suggested name, and then type in a descriptive name for the e-mail account.

5. Touch the Next button to display the Enter Email screen.

Figure 6-14. Touch the Install button on the Install Profile screen to start installing the profile.

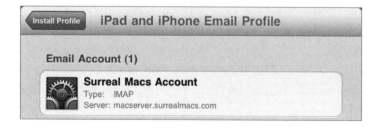

Figure 6-15. Open the profile's screen if you want to see what the profile contains.

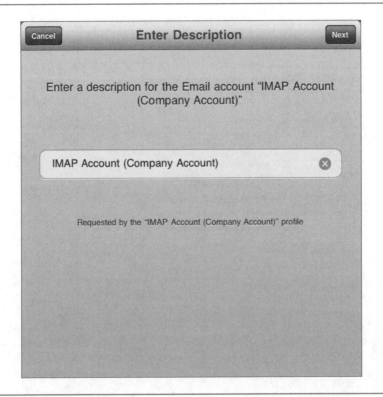

Figure 6-16.   On the Enter Description screen, type a descriptive name for the e-mail account you're adding to the iPad or iPhone.

6. Type in the e-mail address for the account.

7. Touch the Next button to display the Enter Username screen for the incoming mail server.

8. Type the username for the incoming mail server in the text box.

9. Touch the Next button to display the Enter Password screen for the incoming mail server.

10. Type in the password for the incoming mail server.

11. Touch the Next button to display the Enter Username screen for the outgoing mail server.

12. Type the username for the outgoing mail server in the text box.

13. Touch the Next button. iOS checks in with the mail server and verifies the settings, and then sets up the account.

> *NOTE* If iOS displays the Enter Password screen for the outgoing mail server, type in the password and touch the Next button. iOS prompts you for the password only if the Email payload is set to require a different password for the outgoing mail server than for the incoming mail server.

14. When the iPad or iPhone displays the Profile Installed screen (see Figure 6-17), touch the Done button. You can then go to the Mail app and make sure the account can send and receive e-mail.

Setting Up E-Mail to Another Server Manually

When you don't want to—or can't—set up a particular e-mail account by using a configuration profile, you can set it up directly on the iPad or iPhone. You may also need to manipulate the settings on the device directly to troubleshoot e-mail problems.

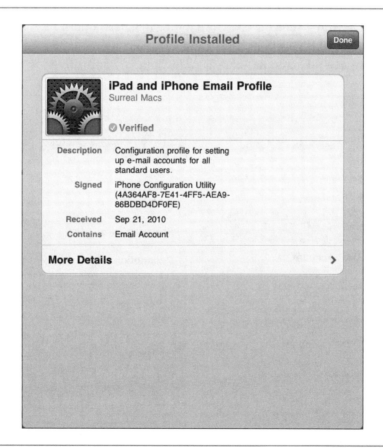

Figure 6-17. The iPad or iPhone displays the Profile Installed screen when you have finished setting up the e-mail account (and any other items the profile contains). Touch the Done button.

To set up an e-mail account, follow these steps:

1. From the Home screen, choose Settings | Mail, Contacts, Calendars to display the Mail, Contacts, Calendars screen.

2. In the Accounts area, touch the Add Account button to display the Add Account screen (shown in Figure 6-6, earlier in this chapter).

3. Touch the Other item to display the Other screen (shown on the left in Figure 6-18).

4. Touch the Add Mail Account button to display the New Account screen (shown on the right in Figure 6-18 with settings entered).

5. Enter the details for the account:

   ■ **Name**   Type the user's name the way you want it to appear—for example, Ann Smith or Bill Jones.

   ■ **Address**   Type the e-mail address.

   ■ **Password**   Type the password for the e-mail account.

   ■ **Description**   Type the description you want the user to see for this account in the list of accounts—for example, Company E-mail.

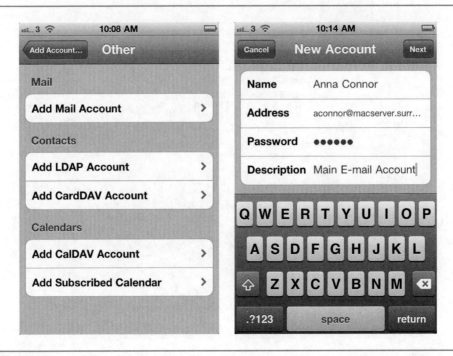

Figure 6-18.   Touch the Add Mail Account button on the Other screen (left) to display the New Account screen (right).

6. Touch the Next button. The iPad or iPhone connects to the server and verifies the account; you'll see the Verifying screen (shown on the left in Figure 6-19) briefly as the device scopes out the server. The device then displays the New Account screen (shown on the right in Figure 6-19).

7. On the New Account screen, choose the account type by touching the IMAP button or the POP button. The device displays the tab for the button you touch.

8. Enter any missing details for the account. How much you need to fill in here depends on how friendly iOS finds the mail server, but you'll often need to enter the details of the mail servers. When you're done, touch the Next button (for an IMAP account) or the Save button (for a POP account).

NOTE   If the iPad or iPhone cannot connect to the mail server, see the section "Troubleshooting Errors When Setting Up Other E-Mail Accounts," later in this chapter.

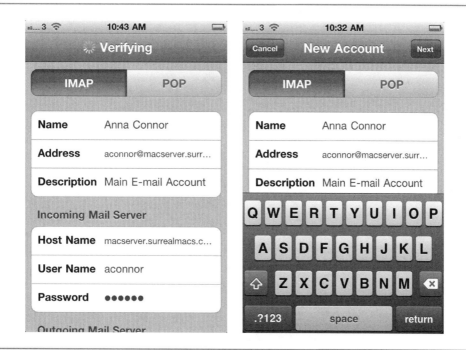

Figure 6-19.   The iPad or iPhone displays the Verifying screen (left) as it connects to the server and checks out the account details. It then displays the New Account screen (right), on which you enter any server and account details that iOS can't grab from the server.

9. If you're setting up an IMAP account, iOS displays the IMAP screen (see Figure 6-20). Use the Mail switch and the Notes switch to choose which items to synchronize. Normally you'll want to make sure the Mail switch is in the On position; if you want to synchronize notes as well, move the Notes switch to the On position too.

10. Touch the Save button. iOS configures the sync, and then displays the Mail, Contacts, Calendars screen with the new account added.

You can now go to the Mail app and start using the new account—for example, to make sure it's working.

Configuring Advanced Settings for an E-Mail Account

After you set up an e-mail account on an iPad or iPhone, you may be done and dusted— or you may find that you need to return to the device and tweak further settings. This section shows you how to configure the advanced settings, first for an IMAP account and second for a POP account.

Figure 6-20. For an IMAP account, choose whether to synchronize Mail and Notes.

Configuring Advanced Settings for an IMAP Account

To configure advanced settings for an IMAP account, follow these steps:

1. Choose Settings | Mail, Contacts, Calendars to display the Mail, Contacts, Calendars screen.

2. In the Accounts list, touch the IMAP account you want to affect. The iPad or iPhone displays the screen for that account.

3. Touch the Advanced button (near the bottom of the screen) to display the Advanced screen (see Figure 6-21).

4. In the Mailbox Behaviors area, check that Drafts Mailbox, Sent Mailbox, and Deleted Mailbox show the folders you want to use for draft messages, sent messages, and deleted messages. If not, change a folder like this:

    a. Touch the button for the appropriate mailbox to display its configuration screen. For example, touch the Drafts Mailbox button to display the Drafts Mailbox screen (see Figure 6-22).

Figure 6-21. On the Advanced screen of the account settings for an IMAP e-mail account, you can set a path profile to tell the iPad or iPhone where to find the folders.

Figure 6-22.   Use the Drafts Mailbox screen to move your Drafts Mailbox to a different folder, either on the iPad or iPhone or on the server. Similarly, you can move the Sent Mailbox and the Deleted Mailbox.

 NOTE   You can choose to place your Drafts Mailbox, Sent Mailbox, and Deleted Mailbox on your iPad or iPhone or on the mail server. Put a folder on the iPad or iPhone if you need to be able to work with drafts, sent items, or deleted items while you don't have an Internet connection. Otherwise, put these mailboxes on the server so that you can access their contents from whichever computer you happen to be using.

    b.   Touch the folder you want to use.

    c.   Touch the Advanced button in the upper-left corner to return to the Advanced screen.

  5.   In the Deleted Messages area, make sure the Remove setting shows when you want to remove deleted messages from the server. To change the setting, touch the Remove button, and then touch the appropriate button on the Remove screen: Never, After One Day, After One Week, or After One Month. Touch the Advanced button to return to the Advanced screen.

6. In the Incoming Settings area, choose settings as needed:

   ■ **Use SSL**   Move this switch to the On position to encrypt your incoming mail with SSL. This is usually a good idea, but if the mail server doesn't offer SSL connections, you'll need to turn SSL off.

   ■ **Authentication**   Check that this readout shows the correct type of authentication. If not, touch the Authentication button to display the Authentication screen, touch the authentication type—MD5 Challenge-Response, NTLM, HTTP MD5 Digest, or Password—and then touch the Advanced button to return to the Advanced screen.

   ■ **IMAP Path Prefix**   In this field, enter the path prefix the IMAP server requires.

   ■ **Server Port**   In this field, make sure the correct server port appears. The normal ports are 993 for SSL IMAP or 143 for unencrypted IMAP.

7. When you've finished choosing settings on the Advanced screen, touch the Done button to return to the Mail, Contacts, Calendars screen.

Configuring Advanced Settings for a POP Account

To configure advanced settings for a POP account, follow these steps:

1. Choose Settings | Mail, Contacts, Calendars to display the Mail, Contacts, Calendars screen.

2. In the Accounts list, touch the POP account you want to affect. The iPad or iPhone displays the screen for that account.

3. Touch the Advanced button (near the bottom of the screen) to display the Advanced screen (shown on the left in Figure 6-23).

4. In the Deleted Messages area, check that the Remove setting shows the time frame you want. If not, touch the Remove button to display the Remove screen, select the appropriate setting—Never, After One Day, After One Week, or After One Month—and then touch the Advanced button to return to the Advanced screen.

5. In the Incoming Settings area, choose settings as needed:

   ■ **Use SSL**   If the POP server supports SSL, move this switch to the On position to encrypt your incoming e-mail.

   ■ **Authentication**   Check the means of authentication the account is using. If you need to change the means of authentication, touch the Authentication button. On the Authentication screen, touch the means of authentication to use: Password, MD5 Challenge-Response, NTLM, or HTTP MD5 Digest. Then touch the Advanced button to return to the Advanced screen.

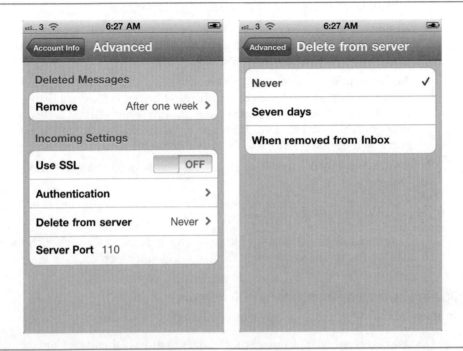

Figure 6-23.   From the Advanced screen (left) for an e-mail account, you can choose settings including when to remove messages from the server (right).

■ **Delete From Server**   Check when the account is set to delete messages from the server. To change the setting, touch the Delete From Server button. On the Delete From Server screen (shown on the right in Figure 6-23), touch Never, Seven Days, or When Removed From Inbox, as appropriate. Then touch the Advanced button to return to the Advanced screen.

■ **Server Port**   Check that the account is using the correct port on the server. If not, touch the field, and then type in the correct port.

6.   Touch the Account Info button when you've finished choosing settings.

Configuring SMTP Settings for an E-Mail Account

As well as configuring settings for incoming mail, you may need to configure settings for outgoing mail to get the iPad or iPhone to send messages correctly. Outgoing mail uses the SMTP server.

To configure SMTP settings for an e-mail account, follow these steps:

1.   Choose Settings | Mail, Contacts, Calendars to display the Mail, Contacts, Calendars screen.

2.   In the Accounts list, touch the account you want to affect. The iPad or iPhone displays the screen for that account.

3. Scroll down to the Outgoing Mail Server area, and then touch the SMTP field to display the SMTP screen (shown on the left in Figure 6-24).

NOTE Check that the Primary Server field shows the SMTP server this account should use. If not, turn off the primary server, and then in the Other SMTP Servers list, turn on the server you want the account to use. The Primary Server readout remains the same, but when you return to the account screen, you'll see that the Outgoing Mail Server box shows the server you turned on.

4. Touch the Primary Server button (the server's name) to display the configuration screen for the SMTP server (shown on the right in Figure 6-24).

5. At the top of the screen, make sure the Server switch is on if you want to be able to use this server. (You may sometimes need to turn a server off temporarily, but usually you'll want the primary server to be on.)

6. In the Outgoing Mail Server area, check or change the server's details as necessary:

    ■ **Host Name** In this field, enter the SMTP server's name.

    ■ **User Name** In this field, you can enter the user name for the SMTP account if it's different from the main account name. (If the user name is the same, you can enter it here anyway if you want.)

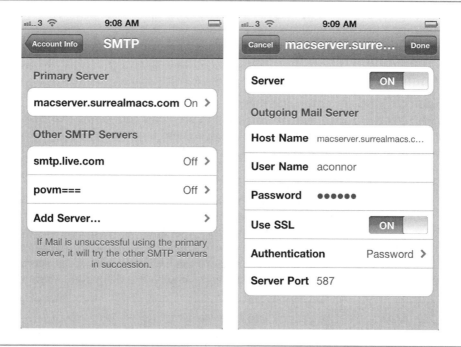

Figure 6-24. On the SMTP screen (left), check that the Primary Server field shows the correct server for this account to use. Touch the Primary Server button to display the configuration screen for that server (right).

- **Password**   In this field, enter the password for the SMTP account if it's different from the main account password. (Again, you can enter the password if it's the same.)

- **Use SSL**   If the SMTP server supports SSL connections, set this switch to On to encrypt the outgoing e-mail with SSL. Otherwise, set this switch to Off.

- **Authentication**   Make sure this field shows the appropriate authentication type—for example, Password. If not, touch the Authentication button, touch the appropriate button on the Authentication screen (Password, MD5 Challenge-Response, NTLM, or HTTP MD5 Digest), and then touch the server's button to return to the server configuration screen.

- **Server Port**   Make sure this field shows the right port for outgoing mail; if not, type in the port number. Normal ports are 587, 465, and 25, in that order of preference, but you can also set a custom port number if necessary.

7. Touch the Done button to return to the SMTP screen.

8. Touch the Account Info button to return to the e-mail account info screen.

Troubleshooting E-Mail Problems

E-mail is great when it works, but it can be murder when it sulks. The world being what it is, chances are you'll run into problems sooner rather than later—so this section presents a round-up of the problems you're most likely to meet.

As before, we'll look at Exchange first, and then go on to other mail servers.

Troubleshooting Microsoft Exchange

This section discusses four problems that can occur when you're using the iPad and iPhone with Microsoft Exchange. We'll start with problems connecting to the Exchange server, deal with an encryption problem that arises, and then look at the primary cause of not being able to send or receive e-mail even though you've connected to Exchange.

Dealing with the "Unable to Verify Account Information" Message

If the iPad or iPhone can't find the Exchange ActiveSync server during setup, it adds the Server field to the Exchange Account screen so that you can enter the server name.

If you enter the server name, and then get the "Exchange Account: Unable to verify account information" dialog box (see Figure 6-25), chances are you've got the wrong server name. Ask an administrator for the name of the Exchange ActiveSync server; most Exchange setups have various servers, so someone may have given you the wrong name.

NOTE   Make sure that the iPad or iPhone has a network connection—for example, use Safari to run through the odds on your favorite sports-betting site. Check also that the server is up—but unless hordes of unhappy employees are converging on your office bearing pitchforks, it probably is.

Figure 6-25.   The message "Exchange Account: Unable to verify account information" usually means that the iPad or iPhone is trying to contact the wrong Exchange server.

If you're certain you've got the right server name, check the SSL setting—you may need to turn SSL off in order to connect.

Choosing the Right Domain

To connect to the Exchange ActiveSync server, you may need to enter the correct domain when setting up the Exchange account—or you may need to leave the Domain field blank.

The best way to get the right domain is to ask an administrator. But if you can't reach an administrator who knows the right domain, and you need to set up the account anyway, first try leaving the Domain field blank. If the mail system is running Exchange Server 2007 or a later version, the iPad or iPhone should be able to pick up the server from the Autodiscover service.

If Autodiscover doesn't round up the Exchange server, and the Exchange system is provided by an external host, try the company's or organization's Internet domain name—for example, surrealpcs.com. And if that's no good, try the domain name without the suffix—for example, surrealpcs.

If you're still stuck at this point, you need to get in touch with an administrator who knows the details of the Exchange system.

Troubleshooting the "Policy Requirement" Error

The message "Policy Requirement: The account *account_name* requires encryption which is not supported on this iPhone" indicates that the iPhone you're using doesn't provide the encryption that the Exchange ActiveSync mailbox policy requires. This is a problem with the iPhone 3G (and the first two generations of iPod touch), not with the iPad, iPhone 4, or iPhone 3GS.

To resolve this problem, either get a better iPhone (here's a good excuse at last!) or remove the encryption requirement from the Exchange ActiveSync mailbox policy for the users with these iPhones. Normally, you'll want to do this by using a different configuration profile for the devices that can't handle encryption than for those that can.

Unable to Send or Receive E-Mail When Connected to Exchange

If you've been able to set up the Exchange account okay, but you're unable to send or receive e-mail using Exchange, make sure that you've entered the correct name in the Domain field for the account. It's possible to set up the account even if the Domain field contains the wrong information—but the incorrect domain setting then prevents you from sending and receiving e-mail.

See the section "Choosing the Right Domain" a couple of blocks north of here for advice on finding out which domain to use. To change the domain name, follow these steps:

1. From the Home screen, choose Settings | Mail, Contacts, Calendars to display the Mail, Contacts, Calendars screen.

2. Touch the button for the Exchange account to display the account's main screen.

3. Touch the Account Info button to display the Account Information screen.

4. Touch the Domain readout, and then either delete its contents (if you need to leave it blank) or type in the correct domain name.

5. Touch the Done button to return to the main account screen.

6. Touch the Done button to return to the Mail, Contacts, Calendars screen.

Troubleshooting Errors When Setting Up Other E-Mail Accounts

This section shows you how to deal with common errors that occur when you're setting up e-mail accounts for mail servers other than Exchange. We'll start by looking at what to do when the server doesn't respond, and then go through problems verifying the server's identity and connecting via SSL.

"The Server Is Not Responding" Error

The message "The IMAP server *server_name* is not responding" (see Figure 6-26) or "The POP server *server_name* is not responding" can indicate any of four problems:

- ■ **Network problems** If the iPad or iPhone isn't connected to a wireless network, it has no hope whatever of prodding the server into responding.

Figure 6-26.   This dialog box can indicate various problems, ranging from network issues to the mail server actually being down.

- **Wrong incoming mail server information**   If you've mistyped the name of the incoming mail server, even a full-scale libation to the deities of the Domain Name System (they are legion) won't enable the iPad or iPhone to reach the server. Check your typing—the soft keyboard is as good as Apple can make it, but it's still a brute for detailed work.

- **Wrong e-mail address**   If you've mistyped the e-mail address (easy enough) or simply typed in the wrong address, that won't work either. But you can easily sort out any problems on this front.

- **The server is down**   If possible, use another mail client—or an administration tool—to make sure that the server is alive and kicking in the right direction.

The dialog box mentions the network connection and the incoming mail server as things to check, but make sure you also check the address—that's a showstopper too.

"Cannot Verify Server Identity" Error

The message "Cannot Verify Server Identity" (shown on the left in Figure 6-27) means that iOS cannot obtain a valid and trustworthy digital certificate from the server. Normally this is because you (or whichever other administrator is guilty) haven't installed a proper digital certificate on the server, but it can also be because the server's digital certificate has expired or been revoked.

Touch the Details button to display the Preferences screen (shown on the right in Figure 6-27). From here, you can take three actions:

- Touch the More Details button to display further details about the server.

- Touch the Accept button to accept the server as being safe.

- Touch the Cancel button to cancel the verification.

"Cannot Connect Using SSL" Error

The "Cannot Connect Using SSL: Do you want to try setting up the account without SSL?" message (see Figure 6-28) is pretty clear: The iPad or iPhone can't establish an SSL connection to the mail server, so iOS is offering you the choice of setting up the account without SSL. Touch the Yes button if you want to see if the device can establish the account without SSL; if so, you can try switching on SSL afterward.

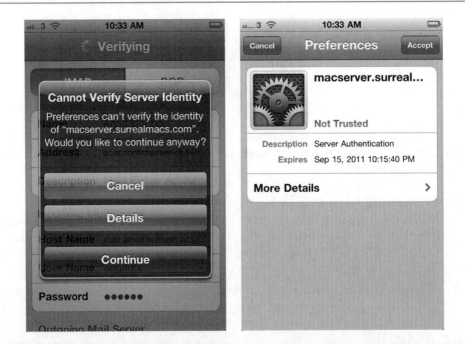

Figure 6-27.   If iOS gives the "Cannot Verify Server Identity" message (left), touch the Details button to display the Preferences screen (right) so that you can decide whether to trust the server.

"Secure Connection Failed: The Certificate May Not Be Valid" Error

The message "Secure Connection Failed: The certificate for *server_name* may not be valid" (see Figure 6-29) usually means that you haven't yet installed a trustworthy digital certificate on your server. For now, if the server address is correct, clicking the Continue button is fine—but you'll want to install a trustworthy digital certificate soon.

Figure 6-28.   If the iPad or iPhone is unable to connect to the mail server using SSL, you may need to open port 993 on your firewall.

Figure 6-29. The iPad or iPhone warns you if the mail server's certificate isn't valid. You can choose to continue—at your peril.

Troubleshooting Problems Sending and Receiving Mail on Other Mail Servers

This section shows you how to deal with some messages you'll see when the iPad and iPhone are having trouble connecting to the mail server and sending and receiving mail.

"The IMAP Server Is Not Responding" Error

If the Settings app on the iPad or iPhone gives the message "The IMAP server is not responding" (see Figure 6-30), check first that the server address is right. If so, you may need to open port 993 on the firewall to allow SSL IMAP traffic to pass.

"The Connection to the Outgoing Server Failed" Error

The message "Cannot Send Mail: The connection to the outgoing server failed" (see Figure 6-31) means pretty much what it says on the tin: iOS couldn't establish a connection to the outgoing server.

So far, so clear—so the question is why iOS can't reach the server. To sort out this problem, try these four general steps:

1. **Check you can connect to the network**   If you've got a network tool (such as those discussed in Chapter 5), use one to make sure the iPad or iPhone is actually connected to the network. If you don't have one of those tools, open Safari and see if it can reach a web site via the network. If the device can't reach the network, deal with the network problem before proceeding.

2. **Try hitting the server again**   The message "The connection to the outgoing server failed" can mean simply that the connection was dropped. So try connecting to the server again, and see if Mail can send the message this time.

NOTE   If this is the first time you've tried to connect to the server, double-check that the server's address is correct; correct any typos. If you've connected to the server before within living memory, the address likely isn't the problem.

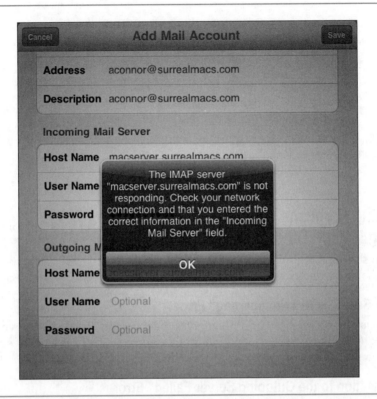

Figure 6-30. The message "The IMAP server is not responding" may indicate that the server address is wrong or that the SSL IMAP port (993) isn't open on the firewall.

Figure 6-31. If you get the message "The connection to the outgoing server failed," check the server address, and make sure port 465 is open on the firewall.

3. **Restart the iPad or iPhone**   The "connection failed" message can mean simply that iOS has got its network connections in a twist. Restarting the iPad or iPhone can clear the problem—so give it a try. It's probably time to shut down all the apps you were using anyway.

4. **Make sure the right port is open on the firewall**   For SSL e-mail, the default is port 465; for unencrypted e-mail, it's port 25. If you've set a custom port, use that number instead.

"The Sender Address Was Invalid" Error

The message "The sender address was invalid" (see Figure 6-32) tends to have two very distinct meanings:

- **The address from which you're sending the message is wrong**   If the mail server doesn't recognize your e-mail address, it'll reject the message. This can happen for any of three reasons:

  - **Your e-mail address has changed**   Normally, you'll be the first to know if this happens, but some administrators take twisted delight in surprising you.

  - **You've changed the e-mail address in the account**   No, I don't know why— but it happens. Maybe your kid decided to "upgrade" your settings for you.

  - **Mail has eaten your settings**   Mail is a friendly puppy, but sometimes it chews your settings just a bit. Like those old slippers that smelled so irresistibly *you*…

- **You're using an old MobileMe address**   At this writing, Apple is still shifting its old .Mac account holders from the .mac e-mail addresses to the new, shiny MobileMe addresses, which use the .me domain. If you're using a .mac address and getting this error, you probably need to heave a nostalgic sigh, take the account with the .mac address outside, and give it a quick and unsentimental double-tap. Have a bracing Jack or Mountain Dew (please don't mix them), and then set up a new .me account for your MobileMe account.

"Cannot Send Mail: The Server Rejected One of the Recipient's Addresses" Error

The message "Cannot Send Mail: The server rejected one of the recipient's addresses" usually means that you've typed an address wrong. You just need to correct the address, and the iPad or iPhone will be able to send it.

Figure 6-32.   The message "The sender address was invalid" may mean that you need to update an old .Mac e-mail address.

Mail puts the message it couldn't send in your Outbox. To send the message, touch the Send And Receive button (the button with the curling arrow).

The iPad or iPhone Can't Receive E-Mail

The message "The account *account_name* is in use on another device" means pretty much what it says: Another e-mail application is accessing the e-mail account, so the iPad or iPhone can't get in. This occurs with POP accounts, which can have only a single connection from any account to the server at once.

If you run into this problem, the easiest fix is to quit the other e-mail application. For example, don't leave your computer checking your POP e-mail account every couple of minutes—quit the e-mail application (or stop checking for new mail) so that the iPad or iPhone can check instead.

Wait five minutes or more for the POP server to notice that the e-mail application has left the scene of the crime; the server will then release the lock on the connection, and the iPad or iPhone can get in.

The iPad or iPhone Can't Send E-Mail

If the iPad or iPhone can't send e-mail, the problem may be that the SMTP server specified in the account's settings is having a quick siesta or is otherwise unavailable.

The first fix for this problem is to wait a few minutes, and then try the server again. If the server is back from its break, all will be well.

The second and longer-term fix for this problem is to turn on other SMTP servers for the e-mail account that's having problems. When you do this, the iPad or iPhone can simply try the next server in the list when the first server proves unavailable.

IMAP Folders All Appear Under the Inbox on the iPad or iPhone

If the folders for an IMAP account all appear under the Inbox on the iPad or iPhone rather than in their correct folder structure, try specifying the IMAP path prefix for the account.

You can specify the path prefix in either of two ways:

- **Configuration profile**   In the Email payload, type the path prefix in the Path Prefix text box. Apply the updated profile to the device, and verify that the problem has gone.

- **On the iPad or iPhone**   To specify the IMAP path prefix, follow these steps:

    1. Choose Settings | Mail, Contacts, Calendars to display the Mail, Contacts, Calendars screen.

    2. In the Accounts list, touch the IMAP account you want to affect. The iPad or iPhone displays the screen for that account.

    3. Touch the Advanced button (near the bottom of the screen) to display the Advanced screen (shown in Figure 6-21, earlier in this chapter).

    4. Touch the IMAP Path Prefix field, and then type in the path prefix.

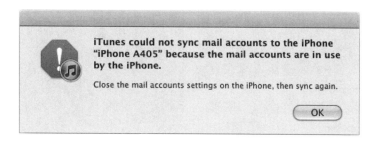

Figure 6-33.   This error message means that you you've left a mail account settings screen open, so iTunes can't sync the mail accounts.

   5.   Touch the account button in the upper-left corner to return to the account screen.

   6.   Touch the Done button to close the account screen.

"The Mail Accounts Are in Use" Error in iTunes

The message "iTunes could not sync mail accounts to the *device* because the mail accounts are in use" (see Figure 6-33) means that you've left a mail account settings screen open when you connected the iPad or iPhone to the computer.

   Click the OK button to dismiss the message box. Then disconnect the iPad or iPhone from the computer, go into the Mail settings, and finish whichever configuration task was underway. Once the device is back at the Accounts screen, you can safely connect the device to the computer and sync the mail accounts.

Deleting an E-Mail Account

When you no longer need a particular e-mail account on the iPad or iPhone, you can delete it. There's one wrinkle: You use a different technique for deleting an e-mail account you've installed using a configuration profile than one you've set up directly on the device.

   Let's start with the easy one—deleting an e-mail account you've set up directly on the iPad or iPhone.

Deleting an E-Mail Account You've Set Up Directly on the iPad or iPhone

If you've set up an e-mail account manually on the iPad or iPhone, you can delete it from the Mail, Contacts, Calendars screen. To do so, follow these steps:

   1.   From the Home screen, choose Settings | Mail, Contacts, Calendars to display the Mail, Contacts, Calendars screen.

   2.   Touch the button for the account you want to delete. iOS displays the screen for that account. The left screen in Figure 6-34 shows an example of this screen on an iPhone.

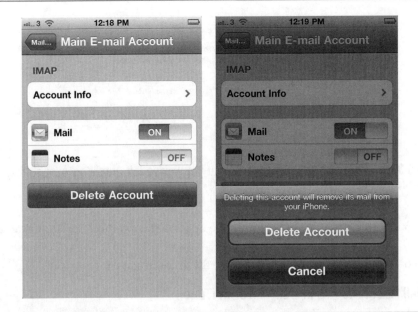

Figure 6-34. To delete an e-mail account, touch the Delete Account button on the account's screen (left). Confirm the deletion in the resulting dialog box (right).

3. Touch the Delete Account button at the bottom. iOS displays a dialog box warning you that deleting the account will remove the account's mail from the device, as shown on the right in Figure 6-34.

4. Touch the Delete Account button to confirm the deletion. iOS deletes the account and then displays the Mail, Contacts, Calendars screen.

Deleting an E-Mail Account You've Set Up Using a Configuration Profile

If you've set up an e-mail account on the iPad or iPhone by using a configuration profile, the only way to delete the e-mail account is to delete the profile that contains it. To do so, follow these steps:

1. From the Home screen, choose Settings | General to display the General screen.

2. Scroll down to the bottom and touch the profile button to display the Profile screen.

3. Touch the Remove button. iOS displays the Remove Profile dialog box.

4. Touch the Remove button. iOS removes the profile and the e-mail account associated with it.

CHAPTER 7 | Putting Documents on the iPad and iPhone

In this chapter, we'll look at how to put documents on the iPad and iPhone and how to remove documents from the devices. Neither operation is as straightforward as you might expect, and the techniques you use depend on what the user needs to do with the documents—simply read them, or edit them and return them to the PC or Mac.

We'll start by going over the way the iPad and iPhone handle documents, because this is substantially different from the way that most PC file systems handle them.

Once you've gotten the hang of how documents work in iOS, we'll look at the tools that Apple provides for putting documents on the iPad and iPhone. Understandably enough, these tools have built-in limitations, so we'll also examine some third-party tools that give you more direct access to the file system at the risk of your wreaking havoc.

What goes up usually comes down (apart from prices), and chances are you'll need to take some documents off the iPad and iPhone as well as putting them on it. Any document that's superfluous to requirements, you can simply delete from the iPad or iPhone; but if it's a document that has been created or edited on the device, you'll probably want to copy it to the PC or Mac. So we'll dig into this too.

Now, I don't know what kind of documents you work with—but chances are pretty high that you'll need to work with word processing documents, spreadsheets, and presentations on the iPad or iPhone. We'll look at how Apple's iWork for iPad applications—Pages, Numbers, and Keynote for the iPad—handle exporting documents to computers. Exporting is both cumbersome and limited, so I'll also mention some alternative apps you may need, especially if you need to share documents with Microsoft Office running on the PC.

Understanding How the iPad and iPhone Handle Documents

As you know, Apple has made iTunes the preferred management tool for iPads and iPhones, handling everything from activation and initial setup to daily synchronization and updates. iTunes is also the preferred tool for adding most types of documents to the iPad and iPhone directly or deleting them from it.

The main exception to this is incoming photos and video, which iTunes doesn't handle. On the Mac, that's iPhoto's job—so if you're on a Mac, iPhoto is the application you'll normally use to copy or remove photos, videos, or screen captures from the iPad or iPhone. (You can also use Image Capture or Preview's File | Import From *Device* command if you want only to copy the items rather than adding them to your iPhoto library.) On Windows, the iPad's or iPhone's photo and video storage area shows up in Windows Explorer as a digital camera, as you can see at the bottom of Figure 7-1. You can then copy the photos to the PC's file system and enjoy them in whichever program you prefer.

Figure 7-1.   Windows detects the iPad's or iPhone's photo and video storage area as a digital camera. To get at the photos or videos, double-click the iPad's or iPhone's entry in the Portable Devices area of a Computer window.

Apart from this digital camera that Windows sees, the iPad and iPhone don't appear in Windows Explorer. On the Mac, Finder acts as if completely unaware of the iPad's or iPhone's presence. This is to encourage you to use iTunes (and iPhoto on the Mac) to manage the device and avoid you stamping around sensitive parts of its file system with hobnailed boots on.

NOTE   If you want to get into the iPad's or iPhone's file system, you can do so with third-party tools such as DiskAid, FileApp, and Air Sharing. We'll meet these tools later in this chapter. (You can wear hobnailed boots if you like.)

Within its file system, iOS gives each app a separate storage area for documents—its own document silo. iOS largely confines each app to its own silo and prevents it from accessing any other silos. But apps that can receive incoming files, such as Mail and Safari, can provide those files to other apps. For example, if you receive a Word document attached to an e-mail message on your iPad, you can choose to open that document in Pages for iPad (if you have it installed) or another app that can handle Word documents. Mail makes the document available to Pages or the app you choose.

iOS doesn't give you a file browser that you can use to browse files and open them in their apps, let alone choose which app to open a particular file in. Instead, you open the app that can handle the document, then open the document from that app's document silo. Or you use Mail or Safari to pick the app you want to open a document stored in one of those apps.

Similarly, when you need to get documents off the iPad or iPhone, you need to use iTunes and the limited sharing capabilities built into specific apps. For instance, to get a Numbers workbook off an iPad, you first export it from Numbers to the File Sharing area, where iTunes can access it. You can then copy the file to your computer using iTunes, send it via e-mail, or upload it to Apple's iWork.com sharing site.

That's the overview of transferring files back and forth. We'll look at the details later in this chapter.

Understanding the iOS File Viewers

iOS has built-in viewers for major file types, including these:

- PDF
- Word (both the .docx and .doc formats)
- Excel (both the .xlsx and .xls formats)
- PowerPoint (both the .pptx and .ppt formats)
- Rich-text format (RTF)
- Text documents
- HTML

Various apps that enable you to transfer files to or from the iPad or iPhone can display the documents using these viewers but cannot open the documents for editing. The viewers display the documents for viewing but don't provide full features. For example, if you open a PDF file for a second time, the viewer doesn't remember the last page you read the first time you opened it; and you can't follow internal links within a PDF file. But as far as straightforward reading goes, the viewers are pretty good.

Transferring Documents to the iPad or iPhone

Given that you can't use Windows Explorer or the Finder to put documents on the iPad or iPhone, you need to use different tools. These fall into two main categories: those that you use with the iPad or iPhone connected to your computer, and those you use across a wireless connection. Some third-party tools work both ways.

We'll start by looking at Apple's preferred solution for transferring documents to an iPad or iPhone connected to your computer: iTunes. We'll then examine the three other main ways of transferring documents: e-mail, downloading from web sites, and downloading from SharePoint sites. After that, I'll show you several third-party tools that access the iPad's or iPhone's file system directly and that you may want to use for transferring documents.

Transferring Documents by Using File Sharing in iTunes

Unless you use third-party apps, the most direct way to add documents to the iPad or iPhone directly is to use the File Sharing capability built into iTunes.

 NOTE   You can also use File Sharing to copy documents from the iPad or iPhone to a PC or Mac. This is useful both for documents you've created on the device (for example, by using the iWork applications on the iPad) and for documents that you're using the iPad or iPhone to transfer from one computer to another.

To transfer documents by using File Sharing, follow these steps:

1. Connect the iPad or iPhone to the computer as usual.

2. If the computer doesn't automatically launch or activate iTunes, launch or activate iTunes yourself.

3. In the Source list, click the entry for the iPad or iPhone to display its control screens.

4. Click the Apps tab to display its contents.

5. Scroll down to the File Sharing area (see Figure 7-2).

6. In the Apps list, click the app to which you want to transfer the files. The list of files for that app appears in the Documents pane to the right.

7. To add documents to the app, follow these steps:

   a. Click the Add button to display the iTunes dialog box (on Windows) or the Choose A File: iTunes dialog box (on the Mac).

   b. Navigate to and select the document or documents you want to add.

   c. Click the OK button (on Windows) or the Choose button (on the Mac).

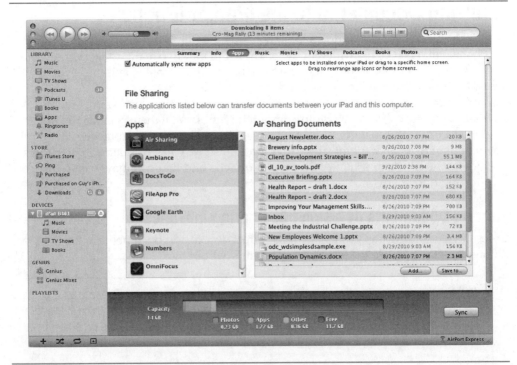

Figure 7-2. The File Sharing area on the Apps tab in the iTunes control screens for an iPad or iPhone lists the apps that can transfer files. Click an app to see its files.

8. To copy documents from the app to the computer, follow these steps:

a. Click the Save To button to display the iTunes dialog box (on Windows) or the Choose A File: iTunes dialog box (on the Mac).

b. Navigate to the folder in which you want to save the document.

c. Click the Select Folder button (on Windows) or the Choose button (on the Mac).

File transfers generally run pretty quickly, as USB 2.0 can handle up to 480 megabits per second (Mbps)—but if you're transferring many large files, it'll take a while. And if you're using a USB 1.x port, its 12 Mbps limit will make things much slower.

Transferring Documents via E-Mail

When you need to get documents onto the iPad or iPhone quickly, you can simply e-mail them to an account on the iPad or iPhone. You can then open the documents directly from the e-mail.

E-mail may seem like a kludgy solution to document transfer, but it's effective both for personal use and enterprise use—up to a point. Because the iPad and iPhone enable you to open a document from Mail in another app, you can easily view or edit documents you've received via e-mail. And if necessary, you can use Mail to send a document back after you've edited it, or send it along to the next person who needs to deal with it.

To get a document out of an e-mail message and into an app's storage area, follow these steps:

1. In the message list, touch the message to display its contents.

2. Touch and hold the document's button in the message until Mail displays a menu (shown on the left in Figure 7-3).

3. If you want to open the basic viewer for the document, touch the Quick Look button; normally, though, you'll do better to open the document in an app. If you want to open the document in the default app (in this example, Pages), touch the Open In "*App*" button (where *App* is the app's name). Otherwise, touch the Open In button to display the Open In menu (shown on the right in Figure 7-3), and then touch the app you want to use.

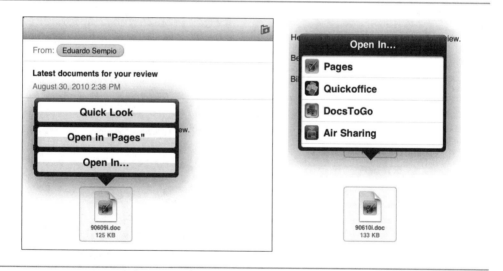

Figure 7-3.   Touch and hold a document's button in an e-mail message until the menu for opening the document appears (left). To use a different app, touch the Open In button to display the Open In menu (right), and then touch the app you want.

That's the most efficient way to copy the document from the message and get it into the app. But what you'll probably want to do often is view the contents of the document so that you can decide which app to open it in. For example, if you receive a Word document on the iPad, you may want to bring it into Pages so that you can use Pages' streamlined layout tools. But if you simply want to edit the document as a Word document, you'll do better to open the document in Documents To Go or a similar app that can maintain the Word document format.

To view a document and then decide which app to use for it, follow these steps:

1. In the message list, touch the message to display its contents.

2. Touch the button for the attached document you want to open. The iPad or iPhone displays the document in the viewer. The left screen in Figure 7-4 shows a PDF document open in the viewer on an iPhone.

3. Touch the Open In button to display the list of apps that can open the document. The right screen in Figure 7-4 shows an example of this list.

4. Touch the app in which you want to open the document.

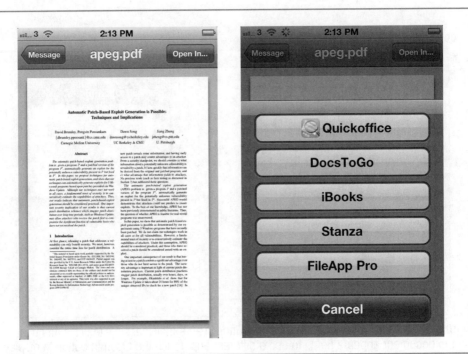

Figure 7-4.   To copy a document from an e-mail message, open it in the viewer (left). You can then touch the Open In button and touch the app to use (right).

This approach leaves the document open in the viewer in Mail. So when you go back to Mail, touch the Message button (on the iPhone) or the Done button (on the iPad) to close the viewer and return to the message.

Once you've opened an attached document in another app, that app stores a copy of the document in its silo. You can now delete the e-mail message and the attached document if necessary; the copy of the document that you've added to the other app's silo remains unaffected.

This is all pretty workable. The main disadvantage of transferring documents via e-mail is that it can choke both mail servers and inboxes. This means it's most effective for transferring documents you know the recipient needs rather than showering the user with a smorgasbord of documents from which the user needs only one or two.

NOTE   If you attach a picture to an e-mail message, the recipient can save the picture to the Photos silo on the iPad or iPhone. But if you attach a music file or video file, the recipient can only play it in the viewer or add it to third-party apps that handle media file types, not add it to the iPod silo on the device.

Providing Documents by Download from a Web Site

Pushing out documents via e-mail works pretty well when you need to make sure that each user receives a particular document. But in many cases you'll need to make documents available only to those who want them. In this case, it doesn't make sense to bombard all users with the documents via e-mail. Not only will your network take a hefty hit, but the users may become swamped by salvos of documents that are useless to them so that they miss the few crucial documents they do need.

In this case, you'll probably want to put the documents on a web site so that users can download those they need and ignore the rest. The web site can be either internal or external, as needed. Let the users know which documents you've posted and where to find them—for example, via e-mail for documents of regular importance or text message for lights-and-siren updates.

Once you've found the document you need, touch its download link to download it. Safari handles the download by opening a new tab containing the document. Figure 7-5 shows an RTF document downloaded from a web site.

From here, you can open the document in a suitable application:

- **Use the recommended app**   Touch the Open In *App* button in the upper-right corner of the screen (where *App* is the app's name).

- **Use another app**   Touch the Open In button in the upper-left corner of the screen, and then touch the app you want to use on the menu that appears.

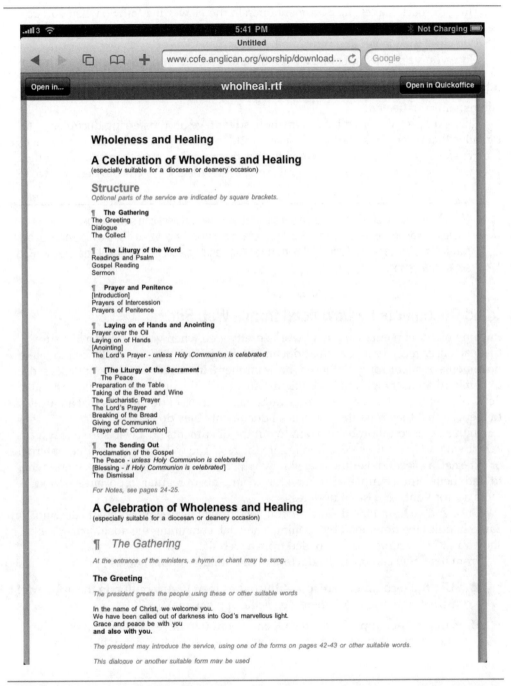

Figure 7-5. After using Safari to download a document from a web site, use the Open In button or the Open In *"App"* button in the viewer to choose the app in which to open the document.

Providing Documents by Download from a SharePoint Site

If your company or organization has a SharePoint site, you can use it to share documents with iPad and iPhone users just as with users of PCs and other devices.

 TIP   If your company or organization doesn't have a SharePoint site, consider using Windows Live SkyDrive for personal use or another hosted site for business use. Such sites can be a great way to get documents onto the iPad and iPhone unless security concerns rule out their use.

The most straightforward way to connect to a SharePoint site using the iPad or iPhone is to open Safari, enter the address of the site, and provide any authentication needed, as shown here.

Once you've logged in, you can navigate the site. What you see depends on which version of SharePoint the site is running:

■ **SharePoint version earlier than SharePoint 2010**   If the site is running a SharePoint version earlier than SharePoint 2010, it doesn't detect that you're using a mobile device, so you're stuck with the usual browser-based interface. On the iPad, navigation is somewhat clumsy, especially opening drop-down lists and choosing commands from them; and on the iPhone, it's that much harder because of the shortage of screen acreage. It does work, but it's fiddly—so you may not want users depending on it as a regular way of getting documents, especially older users with hardening retinas and six-digit salaries.

■ **SharePoint 2010**   If the SharePoint site is running SharePoint 2010, things are much better. SharePoint 2010 detects that you're using a mobile device and gives you the mobile version of the site rather than the standard version. Figure 7-6 shows an iPad accessing the Windows Live SkyDrive site, which runs on SharePoint; as you can see, the controls appear at a good size for the touch interface.

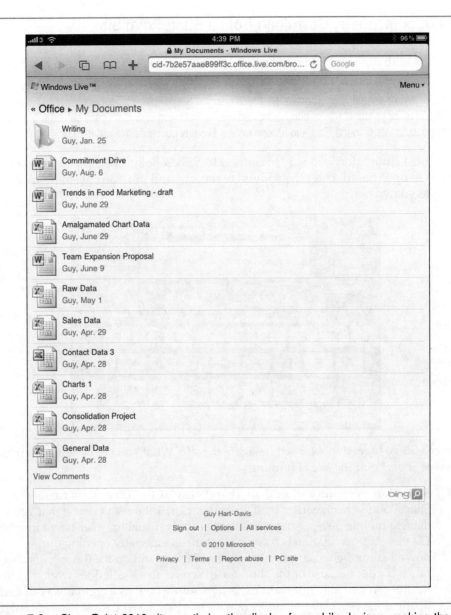

Figure 7-6. SharePoint 2010 sites optimize the display for mobile devices, making the sites easy to use with the touch interface.

If users need easier access to a SharePoint site than Safari can provide, you can also use a third-party SharePoint client instead of Safari. Here are three examples:

■ **SharePlus** SharePlus is a SharePoint client for the iPad that makes connecting to and navigating SharePoint sites much easier. Figure 7-7 shows SharePlus with its Navigator pane open and the Add Site dialog box displayed.

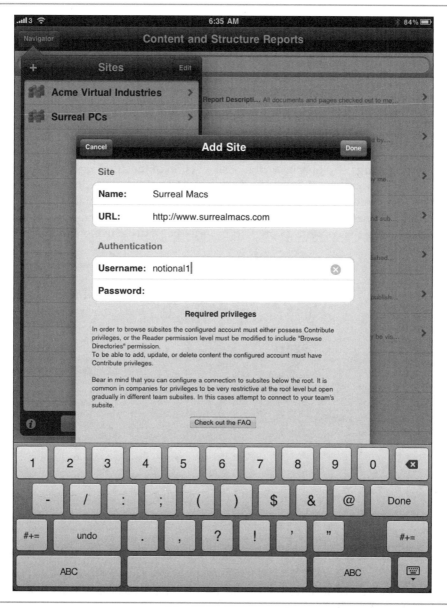

Figure 7-7. SharePlus is an iPad client for SharePoint.

- **Attaché**   Attaché is a SharePoint client for the iPhone but runs on the iPad as well; at this writing, there's no iPad-specific version.

- **Moshare**   Moshare is a SharePoint client for the iPhone that you can also use on the iPad; at this writing, there's no iPad-specific version.

Transferring Documents Using Third-Party Apps

If you need more direct or wider-ranging access to the iPad's or iPhone's file system than iTunes provides, you'll need to use a third-party app instead. This section introduces you to three of the most widely useful apps at this writing: Air Sharing, FileApp Pro (with or without DiskAid), and Documents To Go.

Transferring Documents Using Air Sharing

Air Sharing is an app for transferring documents to and from the iPad or iPhone and viewing them on the device. Air Sharing connects to the iPad or iPhone via a wireless network connection and comes in three different versions:

- **Air Sharing**   Air Sharing is the basic version of the app for the iPhone. You can mount the iPhone as a drive on a PC or Mac (or a Linux box, if you're interested), transfer files both ways, and view or e-mail documents in the formats the iOS viewer supports. Figure 7-8 shows a Finder window displaying the contents of an iPad mounted as a drive using Air Sharing.

Figure 7-8.   With Air Sharing, you can mount an iPad or iPhone as a drive on your computer so that you can easily transfer files.

■ **Air Sharing Pro** Air Sharing Pro adds abilities such as connecting to a Windows PC running a companion program, mounting remote file systems, opening and creating Zip files, and downloading files from the Web.

■ **Air Sharing HD** Air Sharing HD is the iPad version of Air Sharing Pro and provides similar features at the larger screen size. Figure 7-9 shows Air Sharing HD connected to a Mac (named MacServer) and browsing the file system.

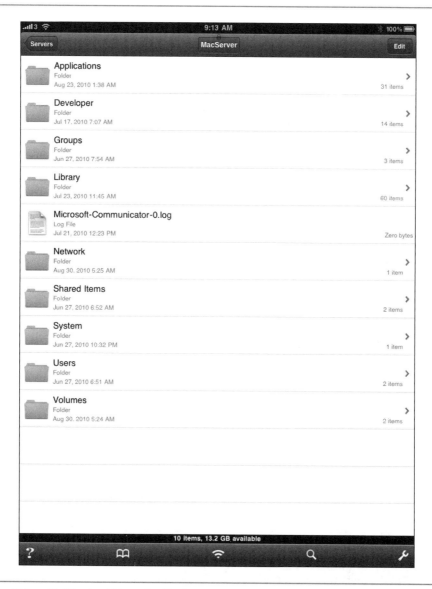

Figure 7-9. Air Sharing HD on the iPad can connect to remote servers so that you can browse their contents.

Transferring Documents Using FileApp Pro

Like Air Sharing, FileApp Pro is an app for transferring documents to and from the iPad and iPhone and for viewing documents on the devices. With FileApp Pro, you can connect to the iPad or iPhone either via the USB cable (which is good for speed) or via a wireless network connection (which is good for flexibility). To connect via USB, you need to either use iTunes's File Sharing feature or run the DiskAid program (from DigiDNA; www.digidna.net) on your PC or Mac.

The left image in Figure 7-10 shows the FileApp Pro interface for manipulating folders on the iPhone. The right image in Figure 7-10 shows the Sharing screen of FileApp Pro, again running on an iPhone. You touch the USB button or the WIFI button to choose the means of sharing, then touch the button for the operating system you're using—Win 7, Win Vista, Win XP, or Mac OS X—to display instructions for connecting.

You can transfer documents by using the FileApp Pro entry in the File Sharing area of the Apps tab in iTunes, but if you want to transfer many files easily and choose the folders to put them in, it's worth getting DiskAid and installing it on your computer. Once you've set up sharing on the iPad or iPhone, you can connect via DiskAid and transfer files easily back and forth. Figure 7-11 shows DiskAid in action with an iPhone.

Figure 7-10.   FileApp Pro lets you choose between USB and Wi-Fi connections (left) and create and manipulate folders easily on the iPhone (right) or iPad.

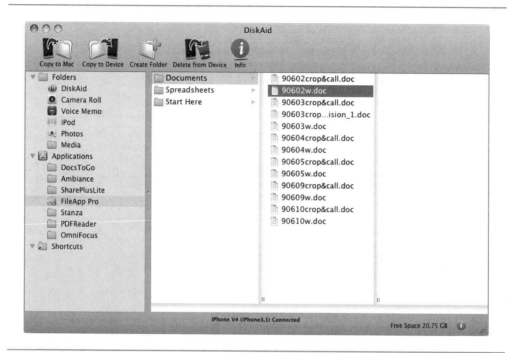

Figure 7-11.   DiskAid is a companion program for FileApp Pro that makes it easy to transfer files to and from the iPad and iPhone. You can also use DiskAid on its own.

Apart from managing files, FileApp Pro also makes it easy to browse and view your files. FileApp lets you create text documents, play audio and video, and show slideshows of images.

TIP   DiskAid is a handy tool if you want to simply store files on your iPad or iPhone—for example, to transfer them from one computer to another—rather than open the files on the iPad or iPhone. With DiskAid, you can create your own folders on the iPad or iPhone, enabling you to use it as an external disk.

Transferring Documents Using Documents To Go

If you need to work extensively with Microsoft Office documents—for example, Word documents or Excel workbooks—you'll probably find the iWork apps too cumbersome. Instead of struggling with frustrating conversions, get a third-party program that can handle the main Office file formats without having to translate them.

At this writing, Documents To Go is the best app for working with Microsoft Office documents on the iPad or iPhone. Documents To Go isn't perfect, but it can display most of the essential parts of Word documents, Excel workbooks, and PowerPoint presentations so that you can edit them. Figure 7-12 shows Documents To Go working on a Word document.

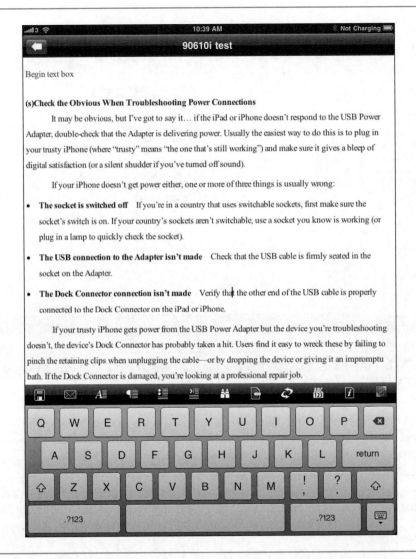

Figure 7-12.   Documents To Go can open Word documents so that you can edit them.

You can load documents into Documents To Go by using the Documents To Go entry in the File Sharing area of the Apps tab in iTunes, but for regular use, download the free companion desktop program that runs on your PC or Mac to synchronize documents with the iPad or iPhone. To get the program, go to the DataViz web site (www.dataviz.com), click the iPad or iPhone link, and then click the Download button.

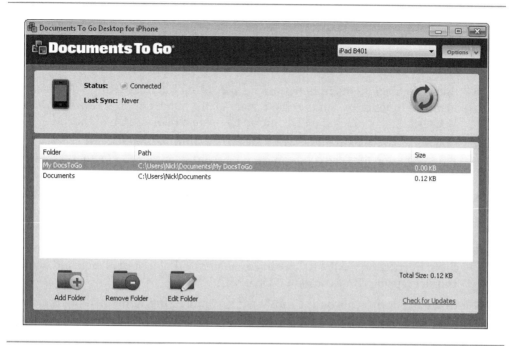

Figure 7-13.   The Documents To Go desktop program runs on your computer and connects to the iPad or iPhone.

Once you've installed the program, you go through a HotSync setup process to pair the iPad or iPhone with the desktop program. You can then use the desktop program to transfer files to and from the device (see Figure 7-13).

> **NOTE**   Documents To Go Premium can access documents in an online storage account such as Google Docs, Box.net, Dropbox, or iDisk.

Transferring Documents from the iWork Apps on the iPad to Your Computer

If you create or edit documents using Pages, Numbers, or Keynote, you'll probably want to get them back onto your PC or Mac. You can transfer them by using iTunes' File Sharing feature on the computer that the iPad or iPhone usually syncs with, by putting them on the iWork.com site, or by using sending them via e-mail to any computer with an Internet connection.

Which method you'll find works best depends on what you need to do:

- **Work with the documents in iWork on the Mac** Transfer the files using iTunes or by sending them via e-mail. Keep the files in their native formats—for example, keep a Pages document in the Pages file format.

- **Share the documents in PDF format for reading but not editing** Transfer the files via iTunes or by sending them via e-mail. On the Export screen or the Send Via Mail screen, touch the PDF button to create a PDF version of the file.

- **Share a Pages document in Word format for editing in any word processor** From Pages on the iPad, you can create a Word document and either transfer it using iTunes or send it via e-mail.

- **Share a Numbers document in Excel format for editing in any spreadsheet application** From Numbers on the iPad, you can create an Excel workbook and either transfer it using iTunes or send it via e-mail.

- **Share a Keynote document in PowerPoint format for editing in PowerPoint** From Keynote on the iPad, you can create a PowerPoint presentation and either transfer it using iTunes or send it via e-mail.

- **Share the documents online for viewing, commenting, and downloading** If you need to make the documents available to various people, you can post them on the iWork.com site instead of sending them via e-mail. People can then view the documents online and can download them in their native formats, as PDF versions, as Word documents (for Pages documents), as Excel workbooks (for Numbers spreadsheets), or as PowerPoint presentations (for Keynote presentations).

These methods work reasonably well, but if you need to work exclusively with the Microsoft Office file formats, you will probably prefer a third-party document editor, that can handle the Office file formats natively, to the hassle of importing the Office documents into the iWork applications and then exporting them again.

Transferring Documents from the iWork Apps on the iPad via File Sharing

Usually, the easiest way to get the documents from the iWork apps on the iPad onto a PC or Mac is by using the File Sharing feature in iTunes.

To use the File Sharing feature, you must first export the document from the app. Until you export the document, the app stores it within its own silo, where iTunes can't reach it. Exporting the document places a copy of it in the File Sharing folder on the iPad, where iTunes can access it.

To export a document, follow these steps on the iPad:

1. Open the app to which the document belongs—for example, Pages.

2. If the app launches with a document open, touch the My Documents button, the My Spreadsheets button, or the My Presentations button in the upper-left corner of the screen to go back to the Document Manager screen. This is the screen that shows the My Documents folder, the My Spreadsheets folder, or the My Presentations folder.

Figure 7-14. On the Document Manager screen, touch the Export button (the arrow button), and then touch Export on the menu.

3. At the bottom of the screen, touch the Export button (the rectangle button with the arrow pointing out to the northeast) to display the Export menu (see Figure 7-14).

4. Touch the Export button to display the Export Document screen (see Figure 7-15), the Export Spreadsheet screen, or the Export Presentation screen.

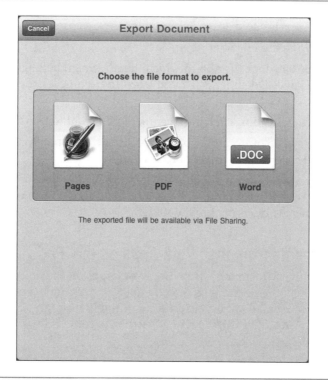

Figure 7-15. On the Export Document screen (shown here), the Export Spreadsheet screen, or the Export Presentation screen, touch the format to use for the exported file.

5.   Touch the format to use for the exported file:

   ■ **Native format**   Touch the Pages button, the Numbers button, or the Keynote button to keep the document in its native format.

   ■ **Office format**   Touch the Word button (from Pages), the Excel button (from Numbers), or the PowerPoint button (from Keynote).

   ■ **PDF**   Touch the PDF button to create a Portable Document File format for viewing on any computer (but not for editing).

6.   The app exports the file in the format you chose, and then displays the Document Manager screen again.

Once you've exported the document to the File Sharing folder, you can use iTunes to copy the file to the PC or Mac. To do so, follow these steps:

1.   Connect the iPad or iPhone to the computer as usual.

2.   If the computer doesn't automatically launch or activate iTunes, launch or activate iTunes yourself.

3.   In the Source list, click the entry for the iPad or iPhone to display its control screens.

4.   Click the Apps tab to display its contents.

5.   Scroll down to the File Sharing area.

6.   In the Apps list, click the app to which the document belongs. Figure 7-16 shows the Pages Documents list you'll see after you click the Pages app in the Apps list.

7.   In the Documents box, click the document you want to transfer.

8.   Click the Save To button to display the iTunes dialog box (on Windows) or the Choose A Folder: iTunes dialog box (on the Mac).

9.   Navigate to the folder in which you want to save the document, and then click the Select Folder button (on Windows) or the Choose button (on the Mac). iTunes saves the document to the folder.

Transferring Documents from the iWork Apps on the iPad via E-Mail

When you need to share documents from the iWork apps on the iPad with specific people, you can e-mail the documents directly to them. Sharing via e-mail works well for documents that are small enough to pass comfortably through mail servers; for any huge documents (over, say, 5MB), it's best to use iWork.com, as described in the next section.

Figure 7-16.   To transfer an exported document to your computer, click the appropriate app in the Apps list, and then click the document.

To share documents from the iWork applications via e-mail, follow these steps:

1. Open the app to which the document belongs—for example, Numbers.

2. If the app launches with a document open, touch the My Documents button, the My Spreadsheets button, or the My Presentations button in the upper-left corner of the screen to go back to the Document Manager screen.

3. At the bottom of the screen, touch the Export button (the rectangle button with the arrow pointing out to the northeast) to display the Export menu.

4. Touch the Send Via Mail button to display the Send Via Mail dialog box.

5. Touch the file format you want to use, as discussed in the preceding section. The app creates a new e-mail message with the document attached.

6. Address the message as usual, type any explanatory text, and then touch the Send button to send it on its merry way.

Transferring Documents from the iWork Apps on the iPad via iWork.com

Apple's iWork.com site is a means of sharing files you've created in the iWork applications, either on the iPad or on the Mac. From one of the iWork applications, you share the file to the iWork.com site so that other people can view it or download it.

To use iWork.com, you buy iWork for Mac OS X or one of the iWork apps for iPad, and then sign up for it with an Apple ID (for example, the one you use for the iTunes Store). The iWork application you're using prompts you to create an account the first time you go to share files on iWork.com.

NOTE At this writing, iWork.com is in beta—as it has been for the best part of two years. The site seems stable, but you may want to wait until a non-beta release before entrusting it with documents you care about.

Once you've signed up, you can place files on the site. When you place a file on iWork.com, you choose who to share it with by sending e-mail invitations. You can send invitations to anyone who has an e-mail account, but each person needs to set up an iWork.com account before they can view the document you're sharing with them.

To use iWork.com to transfer and share files, follow these steps:

1. Open the app to which the document belongs—for example, Keynote.

2. If the app launches with a document open, touch the My Documents button, the My Spreadsheets button, or the My Presentations button in the upper-left corner of the screen to go back to the Document Manager screen.

3. At the bottom of the screen, touch the Export button (the rectangle button with the arrow pointing out to the northeast) to display the Export menu.

4. Touch the Share Via iWork.com button. The app displays the Apple ID Sign In screen (see Figure 7-17).

5. If you need to create a new Apple ID for iWork.com, touch the Create A New Apple ID link, and then follow through the process for creating the ID. Otherwise, type in your Apple ID and password, and then touch the Sign In button.

NOTE The first time you use iWork.com with an existing Apple ID, you may need to go through an e-mail verification process.

6. Once you've signed in, the app creates a new e-mail message containing details of the shared document. The message uses a default subject line such as *View "Document" on iWork.com,* where *Document* is the document's name. Figure 7-18 shows an example in Keynote.

Figure 7-17. From the Apple ID Sign In screen, you can either enter your existing Apple ID or create a new one.

7. Address the message and change the default subject line as needed.

8. Type any explanatory text the message needs to help the recipients understand why you're sharing this document with them.

9. Touch the Sharing Options link to display the Sharing Options dialog box (shown on the left in Figure 7-19).

10. If you need to change the document's name, touch the name button at the top. In the Name dialog box that opens (shown on the right in Figure 7-19), type the new name, and then touch the Sharing Options button to return to the Sharing Options dialog box.

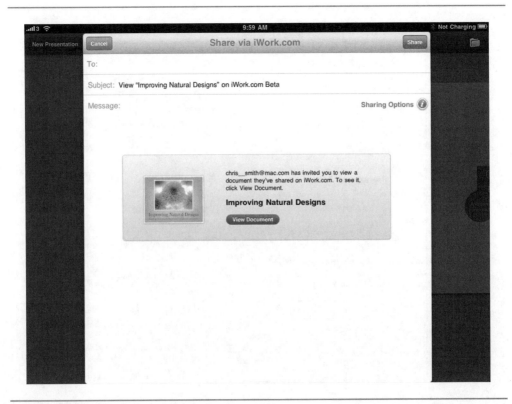

Figure 7-18. The iWork app automatically creates an e-mail message containing details of the document you're sharing on iWork.com. You choose the recipients, set options, and send the message.

11. In the Viewer Options area, choose restrictions on viewers as needed:

■ **Password** To protect the document with a password, touch the Password field, and then type the password.

■ **Allow Comments** Move this switch to the Off position if you don't want viewers to be able to add comments to the document.

12. In the Download Options area, use the On/Off switches to specify which formats the user can download the document in. Move both or all three switches to the Off position if you want people to be able only to view the document online, not download it.

13. When you've finished choosing sharing options, touch outside the Sharing Options dialog box to return to the message.

14. Touch the Share button to send the message.

Figure 7-19.   In the Sharing Options dialog box (left), choose whether to password-protect the document, whether to allow comments, and which download formats to offer. To change the name, touch the name to display the Name dialog box (right), and then type the new name.

In this chapter, we've explored the various ways of transferring documents to and from the iPad and iPhone. You've learned how the iPad and iPhone handle documents—by giving each app its own document silo and providing only limited access to the file system—and how to work with (or around) the limitations Apple imposes.

In the next chapter, we'll go through how to secure the iPads and iPhones under your control. Turn the page when you're ready to start.

CHAPTER 8 | Securing Your Company's iPads and iPhones

As you've seen in the preceding chapters, you can load up an iPad or iPhone with any amount of data—everything from confidential address books and appointments to sensitive documents and financial data. Then you can lose the device—or have it stolen—and put all your data at risk at the drop of a hat or at the pick of a pocket.

In this chapter, we'll look at the measures you can take to keep your valuable and sensitive data safe. Here's your executive-level breakdown:

- First, you'll almost certainly want to protect the iPad or iPhone with a device passcode so that it's armored against casual intrusion when someone lifts it from your pocket; and it's equally likely you'll want to apply auto-locking with a short interval to ensure that the iPad or iPhone is locked when it goes missing, presumed swiped.

- Second, to prevent anyone from getting at sensitive data on the iPad or iPhone, you should apply data protection on the device. You should also set iTunes to encrypt the backups of the device's data so that they're not open to intruders.

- Third, you can configure an iPad or iPhone to wipe its contents automatically if someone keeps entering the wrong passcodes.

- Fourth, you can remotely wipe the contents of an iPad or iPhone if it has strayed beyond your control.

Let's take it from the top.

Protecting the iPad or iPhone with a Device Passcode and Auto-Locking

The first step to keeping the data on the iPad or iPhone safe is to protect the device with a device passcode. This is the sequence of characters you need to tap in to unlock the screen when you turn the device on. You'll also want to make sure the iPad or iPhone locks itself automatically after a short time of inactivity rather than leaving itself unlocked and vulnerable—otherwise, the passcode is about as useful as a screen door on a submarine.

As with many aspects of configuring an iPad or iPhone, you can set a device passcode either by applying policy with iPhone Configuration Utility or by working directly on the iPad or iPhone. Normally, you'll want to use iPhone Configuration Utility to implement device passcodes on all the iPads and iPhones over which you wield dominion, but you may also need to tweak the settings on individual devices manually.

NOTE With iPhone Configuration Utility, you don't set the actual passcode for the device—that'd give you a single passcode per configuration profile and the mother of all security headaches. Instead, you use the configuration profile to specify the passcode requirements—for example, that it must be at least six characters long and must contain some letters. The iPad or iPhone then forces the user to set a passcode that meets the requirements.

We'll look at each approach in turn. But first we'll dig into the types of passcodes you can use on the iPad and iPhone, because there are a couple of twists and subtleties you need to appreciate.

NOTE This section assumes that the iPads and iPhones contain data or connections you want to protect (or—at a stretch—that you want to prevent an outsider from discovering that the devices *don't* contain anything worth protecting). Most iPads and iPhones will contain sensitive information, even if it's just a VPN connection to the corporate network. But if the iPads and iPhones are the users' property, you may need to leave the question of a passcode to the users.

Understanding the Essentials of Passcodes

An iPad or iPhone can use either a simple passcode or a complex passcode:

- **Simple passcode** On the iPad or iPhone, a *simple passcode* is one that uses four digits (for example, 1924). This is what each iPad and iPhone is set to use by default as a consumer device.

NOTE In iPhone Configuration Utility, things are more complicated: Selecting the Allow Simple Value check box in the Passcode screen permits sequences of characters (for example, 1234 or abcd) or repeated characters (for example, 9911 or aaaa); clearing this check box prevents the user from using sequences or repetition. Selecting the Require Alphanumeric Value check box forces the user to include one or more letters as well as numbers. You can then use the Minimum Number Of Complex Characters drop-down list or pop-up menu to force the user to include one or more non-alphanumeric characters (such as symbols) in the passcode.

- **Complex passcode** A *complex passcode* is one that uses more than four characters and that mixes letters and other characters with digits.

A complex passcode can provide much greater security than a simple passcode in three mostly obvious ways:

- **You can set a longer passcode.** A longer passcode is harder to crack because it contains more characters (even if it consists only of numbers rather than letters and non-alphanumeric characters).

- **You can require the passcode to include letters.** Including letters as well as numbers greatly increases the strength of the passcode even at short lengths.

- **You can require the passcode to include non-alphanumeric characters.** Including non-alphanumeric characters (such as symbols) increases the strength of the passcode even further.

When the iPad or iPhone demands the passcode, the Enter Passcode screen indicates whether the device is using a simple passcode or a complex passcode. For a simple passcode, the Enter Passcode screen displays four boxes and a numeric keypad, as shown on the left in Figure 8-1. For a complex passcode, the Enter Passcode screen displays a text box and the QWERTY keyboard, as shown on the right in Figure 8-1.

Choosing between a simple passcode and a complex passcode can be tough, as you need to balance security against the user's need to be able to whip the device out (or open) and get to work without flailing in frustration at the soft keyboard. Keep these points in mind when deciding which type of passcode to use:

- **A simple passcode may be strong enough with auto-erase.**   Given enough time and tries, anyone can break a simple passcode by plodding through all 10,000 possible numbers until they hit the jackpot. iOS makes this harder by automatically disabling the iPad or iPhone for increasing periods of time— 1 minute, 5 minutes, 15 minutes, 60 minutes, and so on—as the wrong passcodes hit in sequence (see Figure 8-2). A determined attacker can keep plugging away, but if you set the iPad or iPhone to erase its data automatically after a handful of failed attempts to enter the passcode, the device's data should be pretty safe—unless the user has chosen a personal number that the attacker can guess (for example, the user's birth year).

Figure 8-1.   The Enter Passcode screen on the iPad or iPhone shows whether the device is using a simple passcode (left) or a complex passcode (right).

Figure 8-2.   If the user enters the wrong passcode, the iPad or iPhone makes the problem clear (left). If the user continues to provide wrong passcodes, the iPad or iPhone disables itself for a while (right).

■ **With a complex passcode, you may not need auto-erase.**   If you require a complex passcode of a certain length (say eight or more characters) and including both alpha and non-alphanumeric characters, you may consider it strong enough that the device doesn't need auto-erase. Your decision will likely depend on whether the iPad or iPhone contains nuclear launch codes, glutinous cookie recipes, or something in between.

■ **A complex passcode can be simpler than a simple passcode.**   Because the Enter Passcode screen for a complex passcode gives no indication of the passcode's length, you may be able to bluff an attacker by setting a short, letters-only passcode (for example, aq) rather than a mashup of the first half of *Moby Dick* and the telephone directory. A short passcode like this is easy for the user to remember and type, so you can set a low number for the Maximum Number Of Failed Attempts setting as a safety net.

Applying a Device Passcode Requirement and Auto-Locking Using iPhone Configuration Utility

If you're managing iPads and iPhones tightly, use iPhone Configuration Utility to apply a device passcode requirement in a configuration profile. To add a device passcode to a configuration profile, follow these general steps; see the section "Creating a Passcode Payload" in Chapter 3 for a detailed discussion of the Passcode payload options.

1. Open iPhone Configuration Utility and click the Configuration Profiles item in the Library category in the Source list.

2. In the list of configuration profiles, click the profile to which you want to add the Passcode payload. If necessary, click the New button on the toolbar to start creating a new configuration profile, and then set its general information in the General payload pane.

NOTE To ensure that the iPads and iPhones remain protected by passcodes, make sure that the user can't turn off the passcode requirement by removing the configuration profile from the device. To prevent the user from removing the configuration profile, set the configuration profile's Security level to With Authorization or Never rather than Always.

3. Click the Passcode item in the Payloads list to display the Configure Passcode box.

4. Click the Configure button to display the Passcode screen (see Figure 8-3).

5. Select the Require Passcode On Device check box to activate the other controls.

6. Choose settings as discussed in the section "Creating a Passcode Payload" in Chapter 3.

NOTE For tight security, set the Auto-Lock drop-down list or pop-up menu to a short interval (such as 1 Minute) and the Grace Period For Device Lock drop-down list or pop-up menu to a similarly short time.

7. Apply the configuration profile to the device. For example, connect the iPad or iPhone to the computer you're using, and then use iPhone Configuration Utility to apply the configuration profile directly. Again, Chapter 3 has the gory details.

Applying a Device Passcode and Auto-Locking Manually

To apply a device passcode manually to an iPad or iPhone, follow these steps:

1. From the Home screen, choose Settings | General to display the General screen (shown on the left in Figure 8-4).

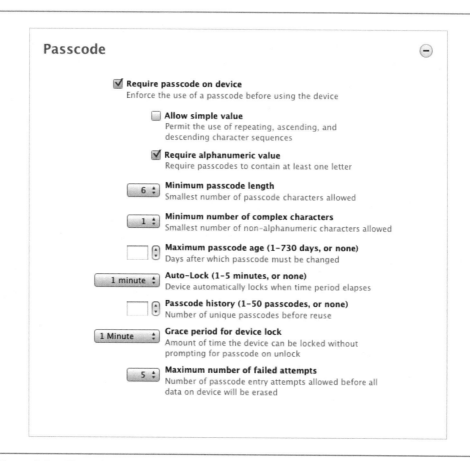

Figure 8-3. To apply a device passcode requirement to an iPad or iPhone automatically, set up a Passcode payload in a configuration profile in iPhone Configuration Utility.

2. Touch the Passcode Lock button to display the Passcode Lock screen (shown on the right in Figure 8-4).

3. If you want to use a simple passcode—a four-digit number—make sure the Simple Passcode switch is set to the On position. If you want to lock the iPad or iPhone down more tightly by using a complex passcode, slide the Simple Passcode switch to the Off position.

4. Touch the Turn Passcode On button to display the Set Passcode screen. For a simple passcode, you'll see the Set Passcode screen shown on the left in Figure 8-5; for a complex passcode, you'll see the Set Passcode screen shown on the right in Figure 8-5.

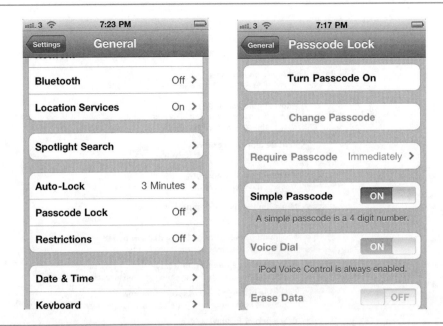

Figure 8-4. On the Passcode Lock screen (left), touch the Turn Passcode On button to display the Set Passcode screen (right).

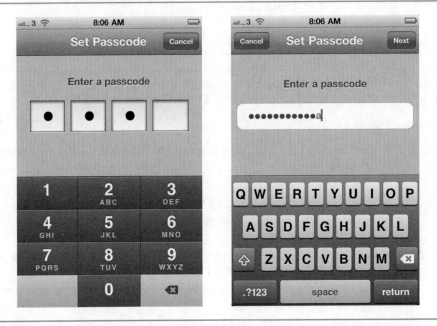

Figure 8-5. On the Set Passcode screen, enter either a simple four-digit passcode (left) or a complex passcode as long as you like (right).

5. Touch the numbers or characters for the passcode:

■ **Simple passcode**   When you've entered four numbers, the device displays the Set Passcode: Re-enter Your Passcode screen automatically.

■ **Complex passcode**   Touch the .?123 button when you need to reach the keyboard with numbers and some symbols. From here, you can touch the #+= button to reach the remaining symbols, punctuation characters, and currency characters. When you've finished entering the passcode, touch the Next button to display the Set Passcode: Re-enter Your Passcode screen.

6. Touch the numbers or characters for the passcode again; for a complex passcode, caress the Done button when you finish. The iPad or iPhone displays the Passcode Lock screen again. This time, all the options are available, as shown in the screen on the left in Figure 8-6.

7. Look at the Require Passcode button to see how quickly the passcode requirement kicks in: Immediately, After 1 Minutes, After 5 Minutes, After 15 Minutes, After 1 Hour, or After 4 Hours. If you need to change the setting, follow these steps:

a. Touch the Require Passcode button to display the Require Passcode screen (shown on the right in Figure 8-6).

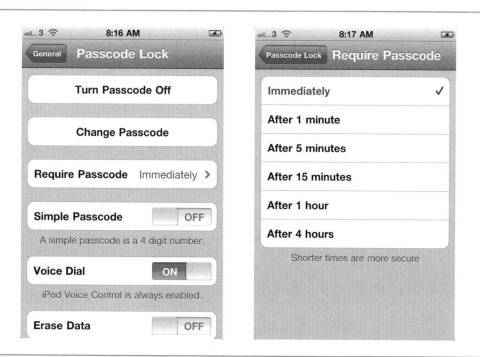

Figure 8-6.   After you set a passcode, the remaining options on the Passcode Lock screen become available (left). Touch the Require Passcode button to display the Require Passcode screen (right), on which you can set the interval after which the device requires the passcode.

    b.   Touch the button for the interval you want.

    c.   Touch the Passcode Lock button to return to the Passcode Lock screen.

8.   Touch the General button in the upper-left corner of the Passcode Lock screen to return to the General screen.

9.   Look at the Auto-Lock setting: 1 Minute, 2 Minutes, 3 Minutes, 4 Minutes, 5 Minutes, or Never on the iPhone, or 2 Minutes, 5 Minutes, 10 Minutes, 15 Minutes, or Never on the iPad. The shorter the interval you can set without making the iPad or iPhone hard to use, the more secure. If you need to change the setting, follow these steps:

    a.   Touch the Auto-Lock button to display the Auto-Lock screen (see Figure 8-7).

    b.   Touch the button for the interval you want.

    c.   Touch the General button to return to the General screen.

After applying a passcode and auto-locking, it's a good idea to give the iPad or iPhone a test drive and make sure that the settings are working as expected.

 NOTE   If you want to configure the iPad or iPhone to erase its data after a number of failed attempts to enter the passcode, turn to the section "Configuring an iPad or iPhone for Automatic Local Wiping," later in this chapter.

Figure 8-7.   On the Auto-Lock screen, choose as short an interval as is practical for the user.

Encrypting the Data on the iPad or iPhone and in Its Backups

To keep your data safe, you can encrypt the data both on the iPad or iPhone and in the backups you keep of it. The iPad and most iPhones have built-in hardware encryption that you can further lock with a passcode, and iTunes lets you protect your backups of a device's data with a password.

Turning on Data Protection on the iPad or iPhone

The iPad, iPhone 4, and iPhone 3GS include hardware encryption that lets you apply data protection to the device. Data protection uses your passcode to protect the hardware encryption keys on the device, which makes the hardware encryption tougher to crack.

NOTE The iPhone 3G and earlier models do not have the hardware encryption required for data protection. (There you go—the perfect excuse to upgrade to an iPhone 4.)

To turn on data protection on the iPad or iPhone, apply a device passcode, as discussed earlier in this chapter. iOS then uses the passcode to encrypt the hardware encryption keys on the iPad or iPhone.

NOTE To implement data protection on an iPhone 3GS that shipped with iOS 3, you must restore the iPhone to iOS 4 rather than simply upgrading it.

To make sure that the iPad or iPhone has data protection enabled, follow these steps:

1. From the Home screen, choose Settings | General to display the General screen.
2. Touch the Passcode Lock button to display the Enter Passcode screen.
3. Enter your passcode (and touch the Done button if you're using a complex passcode) to display the Passcode Lock screen.
4. At the bottom of the screen, verify that the "Data protection is enabled" message appears (see Figure 8-8).

Encrypting the Backups of the iPad or iPhone

To keep your data safe against loss, iTunes automatically backs it up from the iPad or iPhone to a file on your PC or Mac. To prevent anyone who gains unauthorized access to this backup from being able to decipher it, you can encrypt the backup.

To set iTunes to encrypt the backups, follow these steps:

1. Connect the iPad or iPhone to the computer.
2. Launch or activate iTunes if it doesn't launch or activate automatically.

Figure 8-8. To confirm that data protection is on, look for the "Data protection is enabled" readout at the bottom of the Passcode Lock screen.

3. In the Source list, click the iPad's or iPhone's entry to display its control screens.

4. Click the Summary tab to display its contents (see Figure 8-9) if it's not automatically displayed.

5. In the Options box, select the Encrypt iPad Backup check box or the Encrypt iPhone Backup check box. If you haven't yet set a password for encrypting backups (as will normally be the case), iTunes displays the Set Password dialog box (see Figure 8-10).

6. Type the password in the Password text box and the Verify Password text box.

7. On the Mac, select the Remember This Password In My Keychain check box if you want to store the password in the Mac's Keychain. Storing the password means that Mac OS X can enter it for you automatically in the future, but if someone else can access your user account, Mac OS X will happily enter the password for them too.

8. Click the Set Password button to close the Set Password dialog box. iTunes then backs up the iPad or iPhone, encrypting the contents, and deletes the previous backup (which was not encrypted).

Figure 8-9.   On the Summary tab of the iTunes control screens for the iPad or iPhone, select the Encrypt iPad Backup check box or the Encrypt iPhone Backup check box.

Figure 8-10.   In the Set Password dialog box, type a strong password for encrypting the back-ups iTunes keeps of the data on the iPad or iPhone.

Understanding How and Where iTunes Backs Up the iPad and iPhone

When iTunes backs up an iPad or iPhone, it sometimes takes long enough for you to believe it's copying all the data off the device to the PC or Mac. But in fact iTunes backs up only the settings and the unique data from the iPad or iPhone, not all the music and videos that you've synchronized from iTunes itself. For example, iTunes backs up your Address book and its favorites, your app settings and preferences, and the details of your mail settings—plus content you've created on the iPad or iPhone, such as your Notes and your voice memos.

iTunes stores its backup files in a Backup folder contained in a MobileSync folder deep within your user account. Here are the locations:

■ **Windows 7 and Windows Vista**   \Users*username*\AppData\Roaming\ Apple Computer\MobileSync\Backup\

■ **Windows XP**   \Documents and Settings*username*\Application Data\ Apple Computer\MobileSync\Backup\

■ **Mac OS X**   ~/Library/Application Support/MobileSync/Backup/

If you go looking in these folders, you'll find that the backup folders have cryptic names (for example, af03d697af0f5164e196201cb4331ccce198d9b9) and contain items with similar names. There's not much to gain from digging here, but you may sometimes want to back up your Backup folder (or one of the folders it contains) to give yourself an extra way of recovering from disaster.

If iTunes on your computer syncs only one iPad or iPhone, you'll find it easy to tell which folder belongs to the device. But if iTunes syncs multiple devices, the cryptic names make it hard to tell which is which. To find out, sync the device, look at the date stamps on the folders, and find the one with the right time.

Configuring an iPad or iPhone for Automatic Local Wiping

To minimize the risk that anyone who picks up or filches one of your iPads or iPhones can access valuable data on it, you can configure the device to wipe itself automatically after a particular number of failed attempts to enter the passcode. Before you can set up automatic local wiping, you need to apply a passcode as discussed earlier in this chapter.

As usual, you'll probably want to set up automatic local wiping for most of your iPads and iPhones by using iPhone Configuration Utility. But if necessary, you can set up automatic local wiping on the device itself.

Configuring Automatic Local Wiping with iPhone Configuration Utility

To configure automatic local wiping with iPhone Configuration Utility, set the Maximum Number Of Failed Attempts setting in the Passcode screen of the configuration profile to the appropriate number. (You can see the Passcode screen in Figure 8-3, earlier in this chapter.) You can choose any number from 4 to 16; if you want to turn off automatic local wiping, choose the -- setting at the top of the drop-down list or pop-up menu.

Configuring Automatic Local Wiping Manually

On the iPad or iPhone itself, you can set up automatic local wiping to run only after ten attempts—you can't change the number.
Follow these steps:

1.   From the Home screen, choose Settings | General to display the General screen.

2.   Touch the Passcode Lock button to display the Passcode Lock screen. (Enter your passcode when the device prompts you for it.)

3.   At the bottom of the screen, move the Erase Data switch to the On position. The iPad or iPhone displays a confirmation dialog box, as shown here.

4.   Touch the Enable button to turn on the automatic wiping.

NOTE   When an intruder hits the limit for incorrect passcode attempts, the iPad or iPhone momentarily flashes the Wrong Passcode screen. Then it shuts down, restarts, and wipes out all the data it contains.

Remotely Wiping an iPad or iPhone

After you've set up an iPad or iPhone for remote wiping, you're ready to spring into action to protect your valuable data.
You can remotely wipe an iPad or iPhone either by using Apple's MobileMe service or by using Microsoft Exchange. We'll start with MobileMe, as this method of wiping works for end users as well as administrators.

Plug the Original iPhone or iPhone 3GS into Power When Wiping—If You Can

On the iPad, iPhone 4, and iPhone 3GS, Remote Wipe simply removes the encryption key for the device, rendering its data unreadable. The key is tiny, so the Wipe happens almost instantly.

By contrast, on the iPhone 3G and original iPhone, Remote Wipe actually overwrites the data on the device. This bit-by-bit stomping takes about an hour for each 8GB of device capacity—for example, a 16GB iPhone 3G may take two hours to wipe fully. That means the iPhone may run out of power.

If you have control of the iPhone 3G or original iPhone you're wiping, make sure it's plugged into a power supply. For example, if you're using Remote Wipe to restore the device to factory settings for an employee off site, have the employee plug the device into power before you give the Kill command.

If the iPad or iPhone is beyond your control, don't worry—if the device runs out of power during the Remote Wipe, the Wipe resumes when someone connects the device to power again. So your data should be safe even if power loss causes it to be smeared rather than fully wiped at first.

Implementing Remote Wipe Through MobileMe

If you have a MobileMe account, MobileMe can be a great way to remotely wipe an iPad or iPhone. You can run the Wipe operation in just about any web browser that has Java enabled, so you can do the dirty deed from almost anywhere in the world. First, though, you need to set up the device with the Find My iPhone feature—otherwise, MobileMe isn't interested.

Setting Up an iPad or iPhone with the Find My iPhone Feature

Before you can remotely wipe an iPad or iPhone through MobileMe, you must set it up with MobileMe's Find My iPhone feature. To do so, follow these steps:

1. From the Home screen, touch Settings | Mail, Contacts, Calendars to display the Mail, Contacts, Calendars screen.

2. In the Accounts list, touch the MobileMe account you want to link to the Find My iPhone feature.

3. At the bottom of the screen, move the Find My iPhone switch to the On position (as shown on the left in Figure 8-11).

Once you've done this, the account shows Find My iPhone below the name in the Accounts list, as shown on the right in Figure 8-11. You're good to go.

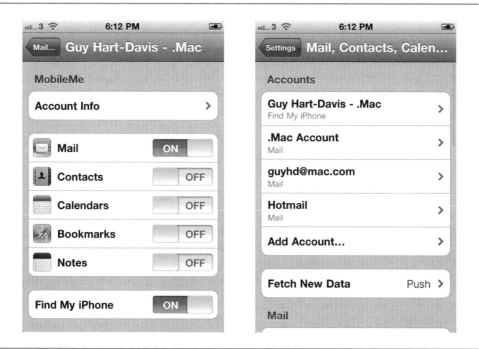

Figure 8-11.   Move the Find My iPhone switch to the On position on the screen for the MobileMe account for which you're activating the feature (left). In the Accounts list (right), you'll see Find My iPhone under the name of the linked account.

Remotely Wiping an iPad or iPhone via MobileMe

To remotely wipe an iPad or iPhone via MobileMe, follow these steps:

1. Open your favorite web browser and go to the MobileMe web site (www.me.com).

2. Log in to the MobileMe account with which you've associated the iPad or iPhone.

3. Click the Switch Apps button (the cloud icon) in the upper-left corner to display the bar of apps.

4. Click the Find My iPhone button to display the Find My iPhone app (see Figure 8-12).

5. If you've got multiple iPads or iPhones associated with this MobileMe account, click the right iPad or iPhone in the Devices pane on the left.

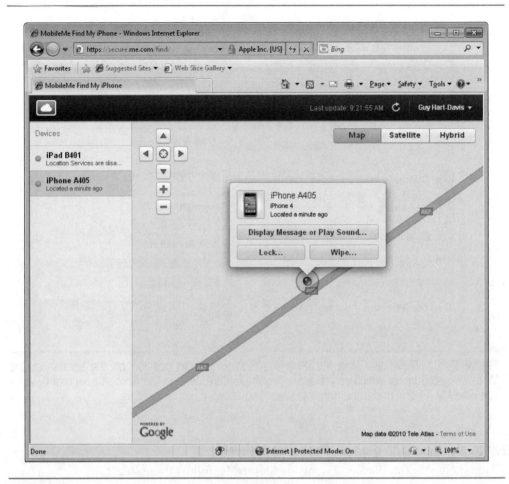

Figure 8-12.   After loading the Find My iPhone app on the MobileMe site, you can display a message or play a sound on the iPad or iPhone, lock it, or wipe it.

6. If you want to display a message on the iPad or iPhone (for example, to encourage whoever has it to contact you about returning it for a consideration), click the Display Message Or Play Sound button. In the Display A Message dialog box that opens (shown on the left in Figure 8-13), type the message, select the Play A Sound For 2 Minutes check box if you want audio accompaniment to gain attention, and then click the Send button. The iPad or iPhone receives the message as soon as MobileMe can deliver it. The screen on the right in Figure 8-13 shows an iPhone receiving the message.

7. To lock the iPad or iPhone, click the Lock button. In the Remote Lock dialog box (see Figure 8-14), click the Lock button.

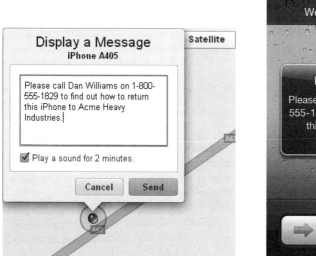

Figure 8-13.   You can use the Display A Message dialog box to display a message on the iPad or iPhone before wiping it.

Figure 8-14.   Click the Lock button in the Remote Lock device if you want to lock the iPad or iPhone.

Figure 8-15. In the Remote Wipe dialog box, make sure you've got the right iPad or iPhone in your sights. Then select the check box and click the Erase All Data button.

 CAUTION Don't rely on remote locking to protect the data on the iPad or iPhone—locking just means that whoever has the device must enter the passcode. For security, you'll want to wipe the iPad or iPhone.

8. To wipe the iPad or iPhone, click the Wipe button. The Find My iPhone app displays the Remote Wipe dialog box (see Figure 8-15).

9. In the title bar of the dialog box, double-check that you've picked the right victim. Otherwise, there may be hell to pay.

10. Select the I Understand That I Cannot Undo Or Stop This Action check box to take responsibility for your deeds.

11. Draw a deep breath, and then click the Erase All Data button. MobileMe sends the command to the iPad or iPhone, which executes it.

Implementing Remote Wipe Through Exchange

If you're using Microsoft Exchange as your e-mail server, you can also use it to implement Remote Wipe on an iPad or iPhone. As an administrator, you'll probably want to use the Exchange Management Console, but you can also use Outlook Web Access, the tool that users can use for Remote Wipe.

NOTE   If you're using Exchange Server 2003, you can use the Exchange ActiveSync Mobile Administration Web Tool to wipe an iPad or iPhone.

Implementing Remote Wipe Through Exchange Management Console

To wipe an iPad or iPhone using the Exchange Management Console, follow these steps:

1. Open the Exchange Management Console.
2. In the left pane, expand the Recipient Configuration item.
3. Click the Mailbox item under the Recipient Configuration item to display the list of mailboxes.
4. In the Mailbox list, click the mailbox that controls the iPad or iPhone you want to wipe.
5. In the Actions pane, click the Manage Mobile Device item to display the Manage Mobile Device screen.
6. In the Managed Mobile Device box, click the iPad or iPhone.
7. In the Action box, select the Perform A Remote Wipe To Clear Mobile Device Data option button.
8. Click the Clear button.

At the next sync, the iPad or iPhone wipes its contents.

Implementing Remote Wipe Through Outlook Web Access

To wipe an iPad or iPhone from Outlook Web Access, follow these steps:

1. Log in to Outlook Web Access as usual on a computer.
2. Click the Options menu in the upper-right corner of the window.
3. In the left pane, click the Mobile Devices item to display the list of mobile devices.
4. In the Mobile Devices list, select the option button for the iPad or iPhone.
5. Click the Wipe All Data From Device link. Outlook Web Access displays a confirmation dialog box.
6. Click the OK button. Office Web Apps changes the device's readout in the Status column to Pending Wipe.

The next time the iPad or iPhone connects to Exchange, Exchange gives it the command to start a secure wipe.

CHAPTER 9 | Giving iPad and iPhone Users Remote Access to the Network

So far in this book, users have been accessing your network from the inside by connecting to a wireless network router within the network. But to get full value out of the iPads and iPhones, you may also need to let some users access the network from outside via virtual private networking (VPN). By using VPN, you can establish a secure tunnel through an insecure public network (usually the Internet), connecting the users securely to your company's network.

This chapter shows you how to connect the iPad and iPhone to your network via VPN. To create the virtual private network (also abbreviated to VPN) connection on the iPad or iPhone, you can either install a configuration profile containing a VPN payload with the correct settings, or set them up on the device manually.

In many cases, you can snap the iPad and iPhone straight into your existing VPN by giving them the right settings. In other cases, you may need to adapt the VPN's setup to suit the iPad's and iPhone's needs. We'll start by looking briefly at these needs, move on to the details of setting up the connection, and then go through several essential troubleshooting moves for VPN connections. We'll also touch upon how to take remote control of computers on the network using the iPad or iPhone.

Planning How to Connect the iPad and iPhone to Your VPN

In this section, we'll look quickly at planning how the iPad and iPhone will connect to your VPN. We'll start by reviewing the VPN technologies the iPad and iPhone support, talk about settings you may need to change to make your VPN friendly to the iPad and iPhone, and finish by considering which users you should grant remote access to the network.

Making Sure Your VPN Uses Suitable Technologies and Settings for the iPad and iPhone

The first step in planning the connection is to make sure your VPN uses one (or more) of the five widely used types of VPN that the iPad and iPhone support:

- **Cisco IPSec** Cisco IP Security is widely used for establishing secure VPN connections. With IPSec, you can use several different methods of authentication, including x.509 digital certificates, RSA SecurID, and CRYPTOCard.

- **L2TP Over IPSec** Layer 2 Tunneling Protocol over IPSec gives good security and is widely used. With L2TP, you can use either a password or a shared secret for authentication.

- **PPTP** Point-to-Point Tunneling Protocol is the weakest of the widely used VPN technologies. Use PPTP only if you can't use any other VPN type. PPTP uses a password to secure connections.

- **Cisco AnyConnect**   Cisco AnyConnect VPN technology uses the Datagram Transport Layer Security (DTLS) protocol to provide security and performance over VPN connections. With AnyConnect, you can use either a password or a certificate for authentication.

- **Juniper SSL**   Juniper Networks' VPN appliances use Juniper SSL to secure the VPN connections. With Juniper SSL, you can use either a password or a certificate to secure the connection.

NOTE   When you use a certificate to authenticate a Cisco IPSec, Cisco AnyConnect, or Juniper SSL VPN, you can enable VPN on demand, which can be a big timesaver. VPN on demand makes the iPad or iPhone automatically establish a VPN connection when the user tries to access any of the domains or host names you add to the connection's list.

If your VPN uses one of those five types, you're halfway there. (Otherwise, you'll need to add one of those five types to your VPN setup.) You should also take these three steps:

- **Check your VPN concentrators**   Make sure they use VPN standards the iPad and iPhone support.

- **Check the authentication path**   Make certain your RADIUS server or VPN authentication server is using iPad- and iPhone-friendly standards.

- **Use suitable certificates**   If you're using certificates for authentication, the iPad and iPhone can use PKCS1 format (files in the .cer, .crt, and .der file formats) and PKCS12 format (files in the .p12 and .pfx file formats).

TIP   To avoid problems, make sure your remote access routers and concentrators are running the latest firmware versions. Update them if they're not.

Deciding Whom to Grant Remote Access to the Network

If you already have a VPN, chances are that you already give some users remote access to the network. Normally, you'll want to manage these users by putting them in a group—for example, a VPN Users group.

To manage your iPad and iPhone users who connect to the VPN, create a similar group. Depending on the setup, you may be able to put all the VPN users in a single group, or you may need to use separate groups to slice and dice their permissions more thinly—for example, to give some users different access permissions than others. For instance, you yourself may need remote access so that you can administer and troubleshoot the network remotely from the iPad or iPhone, but you want to keep other VPN users safely cordoned off from your sensitive servers.

Setting Up the iPad and iPhone to Connect to the VPN

Now that you've made sure the VPN is ready for the iPad and iPhone, it's time to set up the devices to connect to the VPN. You can do this either by creating a VPN payload in a configuration profile you install on the device or by manipulating the settings directly on the device.

As with most other settings, creating a VPN payload is usually the best option if you have more than a few iPads and iPhones to set up. If the devices are only a precious few, or if you need to adjust or troubleshoot the VPN settings, work directly on the device.

Creating a VPN Payload for a Configuration Profile

To set up the virtual private network (or networks) the iPad or iPhone can connect to, create a VPN payload in a configuration profile that you install on the device. As with other payloads, you can include the VPN payload as part of a general profile, or you can create a profile that contains only a VPN payload (along with the mandatory General payload that includes the configuration profile's name). Which is the better approach depends on your circumstances and which users will use the VPN.

Starting a VPN Payload and Entering General Settings

To create a VPN payload and enter general settings, follow these steps:

1. Open iPhone Configuration Utility.

2. In the Library category in the Source list, click the Configuration Profiles item to display the list of configuration profiles.

NOTE If you need to create a new configuration profile to contain the VPN payload, click the New button on the toolbar. In the General pane, type the required name and identifier, and fill in the organization and description if that information will be helpful (as it usually is). In the Security drop-down list or pop-up menu, choose whether the user can remove the profile: Always, With Authorization, or Never.

3. Click the VPN item in the Payloads list to display the Configure VPN box.

4. Click the Configure button to display the VPN pane (shown in Figure 9-1 with some settings chosen).

5. In the Connection Name text box, type the name the user will see for the connection—for example, your company name and **VPN** (or **Remote Connection**).

6. In the Connection Type pop-up menu, choose the security protocol for the connection: L2TP, PPTP, IPSec (Cisco), Cisco AnyConnect, or Juniper SSL.

7. In the Server text box, type the hostname or IP address of the VPN server that the connection accesses.

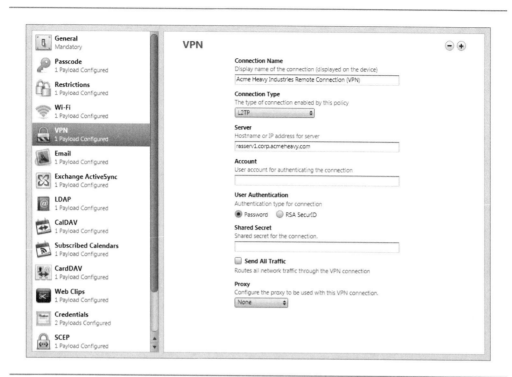

Figure 9-1. Use the VPN pane in iPhone Configuration Utility to create a VPN payload for a configuration profile.

8. In the Account text box, type the user account for the VPN connection if you're setting up the configuration profile for a particular user. Otherwise, leave this text box blank so that each user can fill in his or her username after installing the profile.

Next, specify the authentication for the VPN connection. The settings depend on the VPN type you choose in the Connection Type drop-down list or pop-up menu.

Specifying the Authentication for an L2TP VPN

For an L2TP VPN, specify the authentication by taking the following steps:

1. In the User Authentication area of the VPN pane for an L2TP connection (see Figure 9-2), select the Password option button or the RSA SecurID option button as appropriate.

2. If the VPN uses a shared secret (a passphrase), enter it in the Shared Secret text box.

3. Select the Send All Traffic check box if you need to send all network traffic through the VPN connection.

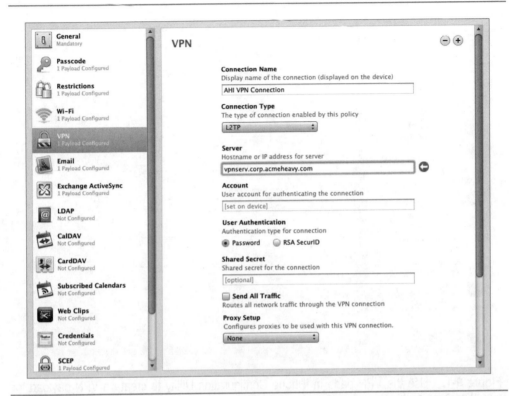

Figure 9-2. The VPN pane for an L2TP connection lets you choose between a password and RSA SecurID for authentication. You can also use a shared secret for the connection and decide whether to send all network traffic through the VPN.

Choosing Whether to Route All Traffic Through the VPN

By selecting the Send All Traffic check box in the VPN pane, you can make the iPad or iPhone route all its traffic through the VPN once it has connected rather than just the traffic sent to addresses within the VPN. For example, with this check box selected, when Safari on the iPad requests a web page, that request goes across the VPN, out through your company's network connection, and back to the iPad the same way. The user gets the benefit (so to speak) of any proxying or filtering you've applied to your company's network connection, but performance tends to suffer because the data is taking a roundabout route and may go through several bottlenecks.

If you don't need to exercise this level of control over users, clear the Send All Traffic check box. Then, when an app requests information from the Internet, the iPad or iPhone sends the request straight to the Internet. When an app requests information from your network, that request goes across the VPN.

Specifying the Authentication for a PPTP VPN

For a PPTP VPN, specify the authentication by taking the following steps:

1. In the User Authentication area of the VPN pane for a PPTP connection (see Figure 9-3), select the Password option button or the RSA SecurID option button as appropriate.

2. In the Encryption Level drop-down list or pop-up menu, choose the level of encryption to use:

   ■ **Automatic** This is normally the best choice. It makes the iPad or iPhone try 128-bit encryption first, then the weaker 40-bit encryption, and then use no encryption.

   ■ **Maximum (128-Bit)** Choose this item to allow only connections with 128-bit encryption.

   ■ **None** Choose this item to turn off encryption. Normally, you'd do this only when you're troubleshooting the VPN and you suspect that encryption may be the problem.

3. Select the Send All Traffic check box if you want the iPad or iPhone to send all network traffic through the VPN connection.

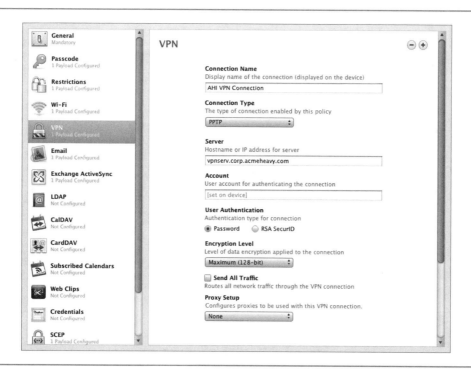

Figure 9-3. The VPN pane for a PPTP connection lets you choose between a password and RSA SecurID for authentication. You can specify which encryption level to use and control whether the iPad or iPhone sends all network traffic through the VPN.

Specifying the Authentication for an IPSec VPN

For an IPSec VPN, you can choose between using a certificate to authenticate the iPad or iPhone and using a group identifier or shared secret. The options available to you depend on which of these two types of authentication you use.

After choosing the basic settings for the VPN, open the Machine Authentication drop-down list or pop-up menu in the VPN pane and choose Shared Secret/Group Name or Certificate, as appropriate.

 NOTE   If you use a certificate for authentication, add the certificate to the Credentials payload as discussed in Chapter 3.

If you choose Shared Secret/Group Name in the Machine Authentication drop-down list or pop-up menu, the VPN pane in iPhone Configuration Utility displays the controls shown in Figure 9-4. To set up the authentication, follow these steps:

1.   Type the connection's group name in the Group Name text box.

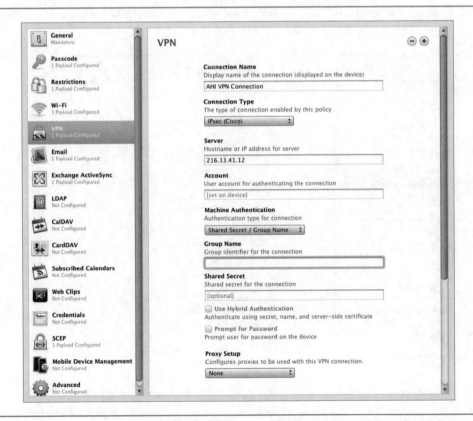

Figure 9-4.   When using a shared secret or group name for machine authentication on an IP-Sec VPN, you can choose whether to use hybrid authentication and whether to prompt the user for a password.

2. Type the shared secret in the Shared Secret text box.

3. Select the Use Hybrid Authentication check box if you want to make the connection more secure by using a server-side certificate for authentication as well.

4. Select the Prompt For Password check box if you want the iPad or iPhone to prompt the user for a password.

If you choose Certificate in the Machine Authentication drop-down list or pop-up menu, the VPN pane displays the controls shown in Figure 9-5. To set up the authentication, follow these steps:

1. Open the Identity Certificate drop-down list or pop-up menu (on the Mac, this pop-up menu is identified only as Credential For Authenticating The Connection at this writing) and choose the certificate to use.

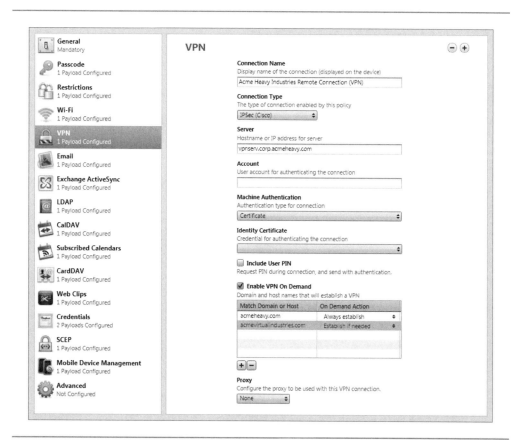

Figure 9-5.   When using a certificate for machine authentication on an IPSec VPN, you can choose whether to include the user's PIN and whether to enable the VPN on demand.

2. Select the Include User PIN check box if you want the VPN to request the user's personal identification number (PIN) during the connection and send it along with the authentication data.

Specifying the Authentication for a Cisco AnyConnect VPN

For a Cisco AnyConnect VPN, you can use either a certificate or password for authenticating the user. To set up the authentication, follow these steps:

1. In the Group text box of the VPN pane (see Figure 9-6), type the group you want to use for authenticating the connection.

NOTE If you use a certificate for authentication, add the certificate to the Credentials payload as discussed in Chapter 3.

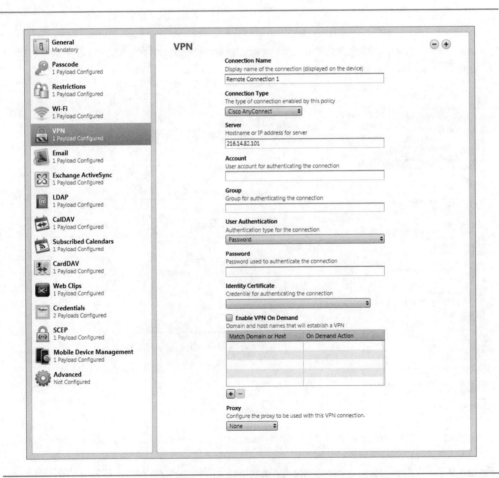

Figure 9-6. For a Cisco AnyConnect VPN, you can use either a certificate or a password for authentication. You can also turn on VPN On Demand.

2. In the User Authentication drop-down list or pop-up menu, choose Password or Certificate, as appropriate.

3. Either type the password in the Password text box, or open the Identity Certificate drop-down list or pop-up menu and choose the certificate.

Specifying the Authentication for a Jupiter SSL VPN

For a Jupiter SSL VPN, you can use either a certificate or a password for authenticating the user. To set up the authentication, follow these steps:

1. In the Realm text box in the VPN pane (see Figure 9-7), type the realm to use for authenticating the connection.

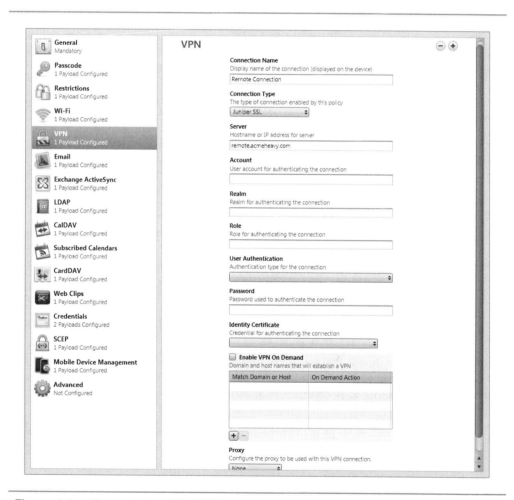

Figure 9-7. For a Jupiter SSL VPN, you can use either a certificate or a password for authentication. You can also turn on VPN On Demand.

2. In the Role text box, type the role to use for authentication.

3. Open the User Authentication drop-down list or pop-up menu and choose Password or Certificate, as appropriate.

 NOTE If you use a certificate for authentication, add the certificate to the Credentials payload as discussed in Chapter 3.

4. Either type the password in the Password text box, or open the Identity Certificate drop-down list or pop-up menu and choose the certificate.

Enabling VPN On Demand for VPN Connections

If you're using a VPN type that uses certificates for authentication, or if you're using Cisco AnyConnect or Jupiter SSL, you can set up the VPN On Demand feature to make the iPad or iPhone automatically establish a VPN connection when the user tries to access a domain or host on a list you supply. This feature is great for making sure that the iPad and iPhone always use VPN connections for connecting to your corporate network.

To set up VPN On Demand, select the Enable VPN On Demand check box in the VPN pane. Then follow these steps to build the list of domains and hosts for which you want to control VPN connections:

1. Click the + (Add) button at the lower-left corner of the Domain And Host Names That Will Establish A VPN list box. iPhone Configuration Utility adds an *Untitled* entry to the list.

2. In the Match Domain Or Host column, type the domain name or host name.

3. Open the corresponding pop-up menu in the On Demand Action column, and choose the appropriate setting:

   ■ **Always Establish**   Choose this setting to make the iPad or iPhone establish a VPN connection for the host or any address in the domain.

   ■ **Establish If Needed**   Choose this setting to make the iPad or iPhone try a DNS lookup for the host or domain and establish a VPN connection if the lookup returns no match.

   ■ **Never**   Choose this setting to prevent the iPad or iPhone from establishing a VPN connection for the host or domain. If the iPad or iPhone has already established a VPN connection, it can use the connection for this host or domain.

4. Repeat those three steps as needed to add other hosts and domains to the list. If you need to remove a host or domain, click it in the list, and then click the – (Remove) button.

Setting Up Proxying for the VPN Connection

If the VPN uses a proxy server, go to the Proxy Setup area at the bottom of the VPN pane and follow these steps:

1. Open the Proxy Setup drop-down list or pop-up menu and choose Manual or Automatic, as needed.

2. Specify the information needed:

   ■ **Manual Proxy Setup**   In the Server text box (see Figure 9-8), type the proxy server's hostname or IP address. In the Port text box, type the port number—for example, 80, 8080, or 8000. If you're setting up the profile for a single user, enter the username in the Authentication text box and the password in the Password text box. Otherwise, leave these text boxes blank so that the user is prompted to fill in their information.

   ■ **Automatic Proxy Setup**   Type the proxy server's URL in the Proxy Server URL text box.

NOTE   After you finish setting up a VPN connection, you can start creating another if necessary. Click the + button in the upper-right corner of the VPN pane to start creating a new VPN connection, and then provide the information as discussed in the preceding pages.

Setting Up a VPN Connection Manually

Setting up a VPN connection by using a VPN payload in a configuration profile usually works pretty well, especially if you're giving many iPads and iPhones access to the VPN.

Proxy Setup
Configures proxies to be used with this VPN connection.

[Manual   ▲▼]

Server and Port
Hostname or IP address, and port number for the proxy server

[proxserv.corp.acmeheavy.com   ] : [0]

Authentication
Username used to connect to the proxy

[[ask during installation]   ]

Password
Password used to authenticate with the proxy

[   ]

Figure 9-8.   If the VPN connection uses a manual proxy server, enter the details in the Server text box and Port text box.

But other times you may need to set up a VPN connection manually, or go in and tweak the settings you've applied with the configuration profile. This section shows you how to do so.

To create a new VPN connection, follow these steps:

1. From the Home screen, touch Settings | General | Network to display the Network screen. The left screen in Figure 9-9 shows the iPhone's version of this screen.

2. Touch the VPN item (down at the bottom of the screen) to display the VPN screen (shown on the right in Figure 9-9).

3. Touch the Add VPN Configuration button to display the Add Configuration screen. The left screen in Figure 9-10 shows the iPhone's version of this screen; you'll need to scroll down to reach the settings you can't see.

4. Near the top of the screen, touch the button for the security type the VPN uses: L2TP, PPTP, or IPSec. The iPad or iPhone displays a list of the information required for the connection.

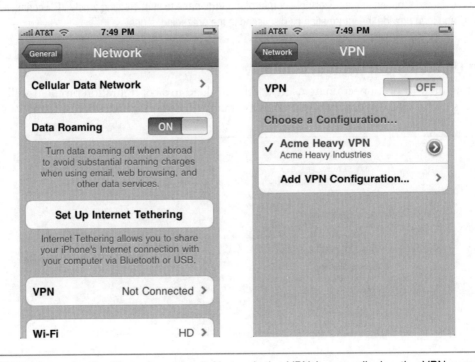

Figure 9-9. On the Network screen (left), touch the VPN item to display the VPN screen (right).

Figure 9-10. On the Add Configuration screen (left), enter the information for the connection. When you've saved the connection, move the slider on the VPN screen (right) to On to start the connection.

5. Type in the details for the VPN configuration on the screen:

- **Description** This is the name under which the VPN appears in the list of VPNs. Choose a descriptive name that will be clear to the user.

- **Server** Type the computer name (for example, vpnserv.acmeheavy.com) or IP address (for example, 216.248.32.88) of the VPN server.

- **Account** Type the user's login name for the VPN connection. Depending on your company's or organization's network, this may be the same as the regular login name, but in most cases it's different for security reasons.

Next, you can set up the authentication as discussed in the following sections.

Specifying the Authentication for an L2TP VPN Connection

After specifying the description, server, and account name for an L2TP VPN connection, set up the authentication by following these steps:

1. Choose whether to use a password or an RSA SecurID token for authentication:

- **RSA SecurID** If the VPN connection uses an RSA SecurID token for authentication, move the RSA SecurID switch to On to use it. The iPad or iPhone then hides the Password field, because the connection uses the token instead of a password.

- **Password** If the VPN connection uses a password rather than a certificate for authentication, you can enter it here and have the iPad or iPhone provide it automatically each time the user connects. For greater security, you can leave the password area blank so that the user must enter the password manually for each connection. This helps prevent unauthorized use of the iPad's or iPhone's VPN connection, but the user will likely find typing in the password laborious, especially if it uses letters, numbers, and symbols (as a strong password should).

2. In the Secret field, type the preshared key, also called the *shared secret,* for the VPN. This preshared key is the same for all users of the VPN (unlike the account name and password, which are unique to the user).

3. Leave the Send All Traffic switch set to On (the default position) if you want to send all the Internet traffic over the VPN connection rather than sending only those parts destined for the network to which you're connected via the VPN. When Send All Traffic is on, all your Internet connections go to the VPN server; when it is off, Internet connections to parts of the Internet other than the VPN go directly to those destinations.

Specifying the Authentication for a PPTP VPN Connection

After specifying the description, server, and account name for a PPTP VPN connection, set up the authentication by following these steps:

1. Choose whether to use a password or an RSA SecurID token for authentication:

   - **RSA SecurID** If the VPN connection uses an RSA SecurID token for authentication, move the RSA SecurID switch to On to use it. The iPad or iPhone then hides the Password field, because the connection uses the token instead of a password.

   - **Password** If the VPN connection uses a password rather than a certificate for authentication, you can enter it here and have the iPad or iPhone provide it automatically each time the user connects. For greater security, leave the password area blank so that the user must enter the password manually for each connection. You'll need to balance security against convenience here, especially if the password is a strong one that will require the user to switch keyboards between letters, numbers, and symbols to type.

2. Leave the Encryption Level setting set to Auto to have the iPad or iPhone try 128-bit encryption (the strongest) first, then weaker 40-bit encryption, and then None. Choose Maximum if you know you must use 128-bit encryption only. Choose None only for testing—for example, when you're struggling to get the VPN working.

3. Leave the Send All Traffic switch set to On (the default position) if you want to send all the Internet traffic over the VPN connection rather than sending only

those parts destined for the network to which you're connected via the VPN. When Send All Traffic is on, all your Internet connections go to the VPN server; when it is off, Internet connections to parts of the Internet other than the VPN go directly to those destinations.

Specifying the Authentication for an IPSec VPN Connection

After specifying the description, server, and account name for an IPSec VPN connection, set up the authentication by following these steps:

1. In the Password field, type the password if you want to store it for the user. Otherwise, leave the Password field blank so that the iPad or iPhone prompts the user to enter it each time they establish the connection.

2. If the VPN connection uses a certificate for authentication, follow these steps:

   a. Move the Use Certificate switch to the On position. The iPad or iPhone displays the Certificate button below the Use Certificate switch, as shown on the left in Figure 9-11.

   b. Touch the Certificate button to display the Certificate screen (shown on the right in Figure 9-11).

Figure 9-11. To set up an IPSec VPN connection to use a certificate for authentication, move the Use Certificate switch to the On position (left). Then touch the Certificate button and choose the certificate on the Certificate screen (right).

c. Touch the certificate to use for authenticating the connection.

d. Touch the Add Configuration button to return to the Add Configuration screen.

3. If the VPN connection uses a group name and secret rather than a certificate, type the group name in the Group Name field and the secret in the Secret field.

Setting Up Proxying for a VPN Connection

If the VPN goes through a proxy server, you can set up the iPad's or iPhone's VPN connection to use the proxy server either manually or automatically.

To set up proxying, scroll down to the Proxy section at the bottom of the Add Configuration screen. Then set up the type of proxying needed:

■ **Manual proxying** When you need to specify a fixed server address and port, follow these steps:

1. Touch the Manual button to display the controls (see the left screen in Figure 9-12).

2. Enter the details in the Server field and the Port field.

Figure 9-12. If the VPN uses a proxy server, you can set up the proxying manually on the Manual tab of the Add Configuration screen (left) or automatically on the Auto tab (right).

3. If the proxy server requires authentication, touch the left side of the Authentication switch to move it from Off to On (as in the figure), and then fill in the Username field and the Password field.

■ **Automatic proxying**   Touch the Auto button, and then enter the server's address in the URL field (shown on the right in Figure 9-12).

Saving the VPN Connection

By this point, you should have entered all the information needed for the VPN connection. Now save the connection by touching the Save button on the Add Configuration screen. The VPN connection then appears on the VPN screen.

You're now ready to connect to the VPN, as described in the next section.

Using a VPN

After you've installed the configuration profile that contains the VPN payload, or you've set up the VPN manually, you can connect to the VPN and use it. When you've finished using it, you disconnect from it.

Connecting to a VPN

To connect to a VPN, follow these steps:

1. From the Home screen, touch Settings to display the Settings screen.

2. Start the VPN connection in one of these ways:

   ■ **If you have only one VPN connection**   Move the On/Off switch on the VPN line to the On position.

   ■ **If you have two or more VPN connections**   Touch the VPN button to display the VPN screen. In the Choose A Configuration list (shown on the left in Figure 9-13), make sure the correct VPN is selected; if not, touch the one you want. Then move the On/Off switch on the VPN line to the On position.

If the VPN requires a password that's not stored in the VPN connection, the iPad or iPhone prompts you to enter it, as shown on the right in Figure 9-13. Type it in, and then touch the Done button. The iPad or iPhone establishes the VPN connection (as shown on the left in Figure 9-14). The VPN icon also appears at the top of the device's screen (as you can see in the Home screen on the right in Figure 9-14) as a reminder that you're using the VPN.

Working on a VPN

Once you've established the connection, you'll be able to work on the VPN. For example, you can access mail, calendars, and other information resources on the network.

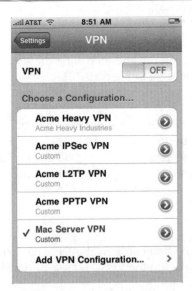 

Figure 9-13. If you have two or more connections, choose the connection on the VPN screen, and then turn it on (left). If the VPN uses a password that's not stored on the iPad or iPhone, type it in (right), and then touch the Done button.

Figure 9-14. The VPN status appears on the VPN screen (left), and the VPN icon appears at the top of the iPad's or iPhone's screen as a reminder (right).

Disconnecting from a VPN

When you've finished using the VPN, close any files that you have been using, and then disconnect like this:

1. From the Home screen, touch Settings to display the Settings screen.
2. Stop the VPN connection in one of these ways:
    - ■ **If you have only one VPN connection** Move the On/Off switch on the VPN line to the Off position.
    - ■ **If you have two or more VPN connections** Touch the VPN button to display the VPN screen. Then move the On/Off switch on the VPN line to the On position.

Deleting a VPN Connection

To delete a VPN connection from the iPad or iPhone, follow these steps:

1. From the Home screen, choose Settings | General | Network | VPN to display the VPN screen.
2. Touch the arrow button for the VPN connection you want to delete. The device displays the Add Configuration screen for the VPN connection.
3. Scroll down to the bottom, and then touch the Delete VPN button. iOS displays the Delete VPN? dialog box for confirmation.
4. Touch the Delete button. iOS deletes the VPN connection.

NOTE If you can't delete a VPN connection from the iPad or iPhone directly, it's normally because the VPN connection has been added using a configuration profile that the user is not permitted to remove. To remove the VPN connection, use iPhone Configuration Utility to remove the profile that contains the connection.

Troubleshooting VPNs

When VPNs work, they can be great; when they don't, they can be a menace to troubleshoot. This section visits several specific problems that you may encounter when using VPN with the iPad or iPhone (or trying to).

iPad VPN Works the First Time but Fails After That

On an iPad, connecting to a Cisco VPN with IPSec works fine the first time you use it after setting up the connection. Thereafter, it fails. At this writing, the only solution is to delete the connection and set it up again.

iPad Can't Connect Through UDP, Only TCP

The iPad's built-in Cisco VPN client only uses TCP, not UDP—so if your VPN uses UDP, the iPad is going to be straight out of luck.

The best fix—okay, you've guessed it—is to open a TCP port on the remote access server to keep the iPad happy.

iPad and iPhone Don't Support IPSec Tunnel with Older PIX Models

If you're having trouble getting the iPad and iPhone to connect via IPSec VPN to a Cisco VPN concentrator, double-check that your concentrator supports the iPad and iPhone as VPN clients.

Cisco routers running Cisco IOS Release 12.4(15)T and later, and Cisco ASA 5500 Security Appliances and PIX Firewalls with Release 7.2.*x* (or, better, 8.0.*x*) or later, do support the iPad and iPhone as VPN clients. The VPN 3000 Series concentrators don't; neither do the Cisco IOS VPN routers.

iPad Fails to Save Password for Cisco VPN

If you find that the iPad fails to save the password for a Cisco VPN (so that the user has to enter the password on each connection), the problem may be that the VPN concentrator is set to not permit the clients to store the password. To solve this problem, use the **password-storage enable** command on the concentrator to permit the clients to store their passwords.

Taking Remote Control of Computers on Your Network

If you're an administrator, one of the things that the iPad and iPhone are great for is taking remote control of computers from wherever you happen to be. Working on a small screen can be awkward, but most people find it far preferable to a midnight drive to the office to sort out the settings on a sickly server.

To connect remotely, use apps such as the following:

- **VNC clients**   If you set up a VNC server on the computer you need to access, you can connect to it by using a VNC client such as Mocha VNC or Jaadu VNC.

- **RDP clients**   Microsoft's Remote Desktop Protocol (RDP) gives good performance even over relatively slow connections. If you need to connect to a Windows server or desktop, set up the Remote Desktop feature to accept incoming connections from your account. You can then use an RDP client such as WinAdmin to connect.

 NOTE   Of the desktop versions of Windows, only the "business" versions include the Remote Desktop feature. These versions are Windows XP Professional; Windows Vista Business, Enterprise, and Ultimate; and Windows 7 Professional, Enterprise, and Ultimate.

- **Third-party solutions**   If neither VNC nor RDP is an option, look at third-party solutions such as LogMeIn Ignition and DesktopDirect. These solutions consist of a remote-access server that you install on the computer and a client that you install on the iPad or iPhone. If you like using the command line, look at third-party SSH clients such as TouchTerm SSH as well.

CHAPTER 10 | Troubleshooting iPad and iPhone Hardware and Software Problems

Apple makes the iPad and iPhone as reliable as possible—but like all hardware and software, they can run into all sorts of problems. Any problem that's not easy to solve, the users will bring to you.

To strengthen your arm and raise your chances of maintaining your heroic status among your network's users, this chapter discusses how to troubleshoot the issues you're most likely to run into with the iPad and iPhone.

We'll spend most of our time dealing with the usual suspects: the iPad or iPhone refusing to turn on, app crashes and system hangs, the PC or Mac refusing to recognize the device, Wi-Fi connections the device can't establish, or iTunes failing to synchronize. By and large, you troubleshoot these problems in the same way for both the iPad and the iPhone, so we'll cover them together, with notes on the differences you need to know about.

Toward the end of the chapter, we'll also go through how to squeeze the most battery life out of the iPad and iPhone—and the best ways to replace the battery when it gives up the ghost. Strictly speaking, this may not be troubleshooting—but it can save you plenty of grief, so I'm guessing you'll want to know about it.

Dealing with a Blank Screen on the iPad or iPhone

If the screen appears blank, the iPad or iPhone will appear to be broken. It may well be, but don't despair yet: The problem may be simply that the battery doesn't have enough charge to turn the device on.

To find out if the battery is the problem, give the iPad or iPhone the Frankenstein treatment: Connect the device to the USB Power Adapter and give it ten minutes or so to see if electricity sparks life. Then try turning the iPad or iPhone on. At this point, you'll find out whether power was the problem:

- **The red battery icon appears**   Give the iPad or iPhone more time to charge, then try turning it on again.

- **The iPad or iPhone starts**   All is well, but keep on charging it.

NOTE   You can connect an iPhone to a USB socket instead of to the USB Power Adapter—as long as you're sure the USB socket gives enough power to charge the iPhone. The iPad won't charge from many USB sockets, so it's best to use the USB Power Adapter. When the iPad has enough power to run the screen, it shows the "Not Charging" readout when connected to a USB socket that can't deliver enough current—but if the iPad is comatose, the screen will stay off, and you won't see this readout.

- **The screen stays blank**   The iPad or iPhone may be dead after all. Give it another ten minutes just in case.

Check the Obvious When Troubleshooting Power Connections

It may be obvious, but I've got to say it: If the iPad or iPhone doesn't respond to the USB Power Adapter, double-check that the Adapter is delivering power. Usually the easiest way to do this is to plug in your trusty iPhone (where "trusty" means "the one that's still working") and make sure it gives a bleep of digital satisfaction (or a silent shudder if you've turned off sound).

If your iPhone doesn't get power either, one or more of three things is usually wrong:

- **The socket is switched off** If you're in a country that uses switchable sockets, first make sure the socket's switch is on. If your country's sockets aren't switchable, use a socket you know is working (or plug in a lamp to quickly check the socket).

- **The USB connection to the Adapter isn't made** Check that the USB cable is firmly seated in the socket on the Adapter.

- **The Dock Connector connection isn't made** Verify that the other end of the USB cable is properly connected to the Dock Connector on the iPad or iPhone.

If your trusty iPhone gets power from the USB Power Adapter but the device you're troubleshooting doesn't, the device's Dock Connector has probably taken a hit. Users find it easy to wreck these by failing to pinch the retaining clips when unplugging the older version of the connector cable—or by dropping the device or giving it an impromptu bath. If the Dock Connector is damaged, you're looking at a professional repair job.

Forcing a Frozen App to Close

If an app stops responding completely, you can normally force it to close without resetting the iPad. Follow these steps:

1. Press and hold down the Sleep/Wake button for several seconds. When the iPad or iPhone displays the red Slide To Power Off slider, release the Sleep/Wake button.

2. Press and hold down the Home button for six seconds.

If that move doesn't force the frozen app to close, restart the iPad or iPhone, as discussed in the next section.

Troubleshooting the iPad or iPhone Freezing or Failing to Turn On

If the iPad or iPhone stops responding to the touch screen, or if it won't turn on at all, turn it off and on. Follow these steps:

1. Turn the iPad or iPhone off. Hold down the Sleep/Wake button until the iPad or iPhone displays the red Slide To Power Off slider.

2. Slide the slider to the right to turn the iPad or iPhone off.

3. Restart the iPad or iPhone by holding down the Sleep/Wake button until the Apple logo appears on the screen. Then wait while it completes the boot process.

Resetting the iPad or iPhone

If turning the iPad or iPhone on and off as described in the preceding section doesn't restore its sunny nature, reset the device. To do so, hold down both the Sleep/Wake button and the Home button for ten seconds. You'll see the screen go dark. When the Apple logo appears on the screen, release the Sleep/Wake button and the Home button. Then wait while the iPad or iPhone completes the boot process.

Restoring an iPad or iPhone

If the iPad's or iPhone's software gets messed up, you can usually fix it by restoring the software. To do so, follow these steps:

1. Back up the iPad or iPhone by connecting it to its regular computer and either allowing automatic synchronization to take place or clicking the Sync button on the Summary screen to force a sync.

2. On the Summary screen, click the Restore button. iTunes contacts the Apple Update server and then displays a confirmation dialog box (see Figure 10-1).

 NOTE   If the restoration includes an update to the iPad's or iPhone's firmware, the button in the confirmation dialog box is called Restore And Update rather than just Restore.

3. Click the Restore button. iTunes downloads the latest version of the software and then installs it. You may need to go through an iPad Software Update assistant (see Figure 10-2) or iPhone Software Update assistant and accept new license terms before you can install the software.

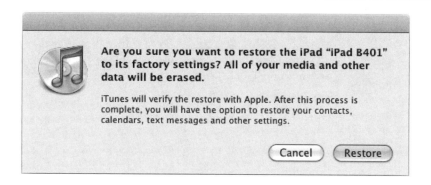

Figure 10-1.   Confirm that you want to restore the iPad or iPhone.

   NOTE   If the restore operation fails when iTunes is verifying the restore with Apple, try restarting your computer. Doing this usually clears the problem that's preventing iTunes from communicating successfully with the Apple servers. If a restart doesn't do the trick, make sure that ports 80 and 443 are open on your firewall and router, and that your computer can reach these sites: phobos.apple. com, albert.apple.com, and gs.apple.com.

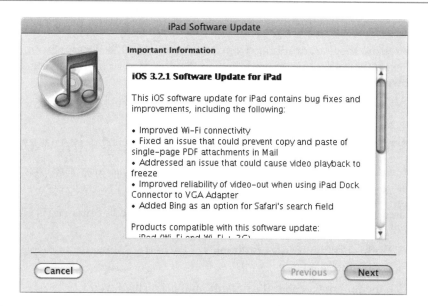

Figure 10-2.   If the iPad Software Update assistant or iPhone Software Update assistant appears, follow through its steps, and accept the license agreement if you want to proceed.

Figure 10-3. iTunes tells you when it has finished restoring the iPad or iPhone.

 NOTE If the restore operation fails with error 9807, iTunes can't access the VeriSign servers it needs to make sure the Russian Business Network hasn't suborned the iPad or iPhone. Configure your firewall to allow access to evintl-ocsp.verisign.com and evsecure-ocsp.verisign.com, and try the restore operation again.

4. When iTunes finishes restoring the iPad or iPhone, it displays a dialog box (see Figure 10-3) to tell you it has done so. Either click the OK button or wait for the countdown to finish and the dialog box to dismiss itself.

5. Next, iTunes displays the Set Up Your iPad screen (see Figure 10-4) or the Set Up Your iPhone screen.

6. To restore the iPad or iPhone from a backup, select the Restore From The Backup Of option button, and then choose the iPad or iPhone in the drop-down list or pop-up menu.

7. Click the Continue button. iTunes restores the device.

Updating the iPad or iPhone with the Latest Firmware

To make sure the iPad or iPhone is up to date, install the latest firmware on it. Follow these steps:

1. Connect the iPad or iPhone to your computer. The computer starts iTunes (if it's not running) or activates it (if it is running).

2. In iTunes, click the iPad's or iPhone's entry in the Source list to display the iPad or iPhone screens.

3. Click the Summary tab if it's not automatically displayed.

4. Click the Check For Update button.

5. If iTunes tells you that an update is available, follow through the prompts to download it and install it.

Figure 10-4. From the Set Up Your iPad screen or Set Up Your iPhone screen in iTunes, choose the backup from which to restore the iPad or iPhone.

Resetting an iPad or iPhone Totally with Recovery Mode

Sometimes an iPad or iPhone can get so messed up that you need to wipe the device clean before you can get it working properly again. This can happen under normal use, but the usual culprit is a user trying to "jailbreak" the device in order to run on it apps that Apple won't approve for the App Store.

CAUTION   Recovery mode is a scorched-earth treatment that wipes out all the data on the iPad or iPhone and replaces the firmware with a fresh copy. Make sure you've backed up any data you need to keep before you use recovery mode.

To reset an iPad or iPhone totally using recovery mode, follow these steps:

1. Make sure the iPad or iPhone has a decent amount of power in the battery—25 percent or more is usually plenty, but more is (as usual) better.

TIP   Recovery mode is also good for a couple of other situations: First, when you need to transfer an iPad or iPhone from one user to another, and you want to make several hundred percent sure that you've wiped any applications, data, or settings that the current user won't want the next user to see. Second, if you're planning to sell or decommission the iPad or iPhone and you want to wipe the slate clean.

2. Boot your PC or Mac if it's not already running. If it's a laptop, plug in the power adapter to make absolutely certain it doesn't run out of juice at a critical moment.

3. Launch iTunes if it's not already running.

4. Connect the USB end of the iPad's or iPhone's connector cable to the PC or Mac. (I know, you probably keep it connected.) Don't connect the iPad or iPhone just yet.

5. Hold down the Sleep/Wake button and the Home button on the iPad or iPhone for about 12 seconds. When the Slide To Power Off slider appears, don't slide it—just keep holding down the buttons as the iPad or iPhone powers right down.

6. Keep holding down both buttons as the iPad or iPhone begins restarting.

7. When the Apple logo pops up on the screen, release the Sleep/Wake button but keep holding down the Home button.

8. When the iPad or iPhone displays the Connect To iTunes screen (see Figure 10-5), plug the cable into the Dock Connector on the bottom of the iPad or iPhone.

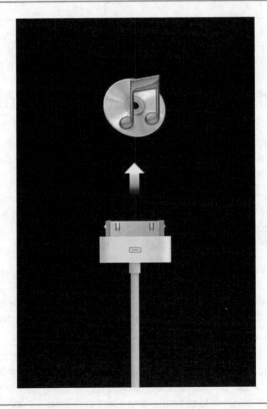

Figure 10-5.   The Connect To iTunes screen indicates that the iPad or iPhone is entering recovery mode.

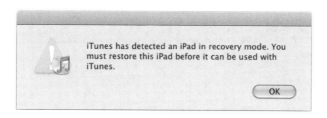

Figure 10-6.   You can finally release the Home button when iTunes detects the iPad or iPhone in recovery mode.

9. When you see iTunes announce that it has detected an iPad or iPhone in recovery mode (see Figure 10-6), release the Home button.

10. Give iTunes time to download the latest version of the device's firmware and install it.

11. When iTunes announces that it has restored the iPad or iPhone, click the OK button.

NOTE   If at this point iTunes claims it can't recognize the iPad or iPhone, unplug the device. Turn it fully off—hold down the Sleep/Wake button until you see the Slide To Power Off slider, and then slide the slider—and then turn it back on again by pressing the Sleep/Wake button. Once Sleeping Beauty has shed its slumbers, plug it back in. By now, the scales will have fallen from iTunes' eyes, and it will recognize the iPad or iPhone.

12. iTunes then displays the Set Up Your iPad screen (see Figure 10-7) or Set Up Your iPhone screen (pick your poison here).

13. Select the appropriate option button:

  - **Set Up As A New iPad** *or* **Set Up As A New iPhone**   Select this option button to complete the process of wiping the iPad or iPhone. Give the iPad or iPhone a name, but don't synchronize any data to it.

  - **Restore From The Backup Of**   Select this option button if you've recovered the device to restore it to health. Open the drop-down list or pop-up menu and choose the backup to use.

14. Click the Continue button. iTunes finishes setting up the iPad or iPhone.

TIP   If the restoration fails with the cryptic message "An unknown error occurred," make sure you're using the iPad's or iPhone's original cable rather than a cable designed for an older model. There's a different pin layout in the older cables that causes trouble only at critical moments like this—it's fine for regular syncing.

Figure 10-7. On the Set Up Your iPad screen or Set Up Your iPhone screen, select the Set Up As A New iPad option button or Set Up As A New iPhone option button if you want to fully wipe the device. Otherwise, select the Restore From The Backup Of option button, and then choose the backup to use.

Troubleshooting Problems Connecting to Wireless Networks

Once you've dealt with iTunes gremlins, the next place you're likely to run into support problems with the iPad and iPhone is wireless networks.

The iPad has notoriously short Wi-Fi range thanks (if that's the word) to its sleek aluminum case, and even the iPhone has much shorter Wi-Fi range than laptops or desktops with full-size antennas. As a result, your wireless network may appear to have dead areas to the iPad and iPhone even though other wireless devices are happy as clams.

In this section, we'll start with signal issues, because you're unlikely to be able to avoid them unless you seat each iPad user within spitting distance of a wireless router. We'll recap what we discussed in Chapter 1 about making your wireless network as friendly as possible to iPads and iPhones. We'll then look at what to do when the Wi-Fi connects but the device can't reach the Internet, how to find the IP address for an iPad or iPhone, and how to reset the network settings if necessary.

Making Your Wireless Network Friendly to iPads and iPhones

If the iPad and iPhone struggle to acquire and retain a wireless signal at certain points within your premises, you may need to take the measures discussed in Chapter 4 to make your wireless network friendlier to the devices:

- Move one or more access points to cover areas that have weak signals.
- Add further access points or repeaters to provide better coverage.
- Add antennas to access points to boost the signal.

NOTE If there are some areas of the building or campus that the wireless network doesn't cover adequately for the iPad and iPhone to connect, make sure the users know where they are and where to go to get a better signal. It's much better to lay out the weak spots and how to avoid them than to claim blanket coverage that doesn't work for some network citizens.

Dealing with iPads and iPhones That Can't Connect to the Wireless Network

When a user can't connect to the wireless network, first make sure that the wireless network is in fact running and happy. Pull out your iPhone and make sure the network is there and that it's working. Check the signal strength; if the iPhone is getting several bars, the iPad ought to be able to sustain a connection. But if even the iPhone is struggling, you may need to reposition the user, the iPad, or the wireless access point.

If you have multiple wireless networks, make sure that the iPad or iPhone is trying to connect to the right network. If the user has wandered beyond the reach of his or her usual wireless network, you may need to turn on the Ask To Join Networks option so that the device will suggest the network that's available. Otherwise, the user can be sitting on top of an access point but not getting a signal.

Fixing the Problem When Wi-Fi Connects but Can't Access the Internet

If the iPad or iPhone can connect to the wireless network but can't access the Internet or other network areas, try renewing the DHCP lease. To do so, follow these steps:

1. From the Home screen, choose Settings | Wi-Fi to display the Wi-Fi screen.
2. Touch the right-arrow button for the network to display its configuration screens.
3. Touch the Renew Lease button. The iPad requests a new IP address from the iPad server, along with the subnet mask, router, and search domain information.

Finding the IP address the iPad or iPhone Is Using

To find the IP address an iPad or iPhone is using, choose Settings | General | About to display the About screen. Scroll down to the bottom, and then look at the Wi-Fi Address readout.

Resetting the Network Settings

Sometimes the network settings on an iPad or iPhone can get so thoroughly confused that you need to reset them in order to get the wireless network going. Don't do this lightly, because resetting the network settings wipes out network passwords and APN (carrier) settings.

To reset the network settings, choose Settings | General | Reset to display the Reset screen (shown on the left in Figure 10-8), and then touch the Reset Network Settings button. In the confirmation dialog box that appears (shown on the right in Figure 10-8), touch the Reset Network Settings button.

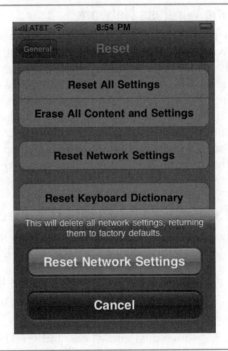

Figure 10-8. You may need to reset the network settings on an iPad or iPhone in order to start a wireless network connection working again.

Dealing with Charging Issues

To get full use out of the iPad and iPhone, the users will need to keep the device's battery charged. They can do this by using either the USB Power Adapter or a USB port that provides a sufficient level of power.

Connecting the iPad or iPhone to the computer via USB is often more convenient, because you can synchronize the device and charge it on the same cable without having to reconnect. But for the iPad, the USB Power Adapter is a better bet for three reasons:

- First, the iPad doesn't charge from a USB connection while its screen is turned on. By contrast, the iPhone does.

- Second, the iPad simply doesn't charge from many USB connections because they don't deliver enough power.

- Third, the iPad charges faster from the USB Power Adapter than from a suitable USB port.

To get the iPad to charge from a USB port, you'll almost always need to connect it directly to a port on the computer rather than one on a USB hub or on a keyboard. Check that the iPad shows the charging symbol in the upper-right corner of the screen; if the Not Charging readout appears instead, you'll know that the port lacks the oomph to charge the iPad.

Dealing with the "Charging Is Not Supported With This Accessory" Message

Once in a while, you may run into the message "Charging is not supported with this accessory" (as shown here) when you plug in the Dock Connector.

This seems to be a puzzler, but it usually just means that someone has dug out a FireWire charger cable or FireWire Power Adapter from the days when iPods used FireWire. The Dock Connector on the FireWire charger cable is the same as the one on the older USB cable for the iPhone, so the problem may not be obvious until you find a FireWire port or a FireWire Power Adapter at the other end of the cable. (The Dock Connector on the USB cable that comes with the iPad and iPhone 4 is shallower from top to bottom than the Dock Connector on older cables, and has no release buttons.)

To deal with this problem, confiscate the FireWire cable or Power Adapter and give the user a USB cable and Power Adapter instead.

Dealing with Problems Connecting to iTunes

For the iPad or iPhone to be a happy camper, it needs to be able to connect to iTunes on the user's PC or Mac and synchronize data. Regrettably often, either the computer doesn't recognize the device, or iTunes refuses to communicate with it.

When this happens, work through the following sections in order until iTunes acknowledges the iPad or iPhone.

Checking That the iPad or iPhone Has Battery Power

Start by turning on the iPad or iPhone and making sure it has at least some battery power. If not, connect it to the USB Power Adapter and give it ten minutes or more to pick up a charge; when it's comatose, it can't make iTunes recognize it.

Checking That the Dock Connector Port on the iPad or iPhone Is Connected and Working

Next, check that the USB cable's Dock Connector is firmly connected to the Dock Connector port on the iPad or iPhone. It's easy enough to get a partial connection with the locking catches not fully snapped home and the connectors not all connected.

If the Dock Connector won't go into the Dock Connector port fully, most likely something else has. Grab your can of compressed air and blast the Dock Connector port free of lint, critters, or other debris. Check that the Dock Connector itself hasn't gotten gunked somehow. Then try inserting the Dock Connector in the Dock Connector port again.

Checking the USB Port the Connection Is Using

Make sure that the USB port is working correctly. Usually, the easiest way to check is to plug in another USB device that you know is working. If the USB device still works, the port should be okay.

Next, double-check that the USB port is a 2.0 port rather than a USB 1.x port. Pretty much every viable computer these days has USB 2.0, but some well-preserved computers may still be staggering along with USB 1.x.

The easiest way to check the speed of a USB port on the PC is to plug the iPad or iPhone in and see whether iTunes or Windows warns you that the port is slow. The Windows warning is usually a pop-up message in the notification area (the system tray) saying "HI-SPEED USB Device Plugged into non-HI-SPEED USB Hub" or "This USB device can perform faster if you connect it to a Hi-Speed USB 2.0 port." The iTunes warning is an easy-to-understand message box.

To check the speed of USB ports on a Mac, follow these steps:

1. Click the Apple menu to open it.

2. Press Option to change the About This Mac item to the System Profiler item.

3. Click the System Profiler item to launch the System Profiler utility, which displays detailed information about the Mac.

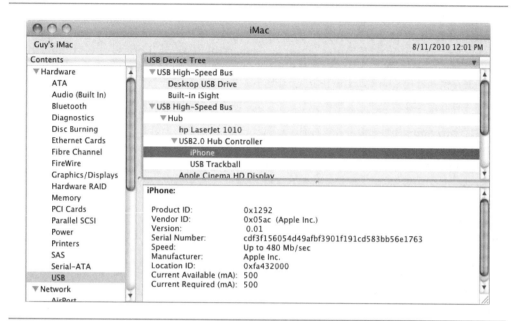

Figure 10-9.   You can use System Profiler to check the speed of USB ports on a Mac.

4. In the Contents pane on the left, expand the Hardware entry if it's collapsed.

5. Click the USB item to display its contents.

6. Click one of the USB Bus items in the USB Device Tree pane, and then check the Speed readout in the lower pane (see Figure 10-9). If the readout says "Up to 480 Mb/sec," the USB bus is USB 2.0 and all is well; if the readout says "Up to 12 Mb/sec," it's USB 1.x, and you've got a problem.

Checking the USB Cable the Connection Is Using

Check that the iPad or iPhone cable is working. For example, try using it to connect the iPad or iPhone to another computer. Or, if you have another cable, try that instead.

Reducing the Load on the USB Bus

The next place where a problem can occur is on the USB bus. This doesn't normally get overloaded, but it can happen now that so many devices use USB.

Unplug any non-essential devices, such as printers, scanners, or hubs. Don't unplug anything vital, such as the keyboard or mouse, just the things you can dispense with for a while.

Then try the iPad or iPhone again and see if iTunes can recognize it.

Updating iTunes to the Latest Version

If you're still stuck at this point, try updating iTunes to the latest version. Sometimes the new version improves iTunes' ability to detect the iPad or iPhone; other times, the process of reinstalling iTunes (by installing a new version) gives Windows or Mac OS X the kick it needs to identify the iPad or iPhone.

To check for updates, choose Help | Check For Updates in Windows or Apple | Software Update on the Mac. (You can also choose iTunes | Check For Updates on the Mac, but doing this launches Software Update, so you might as well go directly to Software Update.)

If an update is available, install it, and then try the connection again.

Restarting the Computer

Next—don't groan—try restarting the computer. A restart is a pain because you need to shut down all the programs you're using, but it can clear up a multitude of niggles.

Closing Down the iTunes-Related Services in Windows

If the restart doesn't clear up matters in Windows, open Task Manager and close the iTunesHelper.exe, AppleMobileDeviceService.exe, and iPodService.exe processes. Follow these steps:

1. Right-click the clock in the notification area, and then click Start Task Manager on the context menu. Windows Task Manager opens.

2. Click the Processes tab to display its contents (see Figure 10-10). At first, the Processes tab discreetly displays only the processes you're running.

3. Click the Show Processes From All Users button to show the system processes and processes that other users are running. Normally, you'll have to click the Continue button in a User Account Control dialog box to proceed; Windows then selects the Show Processes From All Users check box for you. Figure 10-11 shows the Processes tab with all processes displayed.

 NOTE   If you're using Windows XP, there's no Show Processes From All Users button. You just need to select the Show Process From All Users check box.

4. Click the iTunesHelper.exe process, and then click the End Process button. Windows Task Manager double-checks that you want to end the process (see Figure 10-12).

5. Click the End Process button to end the process.

6. Repeat Steps 4 and 5 for the AppleMobileDeviceService.exe process and the iPodService.exe process.

7. Choose File | Exit to close Windows Task Manager.

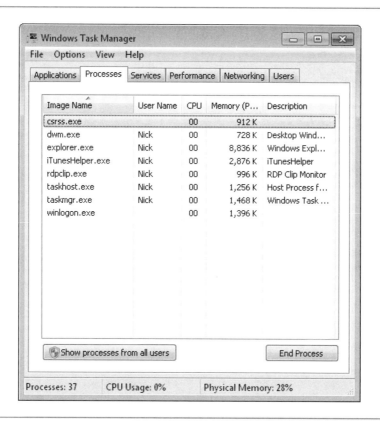

Figure 10-10. From the Processes tab in Windows Task Manager, you can shut down the services related to iTunes. You'll normally need to display all processes by clicking the Show Processes From All Users button and going through User Account Control.

Once you've stopped these services, restart Windows, and then launch iTunes. See if it can now recognize the iPad or iPhone.

Restarting the Apple Mobile Device Service on Windows

If you're still stuck after the previous steps, you may need to restart the Apple Mobile Device Service. Follow these steps:

1. Close iTunes. For example, choose File | Exit.

2. Disconnect the iPad or iPhone from the PC.

3. Click the Start button to open the Start menu.

4. In the Search box, type **services.msc**, and then press ENTER. Windows launches the Services program.

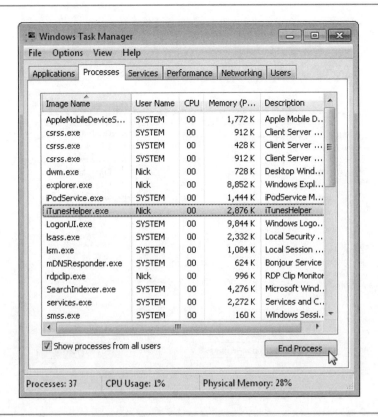

Figure 10-11. Once you've displayed the processes for all users, you can shut down the iTunesHelper.exe, AppleMobileDeviceService.exe, and iPodService.exe processes.

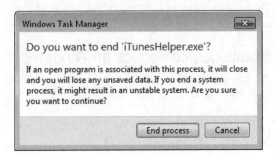

Figure 10-12. In this Windows Task Manager dialog box, confirm that you want to end each process in turn.

NOTE   In Windows XP, choose Start | Run, type **services.msc** in the Run dialog box, and then press ENTER.

5. In the list of services in the Services window, click the Apple Mobile Device service (see Figure 10-13).

6. In the column to the left of the list of services, click the Stop The Service link. Windows stops the service.

7. Click the Restart The Service link to restart the service.

 NOTE   While you have the Services program open, make sure that the Startup Type column shows Automatic for the Apple Mobile Device Service. If not, double-click the service to display its Properties dialog box, choose Automatic in the Startup Type drop-down list on the General tab, and then click the OK button.

8. Choose File | Exit to close the Services program.

Now try the iPad or iPhone again. If iTunes still can't detect the device, read the next section.

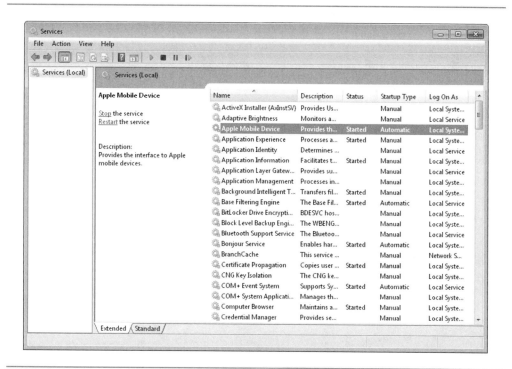

Figure 10-13.   You may need to use the Services program to stop the Apple Mobile Device Service and then restart it.

Removing and Reinstalling iTunes and the Related Software on Windows

The final step in getting iTunes to recognize the iPad or iPhone is to remove iTunes and all its related software from your PC, and then reinstall it.

Close all the programs you're running—you'll need to reboot the PC afterward—and then follow these steps to remove the software:

1. Choose Start | Control Panel to open a Windows Explorer window showing Control Panel.

2. Switch to Category view if the window is using a different view:

   ■ **Windows 7 or Windows Vista** Click the View drop-down list, and then click Category.

   ■ **Windows XP** Click the Switch To Category View link in the upper-left corner of the Control Panel window.

3. Open the Programs And Features window (see Figure 10-14) or the Add Or Remove Programs window (see Figure 10-15) like this:

   ■ **Windows 7 or Windows Vista** Under the Programs heading, click the Uninstall A Program link.

   ■ **Windows XP** Click the Add Or Remove Programs link.

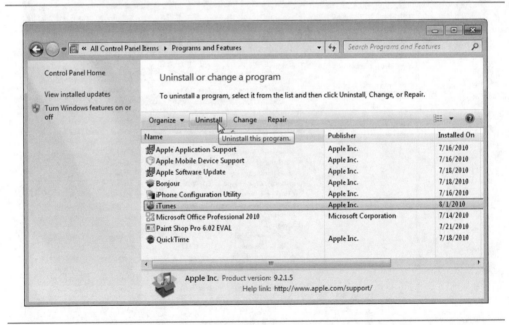

Figure 10-14. To remove a program on Windows 7 or Windows Vista, click it, and then click the Uninstall button.

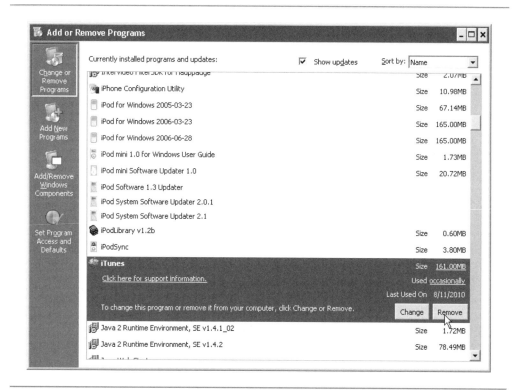

Figure 10-15.   To remove a program on Windows XP, click the program, and then click the Remove button that appears in its listing.

4. Click iTunes in the list of programs, and then click the appropriate button.

   ■ **Windows 7 or Windows Vista**   Click the Uninstall button above the list of programs.

   ■ **Windows XP**   Click the Remove button in the program's listing.

5. In the confirmation dialog box that appears, click the Yes button.

6. When Windows prompts you to restart it, click the No button.

7. Repeat Steps 4, 5, and 6 to remove the following programs in turn:

   ■ Any iPod Updater programs

   ■ QuickTime

   ■ Apple Software Update

   ■ Apple Mobile Device Support

   ■ Bonjour

   ■ Apple Application Support

8. Accept the final invitation to restart Windows. (If you automatically clicked the No button in that dialog box, restart Windows from the Start menu as normal.)

9. When Windows restarts, log in as usual.

10. Choose Start | Computer to open a Computer window on Windows 7 or Windows Vista, or choose Start | My Computer to open a My Computer window on Windows XP.

11. Double-click your PC's system drive (for example, C:) to display its contents.

12. Double-click the Program Files folder to display its contents.

13. Select the following folders and delete them:
    - iTunes
    - iPod
    - QuickTime
    - Bonjour
    - Common Files\Apple

14. Go back to the system drive folder (for example, C:), and then double-click the Windows folder to display its contents.

15. Double-click the System32 folder to display its contents.

16. Delete the QuickTime file and the QuickTimeVR file.

17. Close the Windows Explorer window.

18. Right-click the Recycle Bin on the Desktop, and then choose Empty Recycle Bin.

19. Click the Yes button in the confirmation dialog box.

Now open your browser and go to www.apple.com/itunes/download/. Download the iTunes distribution file for Windows, and then follow through the prompts to install it.

Restart Windows if the installation prompts you to, and then try connecting the iPad or iPhone again.

Removing and Reinstalling the Apple Mobile Device Service on the Mac

If iTunes won't recognize the iPad or iPhone on the Mac after you've checked the connection as described earlier in this chapter, try removing and reinstalling the Apple Mobile Device Service. Follow these steps:

1. Disconnect the iPad or iPhone from the Mac.

2. Click the desktop to activate the Finder, and then choose Go | Applications from the menu bar to display the Applications folder.

3. CTRL-click or right-click the iTunes icon, and then click Move To Trash on the context menu to move iTunes to the Trash.

4. In the Devices list in the Finder window, click the Mac's hard disk to display its contents.

5. Double-click the System folder, then the Library folder, and then the Extensions folder to navigate to the /System/Library/Extensions/ folder.

6. CTRL-click or right-click the AppleMobileDeviceSupport.kext file, and then click Move To Trash on the context menu to move the file to the Trash.

7. Click the Mac's hard disk again to display its contents.

8. Double-click the Library folder, and then the Receipts folder, to display the contents of the /Library/Receipts/ folder.

9. If you find a file named AppleMobileDeviceSupport.pkg, CTRL-click it or right-click it, and then choose Move To Trash to put this file in the Trash as well.

10. Hold down OPTION and choose Apple | Restart to restart the Mac.

11. Log back in as usual.

Now open your browser, go to www.apple.com/itunes/download/. Download the iTunes distribution file for Mac OS X, and follow through the prompts to install it. When the installation is complete, try connecting the iPad or iPhone again.

Squeezing the Most Battery Life Out of the iPad and iPhone

Battery life is the bane of portable electronic devices, and though both the iPad and the iPhone score pretty well in this area, you'll want to make sure that your network's users get as much battery life as possible. This means conditioning the battery at the start of the device's life and teaching the users to treat the battery in a friendly way. It may also mean replacing the battery once it reaches the end of its life span.

Conditioning the Battery

To get the best performance out of a lithium-polymer battery such as those used in the iPad and iPhone, give it three soup-to-nuts charges and discharges at the beginning of its life:

- **Charge the battery all the way up to 100 percent**   Use the USB Power Adapter—it's quicker than a USB cable plugged into your computer, and it doesn't go to sleep.

- **Run the battery all the way down until the iPad or iPhone shuts itself down**   The easiest way to do this is to crank up the screen brightness to full and set a marathon playlist of videos running.

- **Repeat the process twice**   Plug the iPad or iPhone back into the USB Power Adapter; then lather, rinse, and repeat.

This conditioning technique is simple enough to describe, but it's a pain to do in real life, as it takes the best part of three days—for example, ten hours of playback, five hours of charging, plus whatever overhead you need for mundane self-admin such as sleeping and eating. Given that most users will want to use the iPad or iPhone immediately for work or play, you can bet your bottom dollar almost none will perform the conditioning properly.

That means that if you want the battery properly conditioned, you'll need to do it in your workshop or lab during initial setup before providing the iPads or iPhones to the users.

Charging the Battery the Best Way

Once you've performed the initial conditioning, the battery is ready for normal charging. Unless you retain a scary amount of control over your network's users, you'll need to leave normal charging up to them.

Compared to less evolved battery technologies (hello, nickel-cadmium—and goodbye!) lithium-polymer batteries give great performance and are pretty forgiving. For example, the iPad's battery is supposed to retain 80 percent of its battery life after 1000 charge cycles. So if you start off with ten hours of battery life, run the battery down every day, and charge it up all the way overnight, you should still get around eight hours of battery life after three years.

Each time you charge the battery up all the way and run it down all the way, that's one complete charge cycle. If you use just part of the battery, and then charge it up again, that's part of a charge cycle. With lithium-polymer batteries, you don't have to worry about the "memory effect," in which discharging the battery only partially before recharging it could reset the battery's Empty threshold to the point at which you stopped discharging it (for example, resetting the Empty threshold to the 50 percent level would severely reduce the battery life).

Nor do you need to worry about overcharging lithium-polymer batteries: They charge rapidly up to around the 80 percent level, then more slowly for the remaining 20 percent. When full, they stop charging, even if you leave them plugged in.

So—no problems there. What *can* reduce the battery life is when the battery doesn't get a charge in a month or more. This tends not to be a problem, as most users love their iPads and iPhones enough to plug them in every day without chastisement. But you may run into degraded batteries on the occasional sad iPad that spends months untouched in the drawer of an executive's desk and then is expected to perform for the whole of a trans-world flight.

CAUTION   Excessive heat will degrade an iPad's or iPhone's battery far more than leaving the device uncharged for many weeks. Make sure users know not to leave their iPads or iPhones in the sun on a windowsill or in a car—or, worse, in a car trunk or glove compartment. Generally speaking, any ambient temperature that'll cause a human to suffer will give the iPad's or iPhone's battery grief too.

Choosing Settings for Better Battery Life

To get the most battery life out of an iPad or iPhone, you can reduce the power demands in various ways—everything from dimming the screen to collecting data less frequently.

Reducing the Screen Brightness and Locking the Screen

Of all the mouths the iPad's or iPhone's battery has to feed, the screen is by far the most power-hungry—especially on the iPad. So you can improve battery life by turning down the screen brightness and setting the device to lock itself sooner rather than later.

To turn down the screen brightness, choose Settings | Brightness & Wallpaper, and then drag the Brightness slider to the left. If you choose to use the Auto-Brightness feature (by setting the Auto-Brightness switch to the On position), the device tries to automatically set a suitable brightness for the ambient lighting. You can often save more power by setting a lower brightness manually—at the risk of eye strain.

To make the iPad or iPhone lock itself sooner, choose Settings | General | Auto-Lock, and then choose a short interval on the Auto-Lock screen. Figure 10-16 shows the Auto-Lock screen for the iPhone. The iPad offers these settings: 2 Minutes, 5 Minutes, 10 Minutes, 15 Minutes, and Never. The iPhone's settings are: 1 Minute, 2 Minutes, 3 Minutes, 4 Minutes, 5 Minutes, or Never.

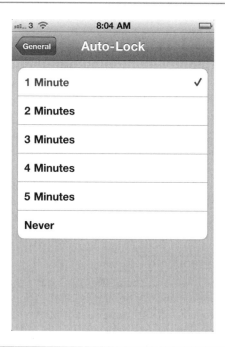

Figure 10-16.   To reduce the demands on the battery, set the iPad or iPhone to lock itself automatically after as short an interval as is practicable.

Turning Off Wireless Services You're Not Using

Both Wi-Fi and 3G can chew through considerable amounts of power, so if you don't need one, the other, or both, turn them off:

- **Turn off Wi-Fi**   Choose Settings | Wi-Fi to display the Wi-Fi Networks screen, and then move the Wi-Fi switch to the Off position.

- **Turn off 3G**   On the iPad, choose Settings | Cellular Data to display the Cellular Data screen, and then move the Cellular Data switch to the Off position. On the iPhone, use Airplane Mode, as discussed next.

- **Use Airplane Mode**   On the iPad or the iPhone, touch the Settings icon to display the Settings screen, and then move the Airplane Mode switch to the On position. AirPlane mode is a quick and easy way of turning off all the cellular and Wi-Fi antennas to keep the flight crew from deplaning you before your destination, but you can use it any time you value battery power over connectivity.

Turning Off Bluetooth

If you don't use Bluetooth for an external device such as a keyboard or a headset, turn it off. Choose Settings | General | Bluetooth to display the Bluetooth screen, and then move the Bluetooth switch to the Off position.

Turning Off Push Notifications

When you don't need to receive push notifications from applications such as the App Store, turn push notifications off to save battery life. To do so, choose Settings | Notifications, and then move the Notifications switch on the Notifications screen (shown on the left in Figure 10-17) to the Off position.

NOTE   If the Notifications item doesn't appear on the Settings screen, the iPad or iPhone doesn't contain any applications that are set to use notifications.

If you want to turn off notifications for a particular app rather than turning them off across the board, touch the app's entry on the Notification screen to bring up its control screen. The right screen in Figure 10-17 shows an example for the app called Ambiance. Then move the switches to the Off position.

Getting Your E-Mail Less Frequently

E-mail is so vital to both business and social life these days that it's a wrench to check it less frequently—but you can reduce the demands on the iPad's or iPhone's battery life by doing so. If your e-mail accounts support push, you can turn that off too.

To turn off push or to change the frequency with which the iPad or iPhone checks for e-mail, follow these steps:

1. Choose Settings | Mail, Contacts, Calendars to display the Mail, Contacts, Calendars screen.

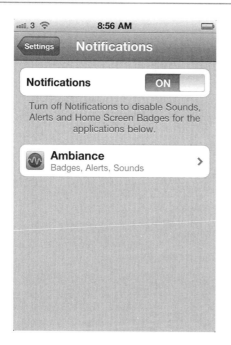
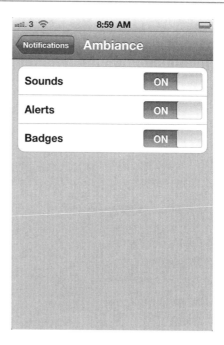

Figure 10-17.   Use the Notifications screen to turn off notifications in general and to see which apps are using notifications. To turn off notifications for a particular app, touch its entry on the Notifications screen, and then use the controls on the screen that appears (right).

2. Touch the Fetch New Data button to display the Fetch New Data screen (see Figure 10-18).

3. To turn off push mail, move the Push switch to the Off position.

4. In the Fetch area, set the schedule for checking for mail: Every 15 Minutes, Every 30 Minutes, Hourly, or (the horror!) Manually.

TIP   If you use some e-mail accounts only occasionally, turn off automatic checking on them. Choose Settings | Mail, Contacts, Calendars to display the Mail, Contacts, Calendars screen, and then touch the account you want to change. On the Account Info screen, move the Account switch or the Mail switch to the Off position. This will help protect you from hauling down a dozen high-resolution snaps of Cousin Grace's snaggletoothed mutt when you least need them.

Culling Power-Greedy Third-Party Apps

Some apps are worth every milliamp of power they consume, but many apps are relentlessly greedy and not worth the juice. As you use the iPad or iPhone, watch out for third-party apps that keep the screen fully lit rather than allowing it to dim, or that

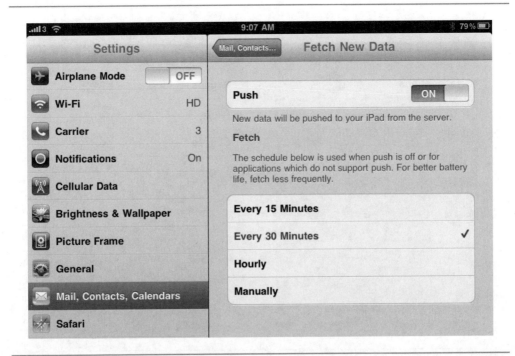

Figure 10-18. On the Fetch New Data screen, you can turn off push mail and change the frequency with which the Mail app checks for e-mail.

prevent the device from locking. Unless any such app is vital, look for a better-behaved alternative, or simply remove it from the devices you manage.

> **NOTE** If you use the iPod feature of the iPad or iPhone frequently, you can save some power by turning off the equalizer. To do so, choose Settings | iPod | EQ, and then touch the Off button on the EQ screen. But most people find the equalizer improves the sound so much that turning it off is too big a sacrifice on the altar of power.

Replacing the Battery on an iPad or iPhone

When the battery on an iPad or iPhone stops holding enough charge to deliver useful battery life, it's time to get the battery replaced.

If the battery goes bad while the iPad or iPhone is still under warranty or under an AppleCare Protection Plan warranty extension you've bought for it, you can get Apple to replace it for free. Otherwise, you're looking at $99 for an iPad battery or $79 for an iPhone battery, plus a $6.95 shipping fee. Third-party companies offer better prices; search for **iPad battery replacement service** or **iPhone battery replacement service**, as needed.

NOTE If you're not sure whether the iPhone or iPad is still under warranty, go to the Service and Repair page at https://selfsolve.apple.com/GetWarranty.do, enter the device's hardware serial number and your country, and see what the Service and Repair Assistant says.

With the iPhone, Apple replaces the battery. But with the iPad, Apple actually replaces the device itself. You're responsible for backing up the data to iTunes so that you can restore it to the replacement iPad when it arrives.

Apple considers iPhone and iPad batteries to be "not user replaceable," and the trail of wrecked and bent iPhones and iPads you can pick up for spare parts (and sometimes for spare change) on eBay tends to bear this out. But of course anyone armed with the right tools and sufficient skill and knowledge *can* open an iPhone or iPad and replace the battery—otherwise, Apple's technicians would be as much use as those mythical monkeys industriously hammering out alternative editions of *Hamlet*.

At this writing (Fall 2010), you shouldn't need to replace the battery in an iPad or iPhone 4 unless you've done something horrible enough to invalidate the one-year warranty. But you can find replacement batteries for both these devices, and for earlier iPhones, at any number of places online, including eBay. Search for **iPad replacement battery** or **iPhone 3GS replacement battery**, and you'll find plenty, along with tools to help you attempt the surgery.

TIP Sites such as iFixit (www.ifixit.com) offer both replacement parts and instructions. You can also find video walkthroughs on YouTube that help identify problems that the repair instructions tend to gloss over.

Index

Q

X

Y